SCC Library

DISCARD

3 3065 00388 3299

Santiago Canyon College
Library

ML
4620
.V248
H37
2008

# A Deepe Blue

D0618704

## The Life and Music
## of Townes Van Zandt

### by Robert Earl Hardy

Number 1 in the North Texas
Lives of Musicians Series

University of North Texas Press
ocn579249222
Denton, Texas
Santiago Canyon College
Library

©2008 Robert Earl Hardy

All rights reserved.
Printed in the United States of America.

10 9 8 7 6

Permissions:
University of North Texas Press
1155 Union Circle #311336
Denton, Texas 76203-5017

The paper used in this book meets the minimum requirements of the American National Standard for Permanence of Paper for Printed Library Materials, z39.48.1984. Binding materials have been chosen for durability.

Library of Congress Cataloging-in-Publication Data

Hardy, Robert Earl, 1957–
    A deeper blue: the life and music of Townes Van Zandt / by Robert Earl Hardy.
        p. cm.—(North Texas lives of musicians series ; no. 1)
    Includes bibliographical references and index.
    ISBN 978-1-57441-247-5 (cloth : alk. paper)
    ISBN 978-1-57441-285-7 (paper : alk. paper)
        1. Van Zandt, Townes. 2. Country musicians—United States—Biography. I. Title.
    ML420.V248.H37 2008
    782.421642092—dc22
    [B]

                                                    2007044532

*A Deeper Blue: The Life and Music of Townes Van Zandt* is Number 1 in the North Texas Lives of Musicians Series

**Cover photo courtesy of Roy Tee**

To my favorite Texan, my mother
Frances Mahala Hardy
(1924–2006)

And, with abiding love, to my wife
Marsha

And in fond memory of
Jim Calvin
Roxy Gordon
Johnny Guess
Mickey Newbury
Dale Soffar
Peggy Underwood
and
Townes Van Zandt

# Contents

# List of Photographs

**(appearing after page 172)**

1. Portrait of Townes Van Zandt
2. Townes performing, 1970s
3. Townes and Fran's wedding
4. Guy, Susanna, and Townes
5. Pickin' on the porch
6. Townes and Cindy
7. Townes with Mickey White
8. On the road
9. Amigos Ricardo and Blaze
10. Townes, Jeanene, and Will
11. Townes and the Calvins
12. Claudia Winterer
13. Townes and J.T.
14. Townes performing in Scotland
15. Backstage, Renfrew Ferry
16. Townes with Bo Whitt paintings

# Acknowledgments

I N 1999, I RETURNED TO Texas for the first time in twenty-five years. My mother was celebrating her seventy-fifth birthday and the fiftieth anniversary of leaving her Galveston home and moving east. I was as happy as she was to see Galveston again, where I had spent many hours as a child, collecting shells on the beach, watching the shrimp boats come in, studying old maps and reading old books, and absorbing the quiet charm of my grandmother's bungalow on Avenue S, with the shades drawn against the heat of the day. Galveston, Texas, is the true source of nourishment from which this book springs.

The second or third evening of our return visit to Galveston, while my mother stayed behind at the Galvez, I took my wife, Marsha, out to see the town. We wandered toward the Strand and stumbled into a little place called the Old Quarter Acoustic Café, where it was open-mic night. Along with three or four other patrons, we sat through a couple of average folk singers, then Rex Bell, the proprietor, sat down and played a few songs, including his own "Whiskey Maybe," Blaze Foley's "Oval Room," and Townes Van Zandt's "I'll Be Here in the Morning." As he played a few more Van Zandt songs, I remembered listening in wonderment to "Pancho and Lefty" on my local underground radio station's early-seventies all-night broadcasts, and I recalled that I still had an old vinyl copy of *The Late, Great Townes Van Zandt*. I was intrigued. We sat at the bar and talked with Rex until closing time, listening to stories about his days playing bass with Lightnin' Hopkins and about his exploits with—and his love and respect for—Townes Van Zandt. At some point, somebody mentioned that Townes' story would make a great book. That evening with Rex Bell was the Shiner Bock–fuelled occasion during which the seed for this book was planted.

Over the years since, many individuals have generously and enthusiastically given their time and energies to help the book grow. I especially acknowledge and thank my wife, Marsha, for providing me with the strongest, most unflagging support imaginable. The many hours we spent poring over tapes and transcripts together, talking with friends and colleagues, and discussing the details and patterns of Townes' life and music, plus the hours she spent transcribing interviews, reading the manuscript, offering suggestions, helping compile sources and obtain permissions, and generally staying deeply involved—were hours essential to this book's existence.

Also in the engine room were Anne Bailey, who provided thoughtful research on a number of difficult topics; Ruth Sanders, who was kind enough to share with me the fruits of her unpublished research, including her personal interviews with one of the principals; and Lisa Uhlman, who transcribed interviews and provided research assistance—I thank them all. I also acknowledge with thanks the support of Nick Evans and Jeff Horne of Heartland Publishing in England, the authors and publishers of *Songbuilder: The Life and Music of Guy Clark*, who offered sincere advice and encouragement and shared valuable contacts. Also sincere and heartfelt in the support that they consistently showed for this project are Doug and Susan Darrow of Houston, Texas. In our travels through Texas, Marsha and I enjoyed the hospitality of many friends, old and new, including Bianca DeLeon, who welcomed us into her home, showed us around Austin, and offered friendship and encouragement. In our travels through Tennessee and vicinity, again, many friends helped us on our way, particularly our dear Kentucky friends, Jimmy Gingles and Joan Morgan. Through Jimmy Gingles, we also got to know and love Jimmie McKinney, a great spirit to whose memory I offer a fond toast.

A number of individuals provided audio and video recordings of live performances (as documented in Audio and Video Sources), and I thank them all, especially Len Coop (whose Blue Sky Home Page Web site is the most comprehensive online source of information on Townes), and also Aleksandar Lazarevic, Marilyn Kay, Jess Codd, and Rodney Hamon. Also, Patrick

Hurley has been a loyal correspondent and a valuable source of information and encouragement.

Songwriters have a special kind of affinity for Townes Van Zandt, and songwriters were often able to offer special insight to this inquiry. Foremost among them, closest to my heart, were Guy Clark, Susanna Clark, and Mickey Newbury. Their contributions to this book mean the world to me, and I thank them profoundly. David Olney and Eric Taylor—two of many contemporary songwriters influenced by Townes—were also invaluable sources of insight. In one memorable episode in researching this book, Taylor phoned one night and challenged me to a round of over-the-phone arm wrestling, explaining that he and Townes had engaged in this activity more than once. In addition, for her encouragement as well as her work in the field, I thank Kathleen Hudson of Schreiner University in Kerrville, Texas, founder and director of the Texas Heritage Music Foundation and author of *Telling Stories, Writing Songs: An Album of Texas Songwriters*. I also offer acknowledgment and thanks to the many contemporary journalists, writers, and photographers who took Townes as their subject during his lifetime and whose work informed my work.

Finally, I want to give special acknowledgment to the people who spent significant parts of their lives with Townes Van Zandt and—believing it was important that his story be told fully and truthfully—willingly, tenderly, and forthrightly shared their memories for the sake of posterity: Rex Bell, Vince Bell, Jim Calvin, Royann Calvin, John Carrick, Guy Clark, Susanna Clark, Jack Clement, Bianca DeLeon, Richard Dobson, Steve Earle, Joe Ely, Rex Foster, Marshall Froker, Jimmy Gingles, Joe Gracey, Jimmie Gray, Frank "Chito" Greer, Darryl Harris, Grace Jameson, Crow Johnson, Cindy Van Zandt Lindgram, Fran Lohr, John Lomax III, Bob Moore, Lyse Moore, Todd Musburger, Bob Myrick, Mickey Newbury, David Olney, Danny "Ruester" Rowland, Luke Sharpe, Dale Soffar, Donna Spence, Bob Sturtevant, Eric Taylor, Michael Timmins, Peggy Underwood, Bill Van Zandt, Jeanene Van Zandt, Will Van Zandt, Mickey White, Jeanette "Jet" Whitt, Earl Willis, Nick Wilson, Claudia Winterer, and all those whose off-the-record contributions informed this work.

# Introduction

# High, Low, and In Between

OWNES VAN ZANDT WAS A songwriter and a traveling minstrel—a folk singer, no less—in an era when practicing these crafts had long since become anachronistic, evocative of a long-gone era in American life—of Jimmie Rodgers riding the rails of the great American West; Woody Guthrie tramping the highways from dustbowl Oklahoma to the migrant camps of California; Robert Johnson playing guitar with the devil at a Mississippi Delta crossroads; Hank Williams driving from roadhouse to roadhouse across the South, drinking and singing with the Drifting Cowboys—an archaic art form, a mythic mode of living. But like these other American originals, Townes Van Zandt was fully invested in his craft, and his craft was inextricable from his life, and this investment and integration gave rise to great art, which is timeless.

As an artist, Van Zandt made no compromises; he lived out his destiny on the road, practicing his craft until he simply couldn't anymore—the embodiment of the troubled troubadour. He was certainly a troubled man.

Townes Van Zandt was troubled throughout his life by alcoholism and manic-depressive illness, and he was constantly battling the demons associated with these conditions. He made attempts to settle down into family life, but it was always a struggle. He made attempts to pursue commercial success with his music, but mostly those attempts came up short. He had a spiritual bent that always trumped his material concerns— and, for better or worse, those of his family. He said he lived for the "hum of the wheels," and in hope of hitting "that one note" that would connect with "just one person," and save that person's life. He was deeply serious about this goal—which he believed without question was his life's calling—to the extent that he "blew off everything" to pursue it, refusing to compromise. In an interview published October 17, 2002, in the *Houston Press,* his oldest son, J.T., succinctly summed up his view of the price they both paid for his father's single-minded pursuit of that goal: "As a father he had a lot of unforgivable shortcomings that can't be excused by his music."

The lack of compromise that made family life impossible for Van Zandt made his music possible. For thirty years, he wrote beautiful, deeply inspired, brilliantly integrated lyrical and musical evocations of his inner life. He gave sometimes magical performances in his engaging, insouciant Texas folk-blues style for what must always be described as a cult audience, even though a couple of his songs reached the commercial heights. "If I Needed You" was a number three record for Emmylou Harris and Don Williams in 1981 and "Pancho and Lefty" was number one on the country charts for Willie Nelson and Merle Haggard in 1983. But Townes never got the break that would take his career to the next level. In fact, he seemed to confound commercial success with a determination second only to his determination to make his music honest, meaningful, and lasting, like the music of his hero, Hank Williams, and his mentor, the Texas bluesman Lightnin' Hopkins. At that, it can be argued, Townes succeeded.

When he left this world at age fifty-two on New Year's Day 1997—forty-four years to the day after Hank Williams' death—Townes Van Zandt left behind a solid and lasting body of work, as original and as deeply personal—yet as naturally a part of a great tradition and as all-encompassing and universal—as any created in twentieth-century American music, embodied in beautifully realized songs like "To Live's to Fly," "For the Sake of the Song," "Don't You Take It Too Bad," "Rex's Blues," "Lungs," "Nothin'," "Flyin' Shoes," "Highway Kind," "Snowin' on Raton," "Marie," and of course "Pancho and Lefty" and "If I Needed You," among many others.

In the years since his death, Van Zandt has been repeatedly cited as a major songwriting influence and had his songs covered by a diverse host of respected artists, including Norah Jones, Alison Krauss, Lucinda Williams, Lyle Lovett, Steve Earle, Gillian Welch, John Prine, Nanci Griffith, Cowboy Junkies, Joe Ely, Jimmie Dale Gilmore, Butch Hancock, and Guy Clark, among many others. Steve Earle is famously and repeatedly quoted as saying "Townes Van Zandt is the best damn songwriter in the world, and I'll stand on Bob Dylan's coffee table in my cowboy boots and say that."

So, one might ask, how is it that the "best damn songwriter in the world" was, like Van Gogh, so unheralded in his own lifetime? In fact, Van Zandt himself was a major contributor to—if not the architect of—his own lack of commercial success. "Why is Townes' career in such a sorry state?" wrote his manager at the time, John Lomax; then he answered himself: "Inept, haphazard management, record company ignorance, and [Townes'] own eccentric conduct."[1] By all accounts, that pithy assessment is accurate. At the height of Townes' recording run, he titled his sixth album *The Late, Great Townes Van Zandt*, a dark spoof on the lifeless state of his livelihood that caused many to assume that he was, in fact, dead. In a sense, it was frustrating for him as an artist to know that his work was worthy but was so widely unrecognized. But in another sense, for the initiated, his obscurity—the magical "cult" status—clearly carried the connotation that his work was the kind of high quality, demanding work that might *never* make an impact with the masses. It was an elite obscurity, based on a demanding level of artistic quality that itself precluded commercial success.

But while he had nearly insurmountable obstacles to overcome from a commercial standpoint, from the beginning Townes Van Zandt had a clear vision of his artistic territory, a strong grasp of his tools, and no fear of confronting an ever-present metaphysical darkness. As one writer of the time said, "Townes carries the terror and the sorrow of a sensitive man who has looked into the abyss and seen ... the abyss."[2] This was Van Zandt's territory, which he explored with a highly articulate poetic and philosophic vision, although it was territory into which a mass audience was simply unwilling to venture. Its sources lay clearly in traditional American blues, country, and folk music—with influences as diverse as Shakespeare and Robert Frost—but the depth of Van Zandt's vision was unique. And his vision never faltered, it only deepened. In a way, he didn't have a chance during his lifetime; the public sponge couldn't possibly absorb the tears his songs shed. Ten years after his death, it's starting to sink in. Like Hank Williams, Townes Van Zandt's monument stands firm: a serious body of work by a great American artist.

Besides the work and a compelling story, Townes Van Zandt left behind an enigmatic memory, permeated with the enduring sense of mystery that Americans require of their icons. But Townes Van Zandt can't be understood simply as the mysterious troubled troubadour of American folk mythology, no matter how much he might have played into the myth and no matter how much others might have tried to cast him in that role. Townes Van Zandt was a complex man. It seems worth asking: Isn't there something we can discover about him *as a man* that will help us understand his work?

———◆◆◆———

This is the kind of question to which biographers naturally turn their craft. This book has taken shape as an attempt to tell the story of Townes' life—beginning, middle, and end—to shed some light on his creative process and his work, and to set his life and work in context and in perspective.

More than forty of Townes' family members, friends, colleagues, and contemporaries agreed to be interviewed for this book. Most participated with great interest and enthusiasm, often inviting me into their homes, showing me around town, engaging me in multifarious conversations, enduring meticulous follow-up calls, and introducing me to new sources and new friends. A few principals had reservations. I spent a day visiting and talking with Townes' third ex-wife, Jeanene, at her home in Smyrna, Tennessee, and she was gracious and forthcoming but insisted on a level of control over my manuscript to which I could not agree. However, I was fortunate to be able to accept an offer from Ms. Ruth Sanders to share personal interviews with Jeanene and Will Van Zandt that she conducted for an unpublished project, so their parts in the story are told from those primary sources in addition to secondary sources. Kevin Eggers, of Poppy Records and Tomato Records, agreed to speak only off the record, so his role in the story is delineated through secondary sources. Only one central figure declined outright to participate: Townes' friend and road manager Harold Eggers. His part in the story is also told through secondary sources.

One of his friends described Townes as a "whirlwind that passed through people's lives."[3] A decade after his death, the dust from that whirlwind is only just beginning to settle. This book draws on the voices of the people who were closest to the center of the whirlwind that was Townes Van Zandt. My task has been to gather together the threads of these many individual voices, each with their unique variations and colorings, and weave them into a whole cloth.

A biography is necessarily filled with speculation, too, informed by and woven into the texture of fact and supporting detail that holds the structure firm. This biography weaves the softer threads of informed speculation—abounding in mystery—in with the durable threads of memory and documented fact. Upon backing up and applying the perspective of time and distance, we begin to see how these diverse threads tighten into the warp and weft of a complex man's life.

So, here is the story of Townes Van Zandt, a man, "born to grow and grown to die."

# 1

# Many a River: The Van Zandts of Texas

O F ALL THE SOURCES FROM which Townes Van Zandt drew nourishment and influence, none was more nourishing or more influential than the Texas soil from which he sprang and in which his roots grew so deep.

When Mexico won independence from Spain in 1821, the Mexican government began to encourage settlement in what was then Mexico's northernmost province, Coahuila y Tejas. Within a short time, there was a steady flow of *norteamericano* settlers into the province, led officially by Stephen Austin and his famous colony. By 1830, there were 30,000 American settlers in Texas. Rapidly mounting tensions between the settlers and the Mexican government led to revolution, beginning in 1835 and followed rapidly by Texas' Declaration of Independence on

March 2, 1836, then ending the next month with the surrender of Mexican forces and the capture of General Santa Anna on the battlefield at San Jacinto, with Texas thereby established as an independent republic. Throughout the next decade, Anglo-American settlement of the region continued. From east of the Sabine, more and more men and their families lit out for the new territory, lured by the well-advertised prospect of cheap land and abundant work. Often with little or no notice, these pioneers left their old lives behind them, along with signs saying simply, "Gone to Texas."

One of those pioneers was Isaac Van Zandt, son of Jacob and Mary (Isaacs) Van Zandt. The Van Zandt family originally sailed from Holland prior to the American Revolution, settling in New York then migrating to North Carolina. Jacob took his family to Franklin County, Tennessee, in 1800. Isaac was born there on July 10, 1813.[1] When Isaac married Frances Cooke Lipscomb in December 1833, he and his father were proprietors of a store in Maxwell, Tennessee, near Salem. When Jacob died in 1834, the young couple moved to Coffeeville, in northern Mississippi, where Isaac opened his own store. A daughter, Louisa, was born later that year, and a son, Khleber Miller, was born on November 7, 1836.

Widespread hard times struck in 1837, and the Van Zandt business failed. The family was struggling and in debt, but Isaac was enterprising and intelligent. Having become somewhat accomplished at public speaking through his membership in a local debating society, Isaac decided to take up the study of law. In 1838 he took his examinations and was admitted to the Mississippi bar, and within the next year he had hung his own "Gone to Texas" sign and moved with his family to a small, one-room log cabin in Elysian Fields, in the Red River District (later part of Harrison County).

On January 5, 1840, another son, Isaac Lycurgus, was born. Van Zandt had persuaded a wealthy local landowner to donate land whereon to establish a town and a college, and he became active in laying out the town that was to become Marshall, Texas, which he named after the Chief Justice of the United States. Van Zandt was quickly becoming a civic leader when he was elected to represent Harrison and Panola counties in the House of Representatives of the Fifth and Sixth Congresses of the Republic of Texas, where he served from 1840 to 1842. He soon emerged as an influential voice in the House. In 1842, Isaac bought 200 acres in Marshall and moved his family there, including a new baby, Frances Cooke Van Zandt, born in May of that year.

Van Zandt was experienced and respected enough as a legislator and politician that in July 1842 Sam Houston, by then President of the independent Republic of Texas, appointed him Chargé d'Affairs to the government of the United States. Isaac took his family to Washington, D.C., and began to work for the annexation of Texas to the Union. The Van Zandts remained in Washington for two years, until that goal was achieved. During their time in the nation's capital, in May 1844, a daughter, Ida, was born, the last of Isaac and Frances' five surviving children.

The family returned to Texas in time for Isaac to attend the Convention of 1845, where the delegates considered and approved the joint resolution of the U.S. Congress accepting annexation of Texas. Van Zandt and the other delegates then drafted the Texas Constitution, which was accepted by the United States on December 29. He was also instrumental in drafting such important legislation as the Homestead Law, which protected settlers' homes from seizure by creditors and in which he had been interested since early in his career. Isaac's political star was still rising and he was in the midst of a campaign for the governorship in 1847 when he contracted yellow fever in Galveston and died in Houston on October 11. He was buried in Marshall, and the next year Van Zandt County was christened in his honor.[2]

The Van Zandts' contributions to Texas history, however, were not over. Isaac's oldest son, Khleber Miller, or K.M., was an early graduate of the college his father helped found, Marshall University, and he settled in that town after also attending Franklin College, in Franklin County, Tennessee, where Isaac had been born. In Marshall, K.M. worked in a dry goods store and helped to found the Christian church there before taking a job securing deeds of right-of-way for the Vicksburg, Shreveport, and Texas Railway Company in Louisiana. He went back to Marshall, following in his father's footsteps and becoming a member of the bar in 1858, and he practiced law there until the outbreak of the Civil War.

In Van Zandt County in 1860 there was only a small population of slaves—just over 300 out of the total population of nearly 6,500—but the citizens there voted decisively for secession in 1861, and as they did all over Texas, men began to volunteer in large numbers for service in the Army of the Confederate States.[3] K.M. Van Zandt helped organize one of the many regiments that sprang up almost overnight throughout the South, Company D of the Seventh Texas Infantry, where he was made captain. He fought with his regiment in Mississippi and Tennessee and was taken prisoner during the capture of Fort Donelson. Exchanged in 1862, he was given a certificate of disability and discharged, with the rank of major, in 1864.

Major Van Zandt, his wife Minerva (the first of his three wives, including his second, Minerva's sister Mattie), and their growing family (fourteen children eventually lived to adulthood) moved west in 1865 and settled in Fort Worth, then a frontier town with a population of fewer than 250 and lacking even a proper saloon, as K.M. himself pointed out. There, seeing no market for a law firm, he opened a dry-goods store and was soon successful.

This was only the beginning of the Major's success in business and civic affairs. He served a term in the State Legislature in 1873–74—his only venture into politics—then in 1874 he founded the company that would become the Fort Worth National Bank. In 1875 he formed the construction company that built the Texas and Pacific Railroad roadbed between Fort Worth and Dallas. Van Zandt served as president of these companies for more than fifty years, and was also president of the K.M. Van Zandt Land Company, director of the Fort Worth Life Insurance

Company, and director of the Fort Worth and Denver Railway and the Fort Worth Street Railway Company.

The Major also co-founded the Fort Worth *Democrat,* one of the town's first newspapers, served for two decades on the local school board, and was instrumental in bringing the Texas and Pacific; the Santa Fe; and the Missouri, Kansas, and Texas railroads to Fort Worth, laying the foundations for the area's future as a transportation center. He helped organize the United Confederate Veterans, serving as that organization's commander in chief from 1918 to 1921. He dictated his autobiography to his daughter, then died shortly thereafter, in March 1930, in Fort Worth, at the age of ninety-three.

K.M.'s brother Isaac Lycurgus, known as I.L., received his medical degree from Tulane University in 1866 and moved with his growing family to Fort Worth in 1868, where he opened a practice and is said to have brought the first microscope to the city. He and his wife Sara Ellen (Henderson) had seven children.[4] The fourth was a son, William Lipscomb Van Zandt (1875–1948), who married Bell Williams (1882–1965) and fathered three children: two daughters, Mildred and Martha Ann, then a son, Harris Williams Van Zandt, who was born in 1913.[5]

Harris and his sisters grew up on the family farm in Dido, in the rolling, scrub-covered pasturelands northwest of Fort Worth. When the handsome, athletic young man started high school, the family moved into Fort Worth proper. Harris played football in high school and lettered in it at the University of Texas while studying law. The summer before entering UT, he had worked in the oil fields of West Texas, an exercise he believed would build his character. During the next summer, between semesters, Van Zandt worked at the prominent law firm Vinson and Elkins in Houston, where the father of a good friend of his from UT also worked. Harris' friend was Dorothy Townes, and Dorothy's father was John Charles Townes, Jr.[6]

Born in 1886, John Charles Townes, Jr., was a nationally known oil company litigator, himself the son of a founder of the University of Texas Law School in Austin. John Townes, Sr., served as Dean of the Law School for thirty years, and his son took his place when he died, serving until his own death in 1948. John Jr.'s brother, Edgar, born in 1878, was also a prominent Texas lawyer. In 1917, in Houston, he wrote the original charter for the Humble Oil and Refining Company, which later became Exxon. Edgar was also a founder of the South Texas Junior College, later to become part of the University of Houston.[7]

After graduating from law school Harris married Dorothy Townes in 1940 at the River Oaks Baptist Church in Houston. Van Zandt began practicing corporate law with Vinson and El-kins, where he was hired full time after he passed the bar. He was soon assigned to represent a prominent client, the Pure Oil Company of Illinois. Harris and Dorothy's first child, Donna, was born in Houston in 1941, and six weeks later the family moved to Fort Worth. As World War II raged and the oil business boomed, the Van Zandts managed to maintain a comfortable lifestyle, and the family grew.

On March 7, 1944, John Townes Van Zandt was born to Dorothy Townes and Harris Williams Van Zandt, in Fort Worth, Texas, the city that the newborn's great-grandfather had helped settle. Raised to follow the family path into a professional career in law or perhaps even politics, John Townes Van Zandt ultimately pursued neither, instead following his own muse into a very different world, where he added his own to the historical legacy of his ancestors.

# 2

## No Lonesome Tune

J OHN TOWNES VAN ZANDT GREW up between the end of World
War II and the coming of Elvis Presley, a great cusp of the
old and the new in America. It was on this cusp that the
boy, who went by his middle name, formed his first impressions
of the world, gathered his first memories, and began to try to
make sense of his life.

Harris and Dorothy Van Zandt provided a solid family-cen-
tered environment, strongly rooted in the extended Van Zandt
and Townes families in Fort Worth and Houston. While there
were branches of both sides of the family that were considered
wealthy, Harris and Dorothy lived relatively modestly. "We were
the Dido Van Zandts," says their second son, William Lipscomb
Van Zandt. Bill was born in 1949, namesake of the grandfather
who had originally moved his branch of the family out to the
small farming community of Dido. There always "seemed to be
enough" money for the family to be comfortable, but "there was
never a bunch" of money, sister Donna recalls. "I remember my
dad telling stories about how the Depression had absolutely no
effect on his family, except all of a sudden their neighbors were

as poor as they were." She remembers her father telling the family how he had never had ice cream until he was in college, then adding, "you don't miss it if you've never had it."[1]

Harris was a strongly built man with a set gaze and a well-cropped crew cut. He was a tough businessman, a straight arrow, and by all accounts a compassionate father and a Texas gentleman. Dorothy Townes Van Zandt, tall and slim, with dark hair and dark eyes, had grown up in the upper-middle-class environment of a prominent professional family, living in Houston and also on a ranch near Conroe, north of the city. "The family raised Great Danes," Donna remembers, "and they raised some cattle. In every picture of my grandmother, they are surrounded by Great Danes." Dorothy's sister, Anne, was married to Brownie Rice, Sr., of the prominent Houston family that included the founder of Rice University—"old bluebloods," according to a relative[2]—and they lived in one of the mansions that graced the Montrose area of the city. Mr. Rice also owned a ranch west of Houston, where the young Van Zandt family spent a lot of time. Other members of the Rice clan were among the first developers of the prestigious River Oaks neighborhood, which became the home of a number of Dorothy's relations. "The Townes family had their wealth a lot longer," explains a relative. "The Van Zandts were famous in their own right, but they were always country people and farmers."[3]

The oil business was booming in Texas and throughout the West after the war, as new markets opened and production soared to all-time highs. Harris Van Zandt was doing very well as a corporate lawyer, and the family prospered. The family was also quite mobile. Donna recalls, "We moved a lot in Fort Worth. They never bought a house, just rented. When we would outgrow one they would have to rent one a little bit bigger, as the kids grew up." The family maid, Frances, who started working for the Van Zandts shortly before Townes was born, recalls the household scene vividly, and her memories provide a fascinating window into Townes' childhood.[4] "I remember his first birthday," she says. The family was living at 2130 Stanley Av-

—————•◦•—————

enue, in Fort Worth. "Mrs. Van was out of town. I thought if she was home we might have a party." She asked Mr. Van Zandt to invite his mother and sister over for dinner, and Frances baked a cake. "Mrs. Van had some real silver glasses for drinking water. These were used," she recalls. She remembers Townes as a fast-moving child who loved to play outside with a little dog named Sandy and who would climb the fence and generally roughhouse with a boundless energy.

Mr. and Mrs. Van Zandt—known to friends and family as Van and Dotsie—had an active social life, mostly revolving around the extended family. During football season, Dorothy's two sisters and their husbands and children would often visit, going to a game then coming back to the house for dinner. She recalls a time toward the end of the war, when there were still shortages of soap and she was making her own using bacon grease, young Townes climbed up in a chair, took the wooden spoon from the simmering pot of grease, and burned blisters on his mouth from licking the spoon. Another time, Townes was discovered sitting on the bathroom floor playing with a can of strong bathroom cleanser; "Thank the Lord he hadn't eaten any," Frances says.

The Van Zandts were generous with Frances' family, each Christmas helping them out with food and extra funds, and also helping Frances' sister attend college. At one point the Van Zandts took in a foster child, a small boy named Jimmie, who looked up to Townes, enjoyed playing with his toy guns, and treasured the hand-me-down cowboy shirts Townes would give him.

"Townes was a pistol. I used to say this so much," Frances remembers. "He was so lively, and always busy." She recalls a time when Townes sneaked into his sister's room while she had her twin girlfriends over for the night. He hid under the covers of the bed, and refused to be driven out, laughing and forcing the crying girls to turn to Frances for help. She ended up dragging him from the room, and "he was so tickled." As Frances remembers, Donna said to her, "Frances, I want to get married, or be an actress, and change my name ... I know Townes is going to be a gangster."

From Stanley Avenue, the family moved across town to Water Street, then soon after to Washington Street. Townes had a group of playmates in the neighborhood and enjoyed playing baseball and running around with his little dog, Nemo. As Townes got older, he became fond of cowboy stories, and he had a collection of books from which Frances would read to him. Townes and Bill and Jimmie especially liked to play cowboys and would spend hours shooting their toy guns and practicing dramatic death scenes. "At night [Townes] would go to sleep sometimes downstairs," Frances says. "Donna and I could not wake him up, so we would carry him upstairs. She would carry one end and me the other. We would take off his boots and jeans, and he would still be asleep."

The family also liked to spend time at Uncle Brownie Rice's ranch outside of Houston and Townes thrived on the time they spent outdoors at the ranch. One summer, Townes had a bad brush with poison ivy there. A family member recalls, "One year they burned the area trying to get rid of some scrub, and he breathed it, and he spent two weeks in bed with gloves and strapped down; he had it in his lungs ... it was horrible. But Townes would go to the ranch a lot, and that's where I think his love of horses came from. The ranch was beautiful. There was an old rambling farmhouse, and a big bath-house and a swimming pool."[5]

The oil business took the Van Zandts (along with Frances and Jimmie) from Fort Worth to Midland, Texas, in 1952. Harris left Vinson and Elkins and went to work for a small oil company in Midland, but after about six months there he accepted an upper management position with Pure Oil, the company he had represented and with which he was quite familiar. "That's when we moved to Billings, Montana," Donna recalls.

The summer before Townes started fourth grade, Harris took his family to their new home in Montana, over a thousand miles from their roots in Texas. With all the moves, Donna says, "there were times when our family was kind of the only friends we had. I think we were probably closer than some families because we needed one another more at times." However, she remembers their parents always marveling at Townes' ability to go out into a new neighborhood and quickly make friends. "While they were unloading the truck, Townes would go out and come back with a friend for him and a friend for me and a friend for Bill."

Townes was by all accounts a fairly normal, well-adjusted child. He was very intelligent, and he liked school. There were always a lot of books around the Van Zandt house, and Townes was an avid reader from an early age. "The family had a whole set of Harvard Classics and history books and old west novels and stuff that [Townes'] daddy loved," recalls a relative.[6]

"He was just real bright," Donna says. "School was always easy for him." He was also strong and naturally athletic, and he became involved in sports, playing second base on the local Little League baseball team in Billings, and later playing football and wrestling on his school team. His sister remembers a Little League game where Townes hit a long line drive that went in the window of a car a woman was driving down the street. "She stopped and came over and was just yelling," Donna says. "My dad was nice to her, but he said Townes couldn't have possibly done it on purpose; he couldn't do it again on a bet!"

While Donna and Bill were "straight arrows," Donna describes the young Townes as "the free spirit." Both Donna and Bill recall that Townes always loved practical jokes. Bill recalls a stranger approaching Townes once and asking for directions to someplace. "Instead of admitting he didn't know, he answered in Spanish and said he didn't speak English. He'd do that kind of thing." A family tradition, going back to Dorothy's family when she was a child, was to spend the summer months in the mountains around Boulder, Colorado, at the Chautauqua community. The Chautauqua Institution, founded in the 1870s, sponsored large camp-like communities—billed as cultural and educational retreats—often featuring a symphony, theatre, lectures, and other cultural and recreational activities, all in an idyllic, rural setting. The Boulder Chautauqua site is a twenty-six-acre park in the Flatirons, covered with woodland and gardens and laced with mountain hiking and horse trails. Guests are housed in cottages, and a lodge, and other beautiful, turn-of-the-century buildings dot the grounds. Donna recalls, "My mom and both her sisters and all my cousins and Townes and Bill and I would go. The daddies would drive us all up, leave us here, and then they would come up when they could for a long weekend or for their vacation, and then come back later in the summer and take us home." In the six or eight weeks Townes spent in the mountains each summer were the roots of his lifelong love of nature and the outdoors, and of Colorado in particular. Those summers were times Townes relished, and times when he thrived.

In September 1956, Townes started the seventh grade at Lincoln Junior High in Billings. A friend remembers serving with him as a class officer. "I was president and he was vice-president," says Todd Musburger, who later attended high school with Townes in Minnesota. "Ultimately, we were removed from office, both of us, just for too much goofing around, basically." According to Musburger, Townes "made a real positive impression as a fun, funny, sociable, gregarious guy."[7]

That same fall, something happened that changed Townes Van Zandt's life, changed the lives of young people all over America, and ultimately changed American culture. It was Sunday night, the ninth of September, and Townes' sister Donna could literally feel the excitement. "It was such a big deal," she remembers. "I don't know why we picked my house, but that's where we all ended up. We all watched it. All the girls screamed."

*It* was Elvis Presley's first appearance on Ed Sullivan's television show. Elvis sent a startling jolt through American youth, including the young and impressionable Townes Van Zandt. He later remembered, "I just thought Elvis had all the money in the world, all the Cadillacs and all the girls, and all he did was play the guitar and sing. That made a big impression on me."[8]

Three months later, Townes asked his father if he could have a guitar for Christmas. As Townes later told the story, his father

told him he could have a guitar if he learned to play "Fraulein," a sentimental country hit of the time, as his first song.[9]
Townes readily agreed. He got the guitar for Christmas, and
by New Year's he had learned "Fraulein," which he proudly
played for his father and which he continued to play for the
rest of his life.

# 3

## Where I Lead Me

**W**ITHIN A FEW YEARS, THE guitar became for Townes Van Zandt the key to the form of expression that was to become his life's work. Learning the instrument and playing and singing along with the radio and with records quickly became for him something more than just entertainment. Once he'd learned "Fraulein" for his father, he began diligently soaking up the music around him and seeking out more.

"My musical influences were Elvis, Ricky Nelson, Jerry Lee Lewis, Johnny Cash, and the Everly Brothers … it started off with country, then Elvis and those guys …" Van Zandt said.[1] Later, he started listening to jazz and blues, then to folk music. But his grounding was in the great, vital melting pot of country and western and early rock'n'roll that bubbled with such creative fervor in America in the 1950s and early '60s. Townes had been absorbing it all with great interest and enthusiasm since he was a child and would ride with his father as he drove across the countryside visiting the oil fields, listening to Lefty Frizzell, Ernest Tubb, Hank Williams, and Roy Acuff on the car radio. According to Van Zandt, while Elvis had inspired him to take up the guitar, "In the long run, Hank Williams and Lefty Frizzell probably inspired me more, they probably went in deeper to my consciousness."[2]

Radio in the post-war years was flourishing, as were all kinds of recorded music, and a number of the artists who later inspired Townes were just beginning to make an impact: Hank Williams and Lightnin' Hopkins both made their first commercial recordings in 1946; in 1950, Woody Guthrie's *Dustbowl Ballads* was re-released to a growing new audience of young folk music enthusiasts, the same year that Leadbelly's old chestnut "Goodnight, Irene," recorded by the Weavers, was the most popular song of the year; in 1952, Harry Smith's monumental *Anthology of American Folk Music* was released on the Folkways label and began to seep into the underground consciousness; Hank Williams died at the age of twenty-nine in the back seat of his baby-blue Cadillac on New Year's Day 1953, and his rise to lasting fame was launched in earnest; and Sam Phillips was just starting to record blues, country, and the beginnings of rock'n'roll music at his little studio in Memphis, and was putting the records out on his fledgling Sun label. This was the rich musical milieu into which Van Zandt was stepping and hoping to find his place.

As the early rock'n'roll explosion was peaking, and as Townes was gradually growing more proficient on the guitar and more interested in making his own music, Pure Oil again transferred Harris Van Zandt, this time to Denver, Colorado, and the family moved to Boulder in 1958. The Van Zandts were already familiar with the area, having spent so many summers in the woods of Chautauqua. They all liked the Boulder area—which is about twenty miles northwest of Denver—and they settled in quickly. In September, Townes started at Boulder High School, and his sister Donna started as a freshman at the University of Colorado at Boulder.

As a young teenager, Townes naturally began to display some of the qualities that he would carry with him throughout his life. Along with his high intelligence came an increasingly high degree of sensitivity. "Townes felt things more than the rest of us did. It was deeper, somehow," his sister recalls. "You and I would hear about a starving person and go about our lives, but it would just break his heart."[3] One time, as part of a business trip, Harris took Townes and Bill along on a hunting expedition with a client. As Bill recalls, Townes shot a deer, then, devastated, began to cry. Later, Townes' brother "heard mom and dad trying to console him, tell him things were all right, because it was really upsetting to him."[4]

A similar story, recalled by a friend, goes further back in Townes' childhood. When Townes was five or six years old, his parents took him to a restaurant where there were live lobsters in a tank, and he was told he could pick out his own lobster. "So he thought that he was picking out a pet to take home, and he went, 'Oh, boy.' He was thinking, 'Oh, boy, I've got a new pet. I can't wait. I can't wait.' And when they sat the plate in front of him … he was terribly upset. They were at a big round table with a lot of other people, and his father was sensitive enough to realize what had happened. He leaned over and said, 'I know, Townes, I know. Just try to hang in there.' And Townes would never forget it."[5]

In school in Boulder, Townes also began, typically, to show signs of rebelliousness. It was the rebelliousness of youth, and it was the dawn of an era of rebelliousness, but it was also the seed of a rebelliousness that was to mark Townes' adult personality. His brother remembers an early instance of the relatively innocent variety of rebellion. "When he was in high school, he went out with my mom, shopping for school clothes. And he bought a very, very bright red pair of pants, a bright green pair of pants, and a bright yellow pair of pants. I mean, just real neon colored green, red, and yellow. And he started wearing them…. I don't know why he would do that, because he was kind of shy in a lot of ways." Bill recalls that the colorful pants started a trend. "Other kids started wearing them," he says. "The school got all upset, and one day they called mom and told her to come get him and make him change his clothes and not wear those pants back again. He liked to poke his finger in the eye of authority."[6]

Townes continued to play the guitar and sing—Johnny Cash songs, Hank Williams, some Elvis numbers, some folk songs—

for himself and now more and more for the family and occasionally for friends. "He would go up in the mountains with a friend, and they wouldn't take any food," Donna recalls. "When they got hungry, they would look around for somebody's campfire and they would play their guitars in exchange for food." But mostly his playing was confined to family gatherings, of which there were many. Harris and Dorothy traveled with Donna, Townes, and Bill back to Texas whenever they could, and they always made it for the family gatherings that were a big part of their lives. "They would always have a family talent show. Townes would play the guitar and be at the center of it," notes Bill. Another story has Harris sometimes secretly putting Townes' guitar in the trunk of his car before going to a family get-together. When Townes was approached and asked to play, he'd say he didn't have his guitar with him. "His father would say, 'Yes we do,' which would infuriate Townes, but he would always agree to play."[7]

One summer in these years, Townes fell off a horse while he was camping in the mountains, and he broke his finger. "He said he would have much rather broken a leg," Donna says. "It's very difficult to play the guitar when you have a broken finger."

Townes maintained a solid B average in high school,[8] but before he was able to settle very comfortably into life in Boulder, Harris delivered the news that the family would be moving yet again, this time to Barrington, Illinois, outside of Chicago. This was not a move that anyone in the family wanted to make; nevertheless, in the middle of the 1958–59 school year, Townes started at yet another new school. Donna remained at college in Boulder, now a sophomore, relieved to be staying put. Dorothy, Donna, Townes, and Bill again vacationed in Boulder that summer, joined later by Harris, who was beginning to feel the mounting pressures of his position at the oil company and seemed to really need the vacation.

There is a story that one day Townes came home from school to find his father very upset, weeping, because he had had to lay off thousands of company employees that day.[9] "My dad had that kind of a job, particularly in Illinois," Bill remembers. "When there was dirty work to be done, my dad had to go and negotiate and do things like that. That's the kind of thing that gave dad ulcers. He really loved people, but he had jobs where he had to confront people and do some things that weren't pleasant."[10] This pressure and frustration was to have a predictably negative effect on Harris Van Zandt's health. It also brought a dark element into the life of the family that did not escape the darkly inclined teenaged Townes.

Even with all the upheaval, and even with his growing reputation as something of a rebel, Townes continued to do well in school, had a decent social life, and continued to read widely. He also continued to seek out records to feed his growing interest in music, and he continued to practice the guitar. By the late fifties, the guitar was becoming a very popular instrument with young people all over the country. By 1958, more guitars were being sold in the United States than ever before; the Kingston Trio sold four million copies of their recording of the old folk standard "Tom Dooley"; and the new folk boom—the "folk scare," as some remember it—reached its first early peak. A young University of Minnesota student whose family name was Zimmerman began performing at a coffeehouse in Minneapolis that year, billing himself for the first time as Bob Dylan. The time was ripe, and as a musician, Townes was in a crucial formative phase, internalizing the music, seeking guidance wherever he could find it, and practicing incessantly. That year one of his friends dared Townes to take the stage at an upcoming school talent show and show them all what he could do. With a swagger and a swallow, Townes accepted the dare.

Dorothy Van Zandt drove her son from the Van Zandt house on Biltmore Drive to the school that evening and waited outside in the car while he went inside with his guitar. When his turn came, Townes played three songs, a natural if somewhat eclectic mix of Elvis Presley, Ricky Nelson, and Hank Williams. The girls screamed when he sang, "because it was in vogue at the time,"

Townes figured. "I went through the crowd, everybody patted me on the back, and I got instant acclaim in my junior high," he said. "I fell in with all the best guys and girls immediately."[11] And he had his first taste of what he'd sensed when he first saw Elvis on television: the thrill of stardom. Townes' mother later said that she had secretly observed the performance from outside, looking through the ground-level window of the basement cafeteria on her hands and knees. This was Townes Van Zandt's first public performance.[12]

Townes coasted through his classes at Barrington High School, not particularly inspired. He was getting B's and C's, with a few A's in English, social studies, and physical education, but he was still not well settled—understandably—and, according to his siblings, he was desperately craving stability.[13] "Townes was afraid we were going to move again," Bill recalls, "and he wanted to go to the same school his junior and senior years. So his junior year he made the decision to go to Shattuck, a boarding school." Donna also recalls the decision to attend Shattuck being Townes', and she also says that he was simply seeking some kind of stability.

A classmate and friend of Townes at Shattuck says he couldn't imagine Townes "seeking that kind of rigidity."[14] Another classmate at Shattuck had a similar impression. "I got a feeling that all wasn't well at Barrington High, and they saw the need for more structure for young John Townes. I'm afraid they offered Shattuck up, and Shattuck was good for what it was, but Townes was a pretty hot article."[15]

Founded in 1858, Shattuck Military Academy, in Faribault, Minnesota, was one of the oldest and most respected college preparatory boarding schools in the Midwest, known for rigid military discipline and strong academics, all situated on a classical-looking campus dominated by massive greystone Gothic buildings. In addition, Shattuck administrators were used to dealing with "hot articles": they had, for example, seen fit to expel young Marlon Brando in 1941, his senior year. On the other hand, Hubert H. Humphrey III graduated in the Class of 1961, and a great many graduates went on to positions of prominence.

"Shattuck was a mix of kids that were probably good citizens before they came to Shattuck, and also kids that had had some sort of run-in in their hometown," classmate Todd Musburger recalls. "Nothing real serious, usually, but probably the parents or the school saying, 'we think your son would do better in a military school,' or strict parents saying, 'I'm gonna straighten you out.' ... And some kids were just dropped on Shattuck's doorstep because of parents that had money and sent them away. But when Townes arrived, my thought was, well, maybe something had happened."

Another classmate, Marshall Froker, has a similar recollection. "There were a lot of stories floating around," he says. One was that "Townes had gotten into some kind of trouble back in Barrington. There were various versions of it, that there had been some row with another kid, and it may have involved a girl and it may have involved something that happened on the school property, and may have concerned his family enough, or may have gotten him in the kind of trouble where going off to military school is the way you avoid having a police record or ending up with probation or in some kind of disciplinary situation. But he wouldn't talk about it."[16]

Townes' good friend from college Bob Myrick asked Townes about Shattuck some years later, and Townes told him simply, "I did that for dad."[17]

At any rate, Townes Van Zandt joined the Academy Class of 1962 in the fall of 1960 to start his junior year of high school. The conflicts he was beginning to experience in his life surely became important ingredients in what must have been a very complex decision, however it was taken.

According to Townes, at Shattuck he got "a real serious private prep-school ivy-covered education."[18] He also got an intensive introduction to military discipline. "When we were there," says classmate Froker, "it was a full-bore Army ROTC program. It was 'cadet this' and 'cadet that.'" Junior "new boy" cadet Van

Zandt was assigned to room with a young freshman from Oklahoma named Luke Sharpe, with whom he shared an interest
in athletics. "He was a football player and a wrestler, and I was
both of those things," Sharpe recalls. "So we got along in that
regard. Plus he was from Texas, I was from Oklahoma, and in
Minnesota that's a pretty good bond."[19]

Academically, Townes started out fairly well at Shattuck.
Grades were given on a numbered scale, from 60 up to 100,
and in his first semester, Townes scored an 83 in English and in
Spanish, a 79 in geography, a 73 in algebra, and an 81 in military training.[20] "In classes, we were grouped by perceived ability," says Sharpe. "Townes wasn't a number one. But he wasn't
bad: number two, maybe number three, that would be Townes.
But I have to say, our number ones were pretty good guys. A lot
of Stanfords, a lot of Harvards."

Townes' grades slipped somewhat after his first semester; he
would only receive one more "honor" grade (higher than 80) at
Shattuck, an 85 in sociology and economics. That senior-year
high point came along with a 74 in English and a 72 in trigo-
nometry, among other mediocre marks. He scored 133 on the
Hermon-Nelson IQ test in 1960, and 128 the following year.
Townes took the SATs in January 1962, and scored an impressive
614 on the verbal test and 556 on the math test. When he took
his College Board exams in June 1961, he listed the University
of Texas, the University of Colorado, and Northwestern University as his first choices for college. On a "vocational interest" test
in 1960, Townes' highest rating was for "musician (performer),"
followed by "real estate salesman." Just below that was "artist,"
and below that, "lawyer."

According to Townes' brother, who attended the Academy
years later for his freshman year, Townes was a popular student
who had a number of mentors among the faculty, including the
headmaster, who seemed to take Townes under his wing, and
the football coach. Bill remembers his rebelliousness manifest-
ing itself even on the wrestling team. He recalls a time that all
the wrestlers decided to shave their heads. "Townes went the

opposite route and grew his hair down to his shoulders. And this was before the Beatles and stuff, so it was really outlandish," Bill says. He adds that his brother was also interested in the dramatic arts at Shattuck, and he vividly remembers Townes being in a play, where he sang "Down in the Valley" and played a Snidely Whiplash-style villain.[21]

All of Townes' classmates remember him as a good athlete. His Shattuck records show that he played football and baseball and wrestled, as he had done since junior high school. Froker played football with Townes and recalls, "In his junior year, he was probably still developing and a little bit on the lean side." Luke Sharpe remembers the "tall, rangy, 147-pound or so" Van Zandt as a good, but not great, wrestler as well. "Townes was okay," Sharpe recalls. "He was quick enough. But athletics didn't consume him. Music was the deal, always, with Townes."

Musburger recollects the musical environment at Shattuck at that time: "The guitar was not mainstream music. I think most of us were Miles Davis lovers and Dave Brubeck lovers. Some of the kids from the South would come in with Bo Diddley records, but this is still the time of 'A Summer Place' and the Lettermen and Johnny Mathis. Music had not taken off; there was just a smattering of rock getting through to us." Marshall Froker recalls that Townes "would just play guitar a lot, and I would hang out in his room. He listened a lot to Josh White, and he liked Elvis, and a lot of whatever was going on in blues-based rock'n'roll. He had a very good record collection." As Townes' roommate Luke remembers, "He had an Elvis Presley collection that was unbelievable. And he was my introduction to Leadbelly, whom I had never heard. There was a little bit of Leadbelly, and a lot of Southern blues-type stuff. Ray Charles too...."

Froker recalls:

> In fact, one of my roommates that year, he and I played around with the bongos. Townes heard us once and walked in with his guitar. As I recall, we were sitting around the room and he said "Why don't you play along with me?" He would play some

---

stuff on the guitar, and I would sort of pick it up on the bongos, and it worked. I remember a staple for us was "I Got A Woman," things like that. It was the early sixties, and there was some R&B floating around. And there was a Johnny Cash album freshly out called *Ride This Train*, and Townes covered a few things from that. There was a song he did called "Train I Ride," I think, and he did some Elvis and some Gene Vincent things....[22]

In between songs he didn't want to talk much, he just would sort of look down at his guitar and try to work through the changes. He'd sit there for awhile and there'd just be this silence, and then he'd say, "okay, let's do this one," and he'd try something else.... One time, I actually performed with Townes at some minor social function involving the St. Mary's Hall girls. It was our junior year, and I remember he did "Train I Ride," he did "I Got A Woman," and he did some other things. He was a big hit with the ladies, as you can imagine.

Townes would often discuss music with his friends, and Sharpe recalls one occasion when he became involved in a conversation about folk music. "There was a little bit of folk music around, like the Kingston Trio and the Lamplighters and Peter, Paul & Mary, and someone asked, 'Do you play any folk music?' And Townes didn't answer directly, but he got into how there just wasn't any good cowboy music around anymore, not exactly putting down the folk music that was out there, but quite impassioned about how good that old stuff was, and he mentioned Hank Williams and some others.... Joan Baez was just getting started, and I think he might have been conscious of her, and I think he liked her." Dylan was around as well, but "not in general circulation" yet at Shattuck, he recalls.

Sharpe recalls that while Van Zandt never got into serious trouble at Shattuck, "he was well known as a rebel. Townes didn't care, he learned certainly enough, he was smart enough for that, but he didn't pay any attention to the basic rule of a police state, which is, you obey the little rules, you shine your shoes, look nice, turn out well, hit all your appointments on time, and then you can break the big rules. Well, Townes was a scofflaw at every point. So consequently he was not too highly regarded by those in power. Townes was just a law unto himself," Sharpe says. "The time that we lived together, we were juniors, and they didn't really bear down on you hard until your senior year. But Townes was his own counterculture when I lived with him, certainly. He did lots of drinking, which didn't bother me too much. Then he got into glue sniffing and so forth in his senior year. But always, Townes was a hedonist, first, last, and always...."

Sharpe recalls the rebellious Van Zandt forming a clandestine group called The Syndicate. "I think it was mostly a figment of Townes' imagination," says Sharpe. "But I was a member, nominally. There was a group called the Crack Squad there.... It was a precision drill team kind of deal. They were the crème de la crème of Shattuck society. Well, Van Zandt, ever with the feel for the counterculture, developed The Syndicate, which was his version of the underworld. Who knows how many people were in it...." According to Bill Van Zandt, The Syndicate "would play music, very loud, right next to the Crack Squad practices and try to mess them up. And at the school there was a tradition about the Crack Squad, where new boys couldn't even refer to them. You had to pretend they didn't exist.... And Townes went out of his way to try to violate that rule whenever he could."

"I would sum up Townes' attitude like this," says Marshall Froker. "He was the guy who stood there in formation in his military hat ... and he managed to wear it at just the right jaunty angle so as not to cross the line." Musburger remembers Van Zandt committing various minor infractions, many stemming from the rather repressive social structure the young cadets labored under, but nothing too serious. "If we wanted to go see a girl, we had to write a letter, and the girl had to go down and put us on the list. That was called 'calling.' We went 'calling' to St. Mary's." Froker elaborates: "Basically the interaction was highly supervised, very controlled, but you could sneak around, and a lot of guys did. There was a St. Mary's girl who was really taken with Townes in his senior year. He was a good wrestler, and they had a tournament up in Minneapolis, where she lived. Between matches, the two of them went off to some janitor's closet somewhere and got it on. I heard that from a couple of different people who swore it was true."

Some of Townes' other later proclivities surfaced at Shattuck as well. One of them was gambling. Says Froker, "if you went into Townes' room, it wouldn't be long before he pulled out a deck of cards and said, 'come on.' Most people, including myself, knew that Townes was a pretty good poker player.... Most kids that age, we'd be sort of conservative—even though it was just pennies or whatever, it was real money—but he would just really go for it, and raise and raise again and again. He won a lot because people would generally just back down."

Luke Sharpe recalls driving with Townes to Indiana in Mrs. Van Zandt's Thunderbird in their junior year, and reflects that "he was certainly indulged, and he was offered every opportunity, which Townes, in my opinion, resolutely rejected." Luke and Townes grew apart after their junior year, and for very specific reasons. "I was just more of an organization kind of man. I had done well in the military, been a floor officer, et cetera. I had been there longer than Townes had been. So I was much more of an institutional kind of boy than Townes. Senior year, we lived in different dorms.... And by then he was doing a lot of glue."

Townes had most likely started sniffing glue sometime in his junior year, but as a senior, it became habitual. Glue-sniffing among teenagers in the mid-1960s was not terribly uncommon, especially where alcohol was hard to come by and before marijuana became more widely available. But it was—and is—a dangerous intoxicant, and the pursuit of that kind of a serious "buzz" represented something of a dividing line between students just looking for fun and those with more extreme proclivities.

As Sharpe puts it, "Even among the guys who were not following all the rules, he was still pretty out there. He was pushing it." Somehow, an incriminating photograph of Townes appeared in the Shattuck yearbook at the end of his senior year: "Townes with a tube of Testors [glue] jammed up his nose," as

Sharpe recalls. "He did graduate and move right along, notwithstanding those pictures in the yearbook," but, Sharpe says, "it was trouble." Other classmates recall, similarly, if in less graphic detail, that Van Zandt indeed graduated in spite of some vague, questionable circumstances. Shattuck records show that he graduated ranked at number twenty-two in a class of seventy-six students.

Harris Van Zandt came up with a way to help his son focus his energies that summer: he sent Townes to Pecos, in West Texas, to work with a seismograph crew in the oil fields. Mr. Van Zandt most likely intended to effect in his son what had been effected in him when he worked in the oil fields as a young man: a strengthening of character. But it's possible too that he was testing him. Townes had graduated from military school—an accomplishment about which Harris must have had doubts at some points—but he was still "different"; he had not "hardened." Hence, to Pecos Townes went. He worked with a crew for a few weeks, then, with two weeks left to work, he lit out for Dallas, unannounced and unbeknownst to his parents. He stayed with a friend from Shattuck there, then with another friend in Fort Worth, then he hitchhiked to Oklahoma, to Luke Sharpe's farm. He told his parents of his exploits only after he returned home. Harris knew that he had more work to do.[23]

Some of Townes' friends and classmates at Shattuck reflect the view that Luke Sharpe summed up years later, that Townes had always been a "creative type," and that creative types "can be pretty hard bipolar characters; and that was Townes in a nutshell," says Sharpe. "He was prone to stimulants, prone to bursts of creativity, and then prone to the depths of depression. That's our boy.... But I never saw Townes as a weak person, or as controlled by substances. This was always a clear choice by Townes."

# 4

## No Place to Fall

**A**FTER GRADUATING FROM SHATTUCK AND surviving summer in the West Texas oil fields, much to his relief, Townes Van Zandt was accepted at the University of Colorado at Boulder in September 1962, the fall after his sister Donna graduated. He loved Colorado, loved the Boulder area, and, short of following in his parents' footsteps to the University of Texas, CU was an obvious choice for Townes. The Van Zandts had just moved back to Texas, to Houston, where Harris had accepted a position as vice president of the Transwestern Pipeline Company—something less stressful, hopefully, than his work with the giant Pure Oil—and Townes naturally liked the idea of staying far from home. He signed up for a general liberal arts schedule at Colorado. "I hit that place like a saddle bronc hits the arena—coming right out of military school and all," Townes later said.[1]

His dramatic description is only partially misleading. Before hitting CU "like a saddle bronc," Townes had a false start and quietly withdrew from school on October 8, after barely a month of classes. He had first phoned his parents and told them that he was uncomfortable, and that he was sure he just wasn't ready to get serious about college. They thought they had convinced him to stick out the semester. Instead, Townes dropped out and hitchhiked to Minnesota, where he stayed with an old girlfriend near Shattuck. After a couple of days, Townes wandered onto the Shattuck campus and went to see his old acquaintance, the headmaster, who decided to try to help Townes' cause.

Townes was confused and discontented, but he trusted the headmaster and claimed he wanted to work. With a combination of understanding and indulgence, the headmaster laid out a list of teaching and coaching duties he thought Townes could perform if he were to accept a position there at Shattuck. He then promptly phoned the Van Zandts and explained that Townes was there, that he wanted to work, and that he would give Townes a chance.[2]

Two weeks later, Townes was back at his parents' house at 6322 Deerwood in Houston. Exactly what Townes told his parents about his reticence to either work or start college is unclear. He later told a doctor that he started experiencing increased feelings of depression during this period, but it is not clear that he revealed this to his parents at the time. Harris was apparently willing to give Townes time to get his bearings if he needed to, but there's little doubt that he was somewhat perturbed. It is likely that Harris told his son at this point to make up his mind quickly. Townes spent the holidays in the bosom of his family as he prepared to return to Colorado for a second try at college in the upcoming spring semester.

Now, the saddle bronc hit the arena. Classes almost immediately became secondary to other pursuits. Townes' drinking and substance abuse, at first sporadic and experimental at Shattuck, soon became methodical and habitual, and the pattern of mood swings he had exhibited in his later teen years became steadily more pronounced. As Van Zandt told the story, during his freshman year he would shut himself up in his apartment for days at a time, staying drunk on cheap wine, listening to records, and playing the guitar. "Then," Townes later said to a journalist, "I'd come out at the end of a week of this and throw a giant party."

This is how Van Zandt told the story of his most infamous youthful stunt to that writer:

> I lived on the fourth story of this apartment building, and at one point during one of these parties I went out and sat on the edge of the balcony and started leanin' backwards. I decided I was gonna lean over and just see what it felt like all the way up to where you lost control and you were falling. I realized that to do it I'd have to fall. But I said, "Hell, I'm gonna do it anyway." So I started leanin' back really slow and really payin' attention, and I fell. Fell over backwards and landed four stories down. Flat on my back. I remember the impact and exactly what it felt like and all the people screamin'. I had a bottle of wine and I stood up. Hadn't spilled any wine. Felt no ill effects whatsoever. Meanwhile, all the people had jammed onto the elevator, an' when the doors opened I was standin' there and they knocked me over coming out—an' it hurt more bein' knocked over than fallin' four stories.[3]

Van Zandt's roommate in that apartment was Bob Myrick, a Boulder native and fellow freshman. He and Townes had met at Tulagi's, a popular nightspot on University Hill in Boulder, just off campus, where bands played and students danced and drank 3.2 beer, and where both Van Zandt and Myrick were employed part time, working the door and doing odd jobs. "At that time, Tulagi's was the third-leading beer seller in the nation. Colorado has always been kind of a party school, because of the skiing," Myrick says. "Townes started working at Tulagi's, ... and after a few months we decided to room together, and we moved into this little place called Varsity Manor, a block or so off campus."

Myrick remembers Van Zandt having what he called "a drinking problem" from the earliest days of that first semester. "Actually, Townes was a rather abusive fellow," Myrick says. "Back then we all did a lot of partying, a lot of drinking. But Townes drank every day; every day. And it was horrible rotgut that we used to drink. There were two types of wine, one was called Showboat, and the other Bali Hai. It tastes like Robitussin. We had tons and tons of empty bottles of Bali Hai around." Myrick recalls having a lot of parties at the apartment, most of them less crazed than the one that featured Townes going over the balcony. "He didn't fall; he jumped," Myrick says of the notorious occasion, "and it was the third floor. We were all blasted. I think it was just alcohol. And he was standing on the balcony, and he had his cowboy boots on, and he said 'I wonder if I'd break my leg if I jumped.' We just looked at him like he was nuts. And he did it. He sprained his ankle but he didn't break anything. And the landing was not soft."[4] The story almost instantly assumed legendary status on campus.

Harris Van Zandt had bought a 1961 Chevy Impala 409 for Townes to drive at college that spring, but Townes kept it parked at Varsity Manor. Myrick recalls, "He almost never drove it, because a lot of times he was just too drunk to drive. We'd walk up to Tulagi's, which was only about four blocks." Another thing Myrick recollects is Townes coming out to play softball. "In the early days," he says, "when I was pitching for Tulagi's softball team, he would play on the team occasionally. He was a pretty good hitter, but he played in his cowboy boots, and he always had a bottle of wine with him. Once he hit a home run, but going from third to home he fell down, only about ten feet from home. He was called out, and he had crawled on his hands and knees the last ten feet, and he was just about to put his hand on the plate, and they called him out. We wouldn't let him play a lot, because he was always drunk."

Van Zandt made it through his first year of college much as he had made it through high school: with minimal effort. Townes' report card for his first complete semester (spring 1962–63) shows four C's and an F. The failing grade was in freshman English, which he retook that summer for a B (along with principles of economics 1 and 2, in which he received a B and a D, respectively).[5]

Later that summer, Townes visited his old roommate from Shattuck, Luke Sharpe, in Checotah, in eastern Oklahoma. "He just dropped in, kind of an itinerant, which I would expect from Townes, drifting from here to there," Sharpe says. Sharpe was

———•◆•———

working on a hay crew, and as Sharpe recalls, "When they put up hay, they would put it up in a square bale, which weighs about sixty-six and two-thirds pounds, and they stack this stuff in a barn. So you have hay crews, and it was the standard practice for young kids who want to make a little money, or want to get in shape—which was my particular project, having gotten interested in athletics—to work on a crew. And Townes came down and said, 'yeah, I'll work on the hay crew with you.' So for three weeks or so we worked on the hay crews in Oklahoma."[6]

Van Zandt proved to be a good worker, but, according to Sharpe, "always a smart aleck and always a needle artist. I thought he was gonna get killed by a couple of black guys on the crew, but hey, that's just Townes.... Townes on his best days was certainly loosely wired."

That same summer, Van Zandt and Sharpe went to a dance at the Muskogee Country Club. As Sharpe recalls, "Through his ill-chosen words—although I think he chose them on purpose, actually—we ended up in a fight in the parking lot. But that was just life with Townes. Townes loved to play the edge—first, last, and always." Sharpe also recalls distinctly that Townes was drinking heavily that summer, and that he had a new favorite drink: "cherry vodka; as much as he could handle."

After returning to Boulder in September 1963 for his sophomore year, Townes met Fran Petters, a bright, pretty, seventeen-year-old blonde Southern Baptist girl from Houston. As Fran recalls their first meeting, Townes was working the door at Tulagi's, and as she tried to walk in the front door, Townes stopped her and told her she'd have to give him a kiss to get in. "Then he got embarrassed," Fran says, and shortly afterward, "he sent me flowers to apologize for being fresh. Then he said that if I was from Houston he would marry me. It was kind of instant love."[7]

Fran was working for the president of the university and lived in a garage apartment behind the president's house. "Townes and I were both in the arts and sciences school," she says. "I was studying math and science, and he was just taking the basic curriculum.

Most of the time he was figuring he was going to be in pre-law.... He was always being pointed in that direction, toward a professional career of some kind." That he would follow a professional path was indeed what Townes continued to tell his family, and what he now told Fran. How much he believed it at this point is another question. Townes' classes that semester comprised American government, his second semester of freshman English, general psychology, philosophy, and physical education. He ultimately received a B in government and C's in the other classes.

"Townes was brilliant," Fran says. "He had a genius I.Q. Everything came very easy in studying. He never went to class, but still he'd make whatever grades he decided he wanted to make. But he was always trying to lead his friends astray, to talk them into skipping class. One of the things we would always do," Fran recalls, "all of us would meet at some place on the Hill for lunch. And Townes would always say to one of his friends, 'So, do you want to go to class or do you want a beer sandwich?' And they chose the beer sandwich every time."

Despite her boyfriend's erratic behavior, Fran remembers that semester at Boulder as a period of very good times with Townes. They socialized with other student couples and often engaged in some outdoor activity or other, including numerous climbs up Boulder Canyon. "There was one great picnic we had with this other couple," she recalls. "This guy, when he married this girl in college, his dad disowned him, made him go on his own for awhile. So we always did things that didn't cost any money.... This guy would hunt; that's how he filled his freezer.... So he provided the meat and we brought baked potatoes or whatever it was, and we went up [the canyon]. There was an old abandoned train station up there, and we had a picnic, a cookout."

Another picnic sticks fondly in Fran's memory. "One time Townes asked me to go on a picnic and the weather turned really bad. He said, 'Well, I really want to go on a picnic; come over to the apartment at such and such a time.' So I came over and he had the living room all set up with a stream and a little tree, and the picnic on the floor with wine and cheese and everything. It was really funny."

Fran was not much of a drinker—"I'd barely had a glass of wine before I got to college," she says—but for the most part she tolerated Townes' drinking, figuring that it didn't seem that much more excessive than that of other students they knew. She also knew well the story of Townes' fall from the balcony the previous year—knew a variety of versions of the story, in fact, as it varied depending on who was telling it—and also remembers other instances of Townes' risk-taking. "Townes and his good friend, Tom Barrow, thought of themselves as mountain climbers," says Fran. "But they would only do it after having a few beers. We would all be sitting around after dinner, listening to music, just kind of a typical evening, and somewhere around eleven o'clock all of a sudden one of them would say, 'Let's go climb the Flatiron!'"

"One night I said, 'You all can't go unless I go.' So we wound up climbing the Flatiron. When they put a rope around me, it was probably the safest they ever were, because they were afraid that I was going to get hurt. So they wound up hauling me up with this rope around my waist, then hauling me down. I was scared to death. This was in the middle of the night. It was for the adrenaline rushes that they would get." Townes finally quit, she says, after a nasty fall during a tough climb in Boulder Canyon. "It scared him," she says. "He was taken to the hospital ... and treated for cuts and bruises and a cracked rib."

Other times were less harrowing, but perhaps just as indicative of Van Zandt's later proclivities. "I can remember one time driving up on the Hill. Townes had that Chevy 409, and we were just so cool. We had just been waving at our friends, who were inside one of the little gathering joints up on the Hill. I don't remember him having a drink at all, we were just cutting class, and he drove into the back of a police car. So, my God, what smart-aleck thing did Townes say to the cop? He says, 'What were you doing backing up?'"

Bob Myrick confirms that throughout this time, Townes continued to be immersed in his music. He was listening to Hoyt Axton and Dave Van Ronk records intensely, Myrick remembers, and a lot of Delta blues. "He also played a lot of Jimmy Reed, a lot of John Lee Hooker. He was amazing; he'd hear a song and he could just pick it up in a matter of minutes. He spent a lot of time learning the guitar, drinking Bali Hai and playing at home." Myrick also remembers Mississippi John Hurt, Sonny Terry and Brownie McGhee, Blind Lemon Jefferson, and Lightnin' Hopkins records being objects of intense study by his roommate. By the time the Beatles came along in 1964, "It didn't affect us much," Myrick says. "Townes liked the Beatles, but he never played any of their songs."

It was also during this time that Bob Dylan's first records were making their way onto the scene. "I introduced Townes to Dylan," recalls Myrick.

> I remember the gal I was going with, her name was Hobie ... and she introduced us to Dylan's first album. I took it home, I played it, and Townes and I looked at each other and said, "I don't know." And we started playing it, and playing it, and playing it, more and more. And we loved it. And then we got into the lyrics. One of the first songs off that album that Townes learned was "One Too Many Mornings"; he played that a lot.
>
> Every time Townes would play—sometimes he'd play around Boulder a little bit; I managed a little place later on called Barefoot Charlie's, and he would play there—he'd always play "One Too Many Mornings." Another song that he particularly was interested in on that first album was "In My Time of Dying." He latched onto that like it was an old friend. "In my time of dying, I don't want nobody to mourn ...". And "Gospel Plow," that was another favorite of his. He had started to write some of his stuff by then too. He'd write down lyrics frequently, but it was really more of a collegiate type of thing.

———•◆•———

Myrick remembers hearing the beginnings of some songs that Townes later developed more fully—for example, an early version of what was to become "Tecumseh Valley." "Sometimes I would ask Townes, I'd say, 'What do you really mean by that lyric?' and he'd say, 'Whatever you want it to mean.' He would seldom explain his lyrics."

Of the songs that Van Zandt continued to play throughout his life, his most "collegiate" song was "Fraternity Blues," a funny talking blues piece which is one of Van Zandt's oldest surviving compositions. It is also a model for some of his other early songs: the talking blues form, taken straight from Woody Guthrie by way of Bob Dylan, always featuring droll humor combined with deft timing, good rhythm, and a personal point of view.[8]

"He wrote that while we were roommates," Myrick says of "Fraternity Blues." "Townes' father was a Sigma Nu, and Townes actually pledged Sigma Nu, although that was never something that he really wanted to do. He did it for his father.... And he never got past pledge; he never went active.... Franny was a Kappa Kappa Gamma, pretty much the number-one sorority on campus."

Myrick remembers witnessing one of Townes' most bizarre college pranks. "We were all drinking very heavily," Myrick says.

> Sigma Nu was having a formal dance, and another friend that worked at Tulagi's with us named Woody, and Townes and I, we were drinking right next door in the annex, and we were pretty ripped. We weren't really going to partake in the dance because it was all formal, and we had our grubbies on, and Townes and I went over to the fraternity for the sole reason of getting a pitcher of punch and taking it back to the annex, and the actives started giving him a ration about being a horrible pledge and not giving a shit.... Townes had put his pledge pin in his pocket, and he walked over to the punch bowl, and some of the actives started giving him shit again, and he stuck his pin right into his skin, kind of bent it around and stuck it right in, and it started trickling blood, and he says, "There." At the time, we thought it was funny. Maybe it's a little pathetic now, but it shocked them right into silence.

Van Zandt's roommate also remembers an increasingly clear underlying element in Townes' temperament. "Townes was kind of a dark fellow," he says. "That's the way he looked at life. He *knew* it was that way. It was almost like Tennessee Williams' *Suddenly Last Summer*. He was about that dark. We both liked Tennessee Williams and would talk about him now and then. Townes kind of looked at life through *The Glass Menagerie*." Myrick tended to avoid engaging Townes' darker tendencies, instead focusing on his strong sense of humor. Fran tended to do the same. According to Myrick, Townes' dark pronouncements "often came out, especially with women, as almost pious. We used to call him a pious pig. Franny'd say 'Oh, Townes, don't be such a pig.' But when he played music, it was a different ballgame. He had a lot of feeling. We knew that there was a sacred side of Townes, the inside of Townes, that he seldom revealed. He was able to see life the way it was."

Myrick recalls that starting during this period, when he and Van Zandt went to bars, "Townes wanted to go to the raunchiest, skuzziest dives ever. He was just more comfortable with those people. He was very uncomfortable with college types, although he made some good friends. But if we were in Denver, we would be on skid row.... He liked real people; he couldn't abide with hypocrisy in any way. He wanted nothing but honesty from people, and he found that in aristocrats and in winos, but mostly in winos."

A rift that had long existed in Townes' life was starting to widen that year at Colorado. "He wanted to be faithful to what the family wanted of him," Fran says, but he was also "trying to figure out what he wanted to be himself." She recalls the atmosphere of the times, in the early and mid-1960s, particularly among college students, as being full of philosophical examination of the status quo and serious reevaluation of priorities. But Townes' sensitivity, the depth of his questioning, raised the stakes for him. "It seems like at that time, he knew he was meant to do something else, but he just didn't know what it was," according to Fran. "He wanted to please the family, but he also wanted to stay true to himself. And it was a real battle."

Fran makes clear, as do Townes' siblings, that it wasn't that the family was putting explicit pressure on Townes to pursue any particular course. "He just felt the implicit expectation," Fran says. "There was very definitely etiquette taught to them, but not necessarily that they had to be something or somebody in particular." Bill Van Zandt also says he never felt that kind of pressure from the family. He recalls that their father "would encourage us to find our own way. I got the feeling that Townes put some pressure on himself, like he wasn't living up to expectations in certain areas. And that would really get him down."[9]

This conflict was playing itself out in a number of ways in Townes' life. "Townes was always abusing something," Fran says, dating it back to his glue sniffing at Shattuck. She describes his drinking at college as binge drinking. "It wasn't that he did it all the time," she says. "It was just that when he did it he would go off and really do it." Myrick sees it differently. "Fran didn't really like him drinking like that. She'd go out and have a few drinks, but she wasn't a big drinker. She was a very, very serious student, an A student, and an extremely smart, extremely intelligent woman. So when we got down to the real nitty-gritty, get-down-and-dirty party, she'd usually leave, or she wouldn't even come." It is possible that Fran was simply not aware, because Townes kept it from her and she kept herself from it, that he was in fact drinking every day, a pattern confirmed by his roommate and others.

Also emerging in Townes' life at this same time was the pattern of extended periods of dark depression, of what became complete withdrawal from society, followed by periods of exultation, confidence, and social command. "He would be just very happy, and in real party moods," Fran remembers, "but then he would go off and want to be by himself. He would be overly reclusive." Again, Fran felt that Townes was not so different from many other college students in his behavior; certainly not different in kind, if perhaps more intense in degree. But the trouble came to a head early in the spring semester of 1964 when Townes decided he needed to leave school and travel for a little while.

"Townes wanted to go 'on the road,' as he would say," Fran recalls. "His family called it 'running away.' He called it 'going on the road.' . . He left school in the middle of the semester to do that. For some reason, he loved Oklahoma, and he went to Oklahoma, where another guy [Luke Sharpe] from Shattuck lived.... And there was this thing in him of wanting to know what poor people lived like, you know? Because any time he went out, he was always sort of going among the downtrodden."

Van Zandt's closest friend at college was a formidable, gregarious young man named Tom Barrow, who had also been at Shattuck with him.[10] "Tom was valedictorian at Shattuck," says Myrick, "but he was a real rebel too. I'm not sure why Townes and Tom ended up both at the University of Colorado; maybe that was planned, maybe it wasn't." Barrow graduated with a degree in architectural engineering, "which was a six-year degree," says Myrick, "and he had a 4.0 average. He had the ability to do many things. And it happens that forgery was one of those things. So Tom forged a letter to the dean, from Mr. and Mrs. Van Zandt, saying that it was okay for Townes to drop out of school for the semester. He was just trying to get his parents off his back, and he just wanted to play guitar. He wanted to work at playing the guitar.... And, of course, drink."

Townes withdrew from school on March 6, the day before his twentieth birthday. He was away from school for two weeks, having hitchhiked to Oklahoma and back, and somehow his family got wind of his absence. They were already aware of his drinking binges and his mood swings, and of his prior "running away," and they knew that this behavior was becoming a problem, but now the extent of the problem was becoming clear to them. Townes' sister recalls that a doctor from Boulder had called the Van Zandts, concerned that Townes could be suicidal.[11] At any rate, the Van Zandts made a quick, unplanned trip to Boulder. "They flew in by surprise," Myrick recalls. "We had had a party the night before, and everybody was on the floor, and this and that. I won't get into the party, but he had been sniffing glue. All night. And he had passed out. And suddenly his parents are at the door. I stagger out, and I'm just bewildered. I just can't believe they're in town. But they'd gotten wind that he was trying to drop out of school with the forged letter, and now we're trying to pull Townes off the rug with glue stuck to his sideburns.... So perhaps that explains why they said, 'You're going to the hospital.'"

Harris and Dorothy took Townes back to Houston with them, fearing for his safety. Bill Van Zandt was in the ninth grade at Shattuck, and he recalls that "I thought he came home because he was just kind of burned out, but he was actually suffering from clinical depression of some sort." Fran recalls that Townes' father called her from Houston. "He called me in Colorado because he was really feeling like something was seriously wrong with Townes. He said, 'I don't want to upset you,' but he was telling me that they had put Townes in the hospital. He said, 'I know you love my son, but I want you to think about that, because I'm worried that he is not good enough for you.' We both were bawling on the phone, just crying and crying. I said, 'No. He's too good. I know he is good.' He said, 'I know he wants to be.' He was struggling so much, he was actually crying on the phone with me."

The Van Zandts drove Townes from their house in Houston down to Galveston, on the Gulf of Mexico an hour south of the Bayou City. One of Dorothy's brothers, Townes' Uncle Donny, had a fishing "camp" on Offat's Bayou on Galveston Island, where the family had spent many weekends, but this visit had no such pleasant overtones. Townes' parents took him straight to the Titus Harris Clinic, part of the Division of Child and Adolescent Psychiatry (now part of the Department of Psychiatry and Behavioral Sciences) at the University of Texas Medical Branch, where on March 14 they had him admitted for psychiatric evaluation and treatment.[12]

# 5

# Sanitarium Blues

UTMB-GALVESTON WAS IN THE 1960s and still is one of the best medical and psychiatric facilities in the country. In 1964, the physical plant at UTMB was a collection of Victorian brick buildings mixed with some drab additions from the 1930s and the early 1950s, nestled into a palm-shaded campus in the northeast corner of the city. The old main building, a monumental redbrick known as Old Red, was built in 1891 and survived the Galveston Storm of 1900. Just west of Old Red was the Galveston State Psychopathic Hospital (later renamed the Marvin Graves Building), the first building in Galveston built to house psychiatric patients. Dr. Titus Harris was the first Director of Psychiatry there, and his colleague Dr. Abe Hauser was the Assistant Director. Together, they had established the Titus Harris Clinic for psychiatric inpatients in 1929.[1]

Grace Jameson is a psychiatrist who has been on staff at the Titus Harris Clinic since the early 1950s. According to Dr. Jameson, "By the early 1940s, people all over Texas knew about Dr. Harris and his associates, and the phrase 'gone to Galveston' began to mean that the individual had a psychiatric disorder and the only possible reason someone would come to Galveston would be to consult Dr. Harris or one of his partners."[2]

At the Titus Harris Clinic—one of the first facilities of its kind to serve children and adolescents—a team of doctors (primarily Doctors Ford, Martin, and Wight) evaluated Townes for a few weeks, overseeing the administration of a barrage of physical and psychological tests. According to his psychological report, Townes "attained a full scale I.Q. of 134 which places him in the very superior range of intelligence."[3]

The psychological report, filed by Dr. Charles Gaston, goes on:

> The patient's character structure is predominantly obsessive-compulsive. This is a pleasant, friendly, but quiet, reserved, somewhat shy and aloof individual. His pleasantness and affable unobtrusiveness lend themselves to being quite charming and gracious in most social situations. Though he is quiet and re-served, he has a capacity for great intensity of feeling, and is also prone to mood swing [sic] and depression. He is outwardly quite deferential and respectful to adults and other authority figures, though he feels quite hostile toward them inwardly.
>
> This is a sensitive, artistic, and idealistic youth. His value system emphasizes that he work hard, achieve, be courageous, take pride in himself, be an honorable and somewhat moralistic individual and stand on his own two feet.

While there is nothing too unusual in this assessment, the re-port goes on to describe what the doctor found to be the darker side of Townes' personality: "This youth has a strong paranoid po-tential to his character structure, and this appears to be becoming more prominent at the present time. The sources for this appear two-fold. One, this youth feels quite inadequate in comparison with his successful father and feels he can never compete with him.... Two, there are indications of some feminine elements in his character structure and these feminine elements threaten his whole value system, sense of self, and adequacy as a male."

The doctor believed that Townes' feelings of inadequacy in relation to his father, along with a recognition of his "feminine" characteristics (most likely just his sensitivity and "artistic" nature), formed a conflict that was fomenting paranoia and the development of "grandiose perceptions of himself to bolster his feelings of personal worth." The report continues: "While the overall pattern of this youth's protocol is not floridly psychotic, he is moving in that direction, and his test protocols are reflective of a definite schizophrenic potential and possible current underlying psychotic ideation."

The psychological report concluded with emphasis that Townes had an "obsessive-compulsive schizoid character with strong paranoid trends." The official diagnosis was "Schizophrenic reaction, Schizo-affective type (Depression)."[4] The treatment prescribed was cutting-edge at that time: a regimen of "shock therapies"—both insulin coma therapy and electroshock treatments—to be administered over the course of the next couple of months—nearly forty treatments between early April and early June 1964—during which time Townes was only to leave the confines of the hospital on occasional supervised weekend passes.

One of the original practitioners on staff at the clinic was Dr. Martin Lee Towler, who was a pioneer in the use of electroencephalography and was a strong advocate of the so-called shock therapies, which even then were controversial, but which were considered the most effective treatments available. Insulin coma therapy, which had been introduced in the mid-1930s to treat schizophrenia, consists of injecting the patient with increasing amounts of insulin each morning in order to lower the blood sugar enough to bring about a coma. The procedure was performed in a special treatment room with specially trained nurses and attendants. "The comas were allowed to continue for about thirty minutes," according to Dr. Jameson, "then [were] terminated by injecting fifty-percent glucose intravenously, followed by the administration of sugared orange juice and then breakfast. Acute episodes of schizophrenia did end quite satisfactorily with this treatment in most cases." Electro Convulsive Therapy (also called electroshock), introduced shortly after insulin coma therapy, was used to treat depression and mania. When the two therapies were combined, as Dr. Towler combined them, electroshocks were administered just before the patient was brought out of the insulin coma.

Years after his treatment, Townes became friends with a fellow Texan called Chito, who had been a patient of Dr. Towler's at the clinic, with the same diagnosis as Townes, and they found that they had had the same experiences. Chito describes the experience as "horrifying," but one that he and Townes came to feel they deserved as "punishment" for their misdeeds. As Chito remembers the treatment, "You go in there, and the doctors strap you down. They grease up these wires and they put them on your head in different places, and they also grease up some stuff that they put on your chest with wires. And then they shoot you with sodium pentathol and ask you to count backwards. The next thing you know, you wake up in a room where other people are slowly waking up. And as you wake up, the orderlies take you back to your room. They used to ask me how I felt, and I said, 'well, it made me really, really sick,' which it really, really did. And [Townes] said it made him really, really sick too. And this is something he told me too, but it's pretty much run of the mill for everybody: You can't remember your name. And that's the most important thing in the world to you."[5]

According to Dr. Jameson, the electroshock treatment alone "would probably have ended the episode that Mr. Van Zandt was treated for here. But, at that time, we all felt that, qualitatively, if someone was psychotic, insulin coma therapy gave a better quality of remission."

Van Zandt's extreme behavior—a rash of serious drinking, sniffing glue to the point of unconsciousness, and taking off on spontaneous trips, removed from all responsibilities—was diagnosed as constituting a psychotic state. Townes' mood swings were recognized as manifestations of manic-depressive illness. And as extreme as these methods seem today, Dr. Jameson, for one, is quick to point out that the convulsive therapies seemed a godsend in those days, compared with the alternatives. "Before that, if somebody was manic-depressive they might spend a great deal of their life in a hospital. In this context, the intro-duction of electroshock and insulin coma therapy seemed just revolutionary.... It's really good at ending an episode of acute schizophrenia, and since we didn't differentiate between that and the psychotic type, if you will, of manic-depressive psycho-sis, it would have been prescribed for that too."

Even when shock treatment was successful, though, the suc-cess was qualified. "Shock treatment could end episodes, but it did nothing to prevent recurrences," Dr. Jameson says. Anti-psychotic medications—primarily thorazine and related drugs—had been introduced in the 1950s, and the first antidepressant medications were on the threshold of being brought into use in the early 1960s. Townes probably did have access to some of these new medicines at Galveston, according to Dr. Jameson.

"Obviously, the man wasn't really schizophrenic, because he was able to do as much as he did," Dr. Jameson says unequivo-cally. "Now we would call it 'bipolar with psychotic features.' Manic-depression—bipolar disorder—is basically a mood disor-der, and it sometimes shows some psychotic features. If he was manic, and he probably was when he was psychotic, he couldn't sleep, and just ordinary sleep deprivation can make a person psychotic."

Manic-depressive illness is often complicated by the subject's substance abuse, and Van Zandt clearly was abusing substances, primarily alcohol, prior to his diagnosis and treatment. In fact, it was recognized at the time and is even better understood today that a much greater percentage of individuals with bipolar disor-der are diagnosed as alcoholics than in the general population, and Townes unquestionably was an alcoholic.[6] It is important to note the relationship between the two distinct diseases. "The alcoholism could have started as his own misguided attempt to treat himself, because it would have made him feel better," Dr. Jameson says. "Often we see patients for alcoholism and drug abuse where the underlying cause is that they're manic-depres-sive. And they have to be treated for that before they can be treated for the other."

———◦◦◦———

Dr. Jameson is clear that Van Zandt's treatment was, temporarily, fairly successful. "But where it was not successful," she says, "is that he needed to be convinced to stay under a therapist's care, even traveling around like musicians do; he could have arranged for it, if he knew enough about his own illness, if he knew he needed to see someone and get the appropriate lab work, or whatever. He could have done it, but he chose not to. And the downside is that he treated the symptoms with drugs and alcohol, which was obviously a mistreatment."

Van Zandt was hospitalized at Galveston from March 14 until June 19, 1964, a period that might have been extended from the original regimen because of some relapses on Townes' part. Townes was allowed to have visitors; his parents, Fran, and a friend or two came to see him—Fran later recalled that he had to be reintroduced to her each time she visited—and he was able to talk on the phone. "One of the stories [he told me] on the phone was he had just gotten in trouble that day, because they had caught him with a bottle of wine," Bob Myrick remembers. "One of his friends somehow smuggled a bottle of wine to him. And he told the nurse it was a torpedo, that he was Captain Torpedo, and the bed was a submarine. I said, 'Townes, that's a weird story even for you.'"

Eventually Townes began to exhibit "less depression" and the doctors decided that "his thought content disturbance" was "in remission." Townes was pronounced well enough to try to begin to make his way back into society, and he was discharged to his parents with no medications prescribed. But he was very likely changed forever.[7]

# 6

# Waitin' for the Day

A FTER HIS STAY AT GALVESTON, the Van Zandts took their son back home to Houston. They would not allow him to return to Colorado, but encouraged him to attend school locally, at the University of Houston. Fran had returned to Boulder to finish the year at the University of Colorado, but her and Townes' strong desire to be together was the central tenet of their frequent, ongoing discussions of the future.[1]

And it seemed that the future was all that Townes was equipped to discuss. "He virtually had no memory of his childhood," Fran says. She recalls that Townes' mother, distraught by this unexpected after-effect of his treatment, would go through the family photo albums repeatedly with Townes, telling him stories to reinforce his memories and to help him rebuild them. "When somebody would ask him a question, he would answer and then realize that the only reason he was saying that was because somebody had told him. It was like rote memory, not a picture memory," Fran recalls. "I think it started coming back over time, but he never trusted that it was a real memory." Hence, Townes and Fran did not discuss Galveston. "Townes had total

52

honor for his parents," Fran says. "So there was no resentment, no anger, only the constant sense of not knowing whether he really remembered."

According to Dr. Grace Jameson at UTMB, the electroshock treatments would cause short-term memory loss; indeed, the point was to erase the traumatic memories surrounding the psychotic episode that initiated the treatment. But long-term memory loss, the wiping out of blocks of childhood memories, is not the result of such treatment. Dr. Jameson says, "There may be some other reason that he blocked out some of his childhood."[2] She speculates that his alcoholism could have caused this loss of long-term memory. Others have speculated that Townes pretended to have lost these long-term memories to inculcate guilt in his father and gain sympathy from his mother.

Although Townes was not prescribed any medication, he did go to some follow-up counseling sessions for a few months. By way of providing perspective, Fran adds, "I can remember meeting one of his counselors, months later, one of the young doctors, and he actually quit psychiatry because of Townes' case. He said, 'I didn't think there was anything really wrong with him. I did not agree with the treatment.'"

To Fran, the changes in Townes after Galveston were fairly subtle, but clear. "Townes was needier, always needing reassurance. That was the biggest difference. His sense of humor was still intact, his quick wit, all of that was still there. But he seemed more calm; he wasn't as intense, at least for a while.... He seemed more ..."; she pauses to think, then says, "calmly resolute."

Townes followed his parents' advice and enrolled in the University of Houston's pre-law program in January 1965, transferring thirty-two credits from Colorado.[3] Fran had agreed to return to her home town and take her senior year at the University of Houston, with Townes. "He was a junior and I was starting my senior year," Fran explains. "I picked up a year when he was in Galveston. He was only in Galveston for three months, but you know ... it takes some time for recovery from that kind of treatment." It was during this brief period that, for all intents

and purposes, Townes seems to have decided—either with re-
solve or with resignation—to attempt to walk the straight path
laid out for him by the people who loved him. A friend recalls
Townes as he took up pre-law at Houston. "When he was first
in law school he was pretty straight. He wore long-sleeved white
starched shirts and pressed Levis and boots and a belt, and he
really looked like an up-and-coming attorney."[4]

In February, Harris Williams Van Zandt's mother, Bell Williams Van Zandt, died at the age of eighty-two. Bell Williams was
a strong, matriarchal figure, and she was a favorite of Townes' in
particular, powerful yet benevolent and plainspoken. A family
story illustrating her tough, enduring qualities has Bell being
struck by lightning three times over the course of her life. "She
was always very important to him and to the family," Fran recalls. "She was a central figure."

March brought Townes' twenty-first birthday, which he celebrated quietly with the family at his uncle's fishing camp in
Galveston. At this milestone in his life, it looked to the Van
Zandts as though Townes was at last adjusting and following a
course that they could be comfortable with. Townes was doing
well in school; he would finish the semester with four B's and
one C. And he had reached a decision that made both Mr. and
Mrs. Van Zandt very happy. Townes and Fran had decided to get
married right after the semester was over. And in case Fran's family felt any trepidation about their daughter marrying a young
man so recently released from psychiatric treatment, as Fran recalls, "When Townes asked me to marry him, his dad came over
to my mother and said, 'I would cut off my arm before I would
let them get married if I thought he was going to hurt her.'"

Townes had remained in close touch with his friend Bob
Myrick, who had always encouraged the couple's marriage.
"One of the reasons I became really close with Townes and Fran
is because they were thinking about getting married," Myrick
says. "But a lot of people were against the idea, thinking Townes
would be such a shit to her. Everybody kind of said, 'Holy shit,
you don't want to be married to that guy. That guy's crazy. He'll

be an alcoholic in five years.' But Tom [Barrow] and I totally stood behind him."[5]

In late August, Myrick, Tom Barrow, Tom's wife Joyce, Luke Sharpe, and some other out-of-town friends arrived in Houston for the wedding, which was preceded by a few nights of getting reacquainted and partying. One of those nights, when Fran and her bridesmaids had gone shopping, Myrick recalls that "Townes suddenly said to Tom and Joyce, 'let's play strip poker'; which we did. I think the whole thing was that Townes wanted to have Fran and the girls walk in on us, which they in fact did. Barrow's wife was losing big at the time, and Townes and I had a side bet that the first guy that makes eye contact with Barrow's wife is the loser ... and suddenly Fran walks in, to the general entertainment of all.... Townes was just completely untrammeled by normal rules of decorum."

The night before the wedding ceremony, August 25, 1965, Townes and Fran, along with family members and friends who were to be in the wedding, went to the church for the rehearsal. After running through the ceremony, the preacher signed and dated the marriage license and, according to the plan that both the Van Zandt and the Petters families had agreed to keep quiet, the marriage was made official that night because of a new military draft law taking effect the next day. In 1963, President Kennedy had changed Selective Service regulations so that married men were placed one step lower in the order of call-up than single men, spawning a rush of so-called "Kennedy husbands." Now, Lyndon Johnson's new Executive Order number 11241 stated that "men married on or after August 26, 1965, with no children, are ... considered the same as single men in Class 1-A with regard to order of call...." Townes got in as one of the very last "Kennedy husbands," and remained eligible for draft call-up only in the fourth order of call, after "all delinquents, volunteers, and single and newly married men [age 19 to 26, oldest first] in Class I-A were selected for induction." Had the marriage taken place the next day, he would have been considered the same status as single men in Class I-A and would have been near the top of the list of young men headed for Vietnam.[6] Few at the ceremony the next day knew that Townes and Fran were already officially married. "My mother thought it ruined the wedding," Fran says, "but she got over that quickly."

After the "rehearsal," a large dinner was held at the prestigious Petroleum Club, an oil-industry insiders club in downtown Houston. Fran remembers this as a very special evening, an elegant affair with some fifty guests. "We danced and laughed," she recalls. "I can remember one of our Baptist friends having her very first frozen daiquiri. It was huge, and it looked like a giant snow cone in a dessert glass. She drank it too fast, and when we looked back at her, her nose was in the glass. It was a great evening."

The next day, August 26—a hot, sunny day—Townes and Fran's wedding took place at the River Oaks Baptist Church in Houston. "There were about four hundred guests," Fran remembers. "We had friends from college and from high school, and also lots of relatives stand up with us and as ushers. The whole affair was very nice, and fairly calm; just lots of visiting and laughter. There was no big dinner, dancing, or drinking; it was in a Southern Baptist church, so [there were] just light snacks, cake, and punch.... After the wedding, Townes and I were whisked away in a limo to the Warwick Hotel. It was quite the hotel in the sixties. We had a beautiful suite, champagne in the room, a fruit plate, snacks. It was gorgeous." Photographs from the next day show Fran in a stylish brown suit and pillbox hat and Townes in a maroon blazer and gray slacks, suitcases in hand on their way to their honeymoon. On a side window of their hired limousine, along with tin cans tied to the bumper, someone had scrawled "Bye Mama!" and "Fran and Van."

After a short, quiet honeymoon in Aspen, Colorado, the newlyweds settled into a small second-floor garden apartment on Briarhurst Road, just south of Westheimer Boulevard, less than a mile from the Van Zandt residence in River Oaks, but in considerably more modest surroundings. On a visit years later, Fran points up at the apartment balcony and smiles fondly. "It was a one-bedroom apartment, and it cost a hundred and twenty dollars a month," she says. "We had a little hibachi stove on the balcony where we barbecued a lot."

Fran recalls their early married life vividly, and she recalls it as a happy time. The young couple were attending the University of Houston full time, and they both had friends there and around town, but their lives were very much centered in their families. Fran says, "[Townes] was very much into people. His mom and dad came over all the time, and we went over to their house all the time. We all went to Galveston almost every weekend. We'd go fishing, and every Friday night was game night. His mother liked to play mah jong, and we all hated mah jong. Townes always liked to play hearts or spades, and so did his dad. His mother couldn't cook, so his dad usually was the cook, or all of us chipped in and did something, but we went out to eat as much as anything. My parents and his parents were good friends, so we would all go eat Chinese food on San Felipe."

According to friends and family, Townes seemed happy. According to Fran, though, there were times during this period when "it was like a dark cloud" would pass over him. He would want to be alone for a few days, sometimes for a week, but then his dark moods would pass. Otherwise, he participated fully in and seemed genuinely to enjoy the time with his family. If he was drinking, he was hiding it.

Fran and Townes, both animal lovers, kept an assortment of pets in the small apartment. "We had a dog named Reefus," Fran says. "Reefus was a mutt, and she had a tremendous overbite and was just ugly, but we thought she was beautiful and we loved her." They also had a piranha, which they had tried to give to Townes' brother, but Bill wasn't interested in adding a predator to his tropical fish tank, and they ended up keeping it. Another notable pet was a monkey named Pookens, whose death Townes memorialized in verse. "Townes wrote a poem called 'The Passing of the Pookens,'" Fran remembers. "It was four verses, and at the end of each verse it said how much the monkey loved meal worms. It was real cute. We put him in a shoebox with a cross on top of it, Townes read the poem, then we put him in the dumpster."

Naturally, the young couple struggled to keep body and soul together. But Harris and Dorothy Van Zandt helped considerably, supporting the newlyweds almost completely at first, while both Fran and Townes were still in school, and remained generous always. "They paid for our apartment and food," Fran says. "But there were times we were so poor.... I can't eat macaroni and cheese to this day. Macaroni and cheese was like nineteen cents a box, and we'd have enough money to buy three boxes of it but we didn't have enough for the butter and milk, so it was just water. One time we had about fifteen dollars in the bank. [Townes] was always pretty compassionate. If you said you liked something, whatever he had, he gave it to you. There was a woman we knew, a single mom with a baby, and she was broke. So he wrote her a check for fifteen dollars, which was everything we had. I asked him why he didn't write it for ten dollars, but he wrote it for everything we had."

While Townes was ostensibly attending classes (he failed one class and withdrew from another in the fall semester) and settling into a straight, domestic life, his interest in music was undiminished. Indeed, he played with a renewed passion and discipline, keeping up a regular regimen of practice whenever he could get a few hours alone. He also began more and more to seek out some of the live music that flourished in Houston and throughout the Gulf coast region. Fran recalls a long trip to hear a blues band one night shortly before they were married: "We drove to New Orleans … about a two-and-a-half-hour drive. And we danced and just had a great time and came back very late. It was probably three o'clock in the morning before he got me home. We came home and my mom and his dad were on the phone talking to each other, scared to death."

Before long, the couple's growing need for income converged with Townes' growing desire to play music for a paying public. "That's really why Townes went out and started playing guitar and singing in public," Fran says. "It was to get the ten dollars a night."

The Jester Lounge on Westheimer Boulevard was one of no more than a half-dozen small nightclubs or coffeehouses in Houston that featured folk music. They were small rooms with tiny stages where mostly local acts would play for tips or for five or ten dollars a night. "At the time, the Jester was very cool. It was a real folk music club," recalls John Carrick. Carrick, along with his mother, who was known as "Ma" Carrick, ran another of Houston's seminal folk clubs, the Sand Mountain Coffeehouse, and also was among the group of local regulars who played the few—"three or four," according to Carrick—folk venues in Houston. "What we didn't know then," Carrick says, "was how cool the Jester was. Here's a short list: Townes played there, and he was one of the kids, you know. I think that was the first place in Houston that Jerry Jeff Walker played. K.T. Oslin was a regular there, and Guy Clark. A lot of the blues guys played there, including Mance Lipscomb and Lightnin' Hopkins, and a lot of musicians that people had never heard of but that were just phenomenal. Townes was one of the first around doing any stuff he'd written, although at first they were just kind of goofy talking blues songs, like 'T-Bird Blues' and 'Mustang Blues' and stuff like that."[7]

"[T]he first place I played was a club on Westheimer called the Jester Lounge," Townes later recollected.

> That was the first place I ever got paid real money for singing. This guy, who turned out to be Don Sanders, came up to me in there and said I also oughta try this place called Sand Mountain. I went over there with him and we did a short little set. Mrs. Carrick was at her desk keeping an eye on the proceedings, and the place was almost empty at the time. There was this song I used to do at the time called "The KKK Blues," and I sang it that night. It was a talking blues about dropping out of the second grade to join the Ku Klux Klan, and the guy said "you got too much education." Then I did another one called "The Vietnamese Blues," which had a chorus line about leaving Vietnam to the Vietnamese. Anyway,

> I got through singing and Mrs. Carrick said, "Well,
> that was real good, but we just don't do things like
> that around here." I said, "Well, this is a fine place,
> but I just can't stay here then." Next day she sent
> Don as an envoy again and she said she wanted us
> to come back. That was the beginning.[8]

Townes recalled meeting Guy Clark around this time. "He was at the Jester before I played there, and then [he] joined the Peace Corps. I started playing there, and then he came back [and] we met...."[9] Fran also recalls Townes and Guy meeting sometime in mid- to late-1965. "Guy was just one of these ten-dollar acts like Townes was. It was kind of an immediate friendship. Guy lived not too far from Sand Mountain, in a one-room apartment. Susie, his first wife—Susan—came in to Sand Mountain. She was a little-bitty cute thing, kind of feisty. And Guy just kind of fell for her right off. They started dating and got married and had a baby. So, all of us were just kind of hanging out there."

Since the mid-1950s, the local folk scene had been centered in the Houston Folklore Society and in the powerful personality of its leader, John A. Lomax Jr., the well-known folklorist Alan Lomax's brother, the other son of the legendary patriarch John A. Lomax Sr. The senior Lomax had collected cowboy songs in the 1920s and discovered Leadbelly and made field recordings of dozens of other American roots musicians all over the South, and he remains one of the most important figures in twentieth-century American music scholarship.

As John Lomax Jr.'s son, John Lomax III, recalls, for folk singers in Houston, the Folklore Society "was the only place to go, really." The society met monthly and held events in local clubs and coffeehouses or occasionally at the Jewish Community Center. "The meetings of the Houston Folklore Society consisted of about ten minutes of business, then the rest was essentially what they now call 'pass the guitar,'" says Lomax.

"My dad was extremely democratic, and they were all very democratic, and everyone got a song or two.... No matter if you were wretched or professional; the whole concept was you were doing this for fun, and numerous beverages were served. They used all the members' houses.... My dad would sing some in that setting. He would get up and sing real folk songs *a capella*, and sometimes he'd accompany himself with an axe and a big chunk of wood. He would stroke it with these big *whack* sounds, [singing] 'take this hammer ... *whack*!' With this big fuckin' log, and it would go flying everywhere, to show how it was rhythmic. And he would talk about where the songs came from and how he learned them from his dad, who learned them from whoever.

"Guy Clark came through there when he first came to town," recalls Lomax. "My dad had a show with Lightnin' Hopkins—he managed Lightnin' at the time—and Guy had just showed up in town, and he went to a meeting, and they said, 'Oh, we're having a show day after tomorrow, do you want to play?' And he did, and Lightnin' was there. Guy was a little nervous."[10]

Lightnin' Hopkins was in fact a regular fixture on the Houston club scene throughout the sixties, and it was through the influence of Hopkins and other black musicians like Mance Lipscomb and Josh White that the young Townes Van Zandt left the more purely white, commercial folk path and set a more deep-rooted, blues-oriented course, something that some of the other young, white folk aficionados felt ill-equipped to attempt, but that Townes seemed to take to naturally.

Van Zandt had discovered Hopkins' recordings when he was in high school, then began listening more seriously in college, copying guitar licks, slowly mastering his finger-picking technique, and gradually absorbing the nuances of his style and, critically, his attitude. As he later told the story, one day at the University of Houston, he spotted an ad in the paper for Lightnin's appearance that night at the Bird Lounge. Townes recalled that he was dumbfounded, never imagining that Hopkins was still alive and could actually be seen at a local club. He saw the show, and then met Lightnin', sitting at his table and chatting with him, somewhat in awe.[11]

Rex Bell was another aspiring folk singer, and he played bass with Hopkins during this period, later going on to play a long stint with him. Bell recalls that it was actually he who introduced Townes to Lightnin'. "Mrs. Carrick introduced me to Townes," Bell remembers. "I was her perennial opening act.... I think I got paid six bucks or something. So she introduced me to Townes upstairs there at Sand Mountain, and she left the room. And immediately Townes threw open the window, and he had a gallon of wine on a rope, and he pulled it up, and we both took a swig of wine, and we were friends from then on. It wasn't too long afterward that I introduced him to Lightnin'."[12]

Fran recalls that Townes was a big fan of Lightnin's, and that he got to know him on a personal level to some extent.

> I remember one time it was announced in the paper that Lightnin' Hopkins had died. It was Sunday morning, not even eight o'clock, I don't think. We got the paper and Townes read it and got real upset. We got in the car and drove over. Lightnin' lived in an apartment close to the University of Houston. We knocked on the door, and old Lightnin' always had these bodyguards, these people around, so they opened the door and we went in and Townes said, "Oh, my God, Lightnin'. They said you were dead." And Lightnin' just says, "I don't think so." So we sat there and they played guitars and talked for hours. Lightnin', you know, was drinking white lightning whiskey all the time.

Soon, to save money and to be closer to what there was of a folk music scene, Townes and Fran moved into the tiny apartment above Sand Mountain, and Mrs. Carrick became their landlady. Many of the young folk singers in Houston had lived in that apartment at one time or another, according to John Carrick. "The deal was, you'd live up there, and in return, you'd clean the club and you'd get a little bit of money." Townes became "kind of the house act" at Sand Mountain, opening shows for many of the more well-known acts that passed through, Fran recalls. "That's when he and Guy Clark got real close." Clark had in fact just returned from training for the Peace Corps: "I had a brief fling at it, but I didn't actually go anywhere. I just did the training program," Clark remembers.[13]

"We both started writing about the same time," Clark says. "But Townes just did it in a way that raised it to a level of art, or poetry, whatever you want to call it, rather than just rhyming 'moon, June, and spoon.'" While Bob Dylan's writing was inspiring folk musicians everywhere, Townes' inspiration was more direct. "Townes was right there," Clark stresses, "and while you couldn't be Townes or write like Townes, you could come from the same place artistically."

Darryl Harris was another musician playing the folk clubs of Houston at the time. He had attended Milbey High School in Houston with Fran. "I was a guitar player," Harris recollects. "I played some kind of schlocky flamenco and classical stuff. I was playing at the Jester Lounge, and I went out to the Jester one night, and Townes was playing there. He was with Fran, so that's really how we met.... And when Townes and I met, we were both going to the University of Houston, so we would then run into each other occasionally on campus. We'd run into each other and then we'd sort of talk each other into not going to class."

Harris recalls, "Townes and Guy were probably the most popular guys who played there, but most of the people there were pretty good. Although when I first saw Townes out at the Jester, he was pretty awful, really; pretty drunk. The stuff he was playing made me kind of wonder. Sometimes you hear people play and you wonder how they could ever imagine it being possible to have any kind of career in music. That was really sort of my response the first time I ever heard him."[14]

Another singer on the scene at the Jester and Sand Mountain, who was writing his own songs, was Jerry Jeff Walker. Townes was impressed and inspired by Walker's songwriting; Fran was less enthusiastic. "Jerry Jeff was over at our apartment one day," she recalls. "He was from New York, and back then there wasn't a lot of mixture of the South and the North. Jerry Jeff had such a different sense of etiquette; he really had none." She recalls one day when "He was sitting at our dining room table eating, slumped over, not talking to anybody, and he had his hat on, and Townes' mom and dad came over," she says. "Jerry Jeff didn't stand up, didn't take his hat off, didn't even look up. So Townes' dad wouldn't let his mother sit down, and he called Townes outside and said, 'This guy has insulted your mother. How could you allow that to happen?' That is the sense of honoring women that Townes was brought up with.... [Townes' parents] always wanted to hear Townes sing, but if Jerry Jeff was on the bill too, they wouldn't come."

Fran remembers clearly that it was also during this time that Townes wrote the first few batches of the songs that would make up his lasting body of work. "In the first apartment we lived in there were two walk-in closets," she says. "The little one off the bathroom he decorated with posters, music posters, and made into his own little studio. There was just enough room to have a chair and a little amplifier and a little tape recorder, and a little table. You had to step in sideways to be able to sit down. That is where he started writing his first songs. He loved going in there; he would shut the door and stay there for hours." They had a small antique pump organ in their apartment, and Fran would often help Townes write out his music. "I would sound it out [on the organ] and write it because I knew music, although I could only do the treble.... That was for the first five or six songs."

The songs came quickly. "'Waitin' Around to Die' had to be within the first two or three songs, maybe the second or third," Fran recalls. "It wasn't the first one I heard. He might have written it first, but I think he didn't sing it for a while, he kind of just held it.... 'Turnstiled, Junkpiled' was another early one."

Fran was overjoyed by this creative outpouring, but she was taken aback by "Waitin' Around to Die." She asked Townes where such a song had come from. "He just said he didn't know," she says. "He would often just wake up in the middle of the night and write, and sometimes he described it like it would just tumble out of his brain and down his fingers."

"My first serious song was 'Waitin' Around to Die,'" Townes said in 1977, a statement he repeated many times when performing the song. "I talked to this old man for a while," he continued, "and he kinda put out these vibrations. I was sitting at the bar of the Jester Lounge one afternoon drinking beer, thinking about him, and just wrote it down."[15]

"Waitin' Around to Die" is indeed a serious song for a young man with Townes' early background to have written, but unlike many "serious" songs that young folk singers come up with, it bears the weight of its seriousness almost effortlessly. It takes its subject, a young man, through a life of misfortune, from a childhood marked by his father's beating of his mother and the mother's desertion, to an adolescence of deceit and abandonment at the hands of a woman, to imprisonment for robbing a man, always with the almost offhand refrain, "it's easier than just waiting around to die." Finally, after spending two years in prison, the young man is resigned to a life of destitution with his new "friend," codeine, a drug of poverty and desperation, and he ends, "together we're gonna wait around and die."

This is a bleak vision indeed, but it is handled so deftly that there is no sense of it being maudlin. The simple three-chord progression in a minor key perfectly reflects the direct simplicity of the storytelling, Van Zandt's delivery is entirely straightforward and unaffected, and the poetic sensibility shows an already well-honed maturity—the use of the place names in each verse: Tennessee, Tuscaloosa, Muskogee; the offhand vernacular: "she cleaned me out and hit it on the sly"; "we robbed a man and brother did we fly"; and the fine-tuned balance of the verses—so that all of these things add up to a stunning personal vision of something much deeper than mere folk music. "Waitin' Around to Die" is the blues: starkly personal and universal at the same time. It's the kind of song that instantly differentiated Townes Van Zandt from his contemporaries, and that often left audiences stunned, as Fran had been.

"He had lots of fun ones, too," Fran says of those earliest songs. She recalls his various talking blues numbers as "just so comedic; and he always sang that New Orleans song for me. It just drove me crazy because I thought *his* music was so much better. Every time he sang it I would think, 'oh, don't sing that again.' It was the 'Three Shrimp' song: 'I saw three shrimp in the water ... '. That was from an Elvis Presley movie, *Girls, Girls, Girls*. If he played 'Waitin' Around to Die' he would always play 'The Shrimp Song' afterwards."

This juxtaposition of serious material and more light-hearted songs and banter was from the very beginning a hallmark of Van Zandt's performances that lasted throughout his career. Indeed, the balance between dark and light, exalted and ordinary, sacred and profane, was from the beginning central to Townes' writing as well as his performance.

A recording of one of Townes' earliest performances at the Jester, in 1965, provides a glimpse of exactly what kind of ground Townes was treading in those early days.[16] Townes opens his forty-five-minute set with his own "Black Crow Blues," an early meditation on an early death: "Don't mourn your young life away ... /lower me down with a quick-said goodbye/pour in the black Texas mud." The black crow image is tacked on in the final verse, reminiscent of Van Gogh's *Cornfield with Black Crows*, portentous and somewhat pretentious as well. Townes follows this song immediately with a joke, a somewhat involved story about a nun drinking a martini, deftly clearing away the portentous and the pretentious. Another early original follows, "Badly Mistreated Blues," a vaguely Hank Williams–inspired comedic number with the refrain "As a matter of fact, sweet mama, I'm sick of you." The crowd seems to follow Van Zandt faithfully down the path he lays out for them, and the mood is light enough that he feels that he can bring out another serious number, "Colorado Bound," the earliest of his Colorado songs, wherein his lover leaves him and he retreats to the purity of "some lonesome canyon" in Colorado. He again lightens the mood with "Talkin' Karate Blues," then follows with a traditional Carter Family song, "Cannon Ball Blues."

Townes is fully warmed up at this point in the set, and the recording makes clear that the crowd is as well. His self-deprecation, his humor, his dry tone, and his timing are as much responsible for this as the quality of his lyrics.

Townes continues into the heart of his set with a Lightnin' Hopkins song, "Hello Central." Townes' Hopkins-inspired guitar playing is clearly well studied and fairly well developed, although without the subtlety of his later playing. There's a bluesy crack in his voice reminiscent of Hank Williams, illustrating clearly the mix of styles he's attempting. Next is another early original song, the somewhat undistinguished "Louisiana Woman," a simple, cautionary blues about the women of New Orleans ("Well, I guess I better do a dirty one," Townes says by way of introduction). "Talkin' Thunderbird Blues" is next (with lyrics slightly less developed than they became as Townes performed this throughout his life), then Jimmie Rodgers' "Blue Yodel No. 1 (T For Texas)," where he shows his lack of yodeling skills. Another joke follows, this one about a gorilla catcher, again rather long and involved, then two more forgettable early originals, "Mustang Blues" ("I'm gonna take a Greyhound/leave all the drivin' to them") and "Talkin' Birth Control Blues" ("real life savers … depending on how you look at it").

Van Zandt closes with the well-known "Trouble in Mind" and Hank Williams' "I'm So Lonesome I Could Cry." In forty-five minutes, Townes has covered his ground. His ground would expand and his roots deepen considerably over the years, but he remained centered in roughly the same place we see him this night.

In January 1966, Harris Williams Van Zandt died suddenly of a heart attack. He was fifty-two years old. His unexpected death was a shock to Townes, as it was to the rest of the family, and it seemed like a piling-on of hardships so soon after all Townes had just been through, and after all the family had just been through with Townes. The eldest son took his father's death particularly hard, which in turn compounded his mother's grief. Dorothy had been looking after Townes closely since his return to Houston. She was scared for him, and she felt responsible for what had happened to him, though it almost surely had been her husband's decision to send Townes to Galveston. But she was heartened by his return to school and by his marriage to Fran, with whom she shared a close relationship. Harris Van Zandt's funeral, at River Oaks Baptist Church, was attended by hundreds of people.

"Townes never really talked about how much losing his dad affected him," Fran says. "But he went into a deep depression right afterwards. At first he just clung to me real tight, then it was like he had to get away, like it was unbearable. After that, he decided, 'now I'm going to find out about my music.' After his dad died, he really got committed to writing songs."

It was also at this point—as the war in Vietnam raged and U.S. troop levels were sharply on the rise—that Townes determined that he wanted to join the Army. He went to a recruiter to sign up, Fran recalls, "and one of the things they ask is, 'Have you ever been in a mental hospital?' And of course he had been. So he had to get a clearance from the doctors, and they wouldn't give it to him. That is when they wrote this letter, which said that he was an acute schizophrenic and was only marginally adapting to life.[17] I will never forget that sentence, because Townes looked at that and said, 'I'm crazy.' I said, 'No, you're not. It's just making you 4-F.' It was one of those kind of mixed blessings. We didn't have to worry about his going to war, but at the same time there was some desire to keep him out of trouble, I think. That doctor also said that he thought that Townes should be allowed to wander and find himself, which was kind of counter to what everybody thought, [which was] that Townes needed more structure. Amazing. So Townes took that to mean, 'okay, maybe it's time for us to go on the road.'"

Fran had gone to work for Shell Oil right after graduating from college, in August 1966. Now, early in 1967, she quit her job and prepared to accompany her husband in an old RV they had bought. "Townes was an incredible craftsman, and he had great decorating talent, and he and his mom got in this old thing and redecorated the whole thing. She was just dying that we were doing this, but she kept up this great face. She hired some of her upholsterers and stuff to redo everything. Townes redesigned the inside so we would have maximum space to move around, and so we could have more people in it.... we toured Texas and Oklahoma, all through the Hill Country and Dallas–Fort Worth and Oklahoma, playing lots of little clubs like the Jester, that kind of ten-dollar-a-night thing. We didn't have an agent or anything. There was just this guy, Mack Webster, who knew a lot of the club owners. There was a circuit you could get on. Beaumont, Texas, was a big spot, and a lot of the college towns, because they would always have clubs."

The couple stayed on the road for three or four months, and then it started to wear thin. Fran says, "He had made a real point to try and make it work, really work. We were going to make a living with this. But it wasn't working. It was making him a nervous wreck. Anytime we were doing well financially and he didn't have to worry about that, we were happy. But as soon as he felt that the pressure was on him to feed me, it was too much. So I came back and stayed with my parents for a while, and Townes went back on the road. I was just devastated. I mean, I worshiped him; I just worshiped him. And I was scared for him. Then I went on back to work. I thought the one thing we needed for sure was some income. And he wound up coming back because the Jester and Sand Mountain were really starting to do something."

So they kept at it. "Townes was writing a lot," Fran says, "and he was taking a few courses, and working in the places around town … and I was supporting us. It was still good during that time; we were still having a lot of fun."

One of the songs Townes wrote during this time was "Tower Song." As Fran remembers, "We were living [in the apartment] on top of Sand Mountain when he wrote it, sitting in a chair, and I was laying on the bed reading. As soon as he got through writing it, he said 'listen to this and tell me what you think.' I can remember the conversation; I said, 'It's a beautiful song, but what are you trying to tell me?' And he said, 'I don't know if it's about you or not.' He said 'I never try to tell anybody anything, it's all what they hear.'"

———•◦•———

In "Tower Song," a "poet" speaks—preaches, really—to his lover about her fears, her demanding pride, and her ideas of "faith and love and destiny" which are "as distant as eternity from truth and understanding." The singer seems to set up his righteous "poet's tears" and "drunken smile" against the woman's uptight, conventional ideas of love and responsibility, which he says serve to build a wall between them, between their "lives and all that loving means." "You built your tower strong and tall," he tells her; "Can't you see it's got to fall someday?" "That was funny," Fran says, "because I said to him, 'I wonder whose towers those really are?'"

"Tower Song" is a well-crafted love song, if somewhat pious in its assumptions and outlook. It is much more in the commercial folk tradition than "Waitin' Around to Die," yet still reveals a depth of thought unusual for that tradition. It very clearly shows the influence of Bob Dylan's writing circa *Another Side of Bob Dylan*, and comparing it with the more blues-oriented "Waitin' Around to Die" illustrates a dichotomy in Townes' early songwriting that remained quite solid for some years: it is easy to separate Townes' Dylan-influenced songs from his blues-influenced songs. The clearest sign that Townes' songwriting is maturing comes later, when those two lines of descent merge and become something uniquely his own.

Townes and Fran were clearly growing apart, and it was not only financial strains that were tearing at the relationship. "When he did something, he hid it from me," she says. "That was one of the things that started to become real apparent. He didn't want me to be part of his 'bad' life. I was like the 'good' side, and then he had this dark side that came out other places." She recalls one time that Townes told her that she had to remain "straight" so he'd have someone to come home to.

"He couldn't stand me to say a cuss word," she remembers. "He had this great respect for women, the way I saw him. I would go to parties and stuff, but one time he said he was so proud of me because I sat on the side and I never participated in anything that went on. He thought that I was like this queen there." But problems were arising more regularly in close quarters on the road. "He had trouble because [touring with him] kept me in both sides of his life, as opposed to having me set apart in this other side. That was starting to scare him," Fran says.

"I was getting horrified, because that's when he started smoking marijuana and stuff. And I just didn't do that. I loved the music; I loved hearing him. But it was very different for me to see all these different kinds of people he was involved with. I was far from being a hippie. So, the whole hippie thing, knowing Guy and all that sort of thing.... What I started seeing was lots of waste going on, and that's what I started seeing Townes doing to himself.

"That is also when we met Mickey Newbury and Jack Clement, here in Houston. Mickey Newbury had been at the club and they met, then Mickey introduced him to Jack. So when they signed a record deal, boy, it looked like something really good was going to happen."

# 7

## For the Sake of the Song

STRANGER THINGS HAVE HAPPENED IN the annals of the record business, but the story of Townes Van Zandt's first record deal is bizarre even by industry standards. Mickey Newbury, a native of Houston, was at this time one of Nashville's most prolific and successful songwriters and one of the artists who was breaking away from the staid, straight "Nashville Sound" and paving the way for the more progressive music of Roger Miller, Willie Nelson, Kris Kristofferson, and others. Newbury had been writing songs for Nashville's most prominent publishing company, Acuff-Rose, since 1963, and had had his songs recorded by Elvis Presley, Eddy Arnold, Ray Charles, Tom Jones, Joan Baez, and dozens of others, as well as recording his own albums, first for RCA, then for Mercury, and finally for Elektra. Newbury's success as a songwriter peaked in 1968 with a song not at all characteristic of his work, but one that remains one of his best known: "Just Dropped In (To See What Condition My Condition Is In)," recorded by Kenny Rogers & the First Edition. With his wide experience in the business and a strong artistic ear, Newbury knew a good song when he heard it, and during this period he had the clout to do something about it. In addition to writing and recording, he was producing records with his partner Jay Boyett in Houston at a small facility called Jones Studio.

As Newbury recalls, Van Zandt came to Jones Studio to record a demo record at the beginning of 1968, a step that he decided he needed to take if he were to advance his career beyond small clubs. Newbury recalls, "Jay brought me [Townes'] stuff and asked me if I thought we could do anything with him. I said, 'Hell, I don't know, but he sure deserves it.' When I heard it, it just knocked me totally down. I can remember 'Tecumseh Valley' was one of them.... It seems like, if I'm not mistaken, even that far back, I want to say 'Our Mother the Mountain' was one of them. I know that within that first year or two, he wrote 'Quick Silver Daydreams of Maria,' 'St. John the Gambler,' 'Our Mother the Mountain.' I know those were all written in those early, first years.

"Jay didn't think too much of him, because he was listening to his voice and he didn't think that Townes' singing was very good. I was just the opposite," says Newbury. "I was coming from a completely different place. You know, I liked Bob Dylan's singing. To me, it was the way the song was interpreted, the phrasing and the interpretation. Townes had kind of a sleepy kind of a delivery that really was appealing to me."[1]

Newbury and Townes quickly became friends, and within weeks, Newbury says, "we signed him to a management contract, although Townes never actually knew I was his manager, because I was a silent partner with Jay Boyett. It's hard to maintain a friendship with somebody that you're managing, and I valued our friendship." Newbury says that he told Townes that he should go to Nashville. "I just said 'Sure,' Van Zandt later recalled. "I was a real seriously rambling folksinger in the old sense of the word, you know, guitar over your shoulder. I wasn't even thinking about records or publishing deals. I was just kind of, 'Sure, I'll go anywhere.'"[2]

"I took him to Acuff-Rose first," Newbury explains, "because I felt an obligation to them. It was exactly as I figured it would be; it went right over their heads. I took Kristofferson over to Acuff-Rose, too, and it went right over their heads. So I took him to Bill Hall, who was a really good friend of mine. He was Jack Clement's partner, at Hall-Clement."

Jack Clement was already something of a legend in the recording business. A Tennessee native, he had started out playing bluegrass music as a Marine stationed in Washington, D.C., in the early 1950s. He ended up in Memphis in 1954, where he served as master of ceremonies and sometime-singer with a big band that played at the Eagle's Nest, where Elvis Presley was playing some of his first gigs. Clement soon became involved in recording some Memphis performers, including Billy Lee Riley, whose record he took to Sam Phillips' Sun Studio to be mastered. Phillips ended up hiring Clement as his first staff engineer/producer. Clement recorded Roy Orbison, then his legacy was established when he recorded Jerry Lee Lewis' monumental "Whole Lotta Shakin'." He produced some of the classic Johnny Cash records, and he wrote a number of hits for Cash, including "Guess Things Happen That Way," "Ballad of a Teenage Queen," "It's Just About Time," and "Katy Too" (the last co-written with Cash). In the early 1960s Clement partnered with Bill Hall in a recording and publishing venture in Beaumont, Texas, that found quick success with Dickey Lee's recording of "Patches." Lee also wrote the country standard "She Thinks I Still Care," which was published by Hall-Clement.

Clement moved to Nashville later in the 1960s, where he teamed up with Jim Malloy, built two successful recording studios, and settled into producing records and publishing songs. As Clement recalls, he and Malloy were looking for songwriters and performers, and one of the first things Clement did was go to Houston, where he went to see his old friend Bill Jones, whom he knew from his days in Beaumont, and who owned

Jones Studio in Houston. Clement recalls, "He kept telling us about this writer named Townes Van Zandt, how great he was, and that he'd sit there with a bottle of wine and drink and sing all night, all these wonderful songs. And they played us some tapes that he'd made. Then Townes came in and we met him and we decided, 'Yeah, we like this guy.' Mickey [Newbury], he was in on it too; he was very much supportive of Townes.... So he did have a lot to do with getting us interested in him. But he didn't bring him to Nashville, we went there [to Texas]. And then I came up with this deal with Kevin Eggers, which was a big mistake, to produce a record."[3]

So, whether Newbury brought Van Zandt to Clement in Nashville or Clement came to Houston and found Van Zandt, it was under Newbury's covert but decisive management guidance that Townes signed a publishing contract with Hall-Clement. "He must have had thirty songs at that point," Newbury recollects. "And I'm not talking about just thirty songs, I'm talking about thirty great songs." And Hall-Clement had a valuable advantage, from Newbury's point of view. "The reason I signed him to Hall-Clement was because they said they'd record him." As Van Zandt later told an interviewer, "While we were doing the record, Jack was shopping it around. He had met Kevin Eggers.... [and] Kevin picked up the record."

It was Clement's old friend Lamar Fike who introduced Clement to the young New York businessman who owned Poppy Records, Kevin Eggers. Eggers had worked as an agent and had recently founded the small label specifically to record eclectic, unconventional artists. Clement had known Lamar Fike since his days at Sun, and Fike had gone on to travel with Elvis as one of his assistants and confidants. As Clement remembers, "He called me one day and said that this guy Eggers was coming to town, and he was a really sharp guy, on the level and everything, and he might be interested in signing Townes. So he came to town and that's what happened." Clement and Malloy formed Silver Dollar Music jointly to publish Van Zandt's songs, and Kevin Eggers made ready to record an album.

Eggers recalls that Fike suggested that he meet with Clement, who played him the demo tape of "Tecumseh Valley." "It was love at first listen," Eggers says. "I told Jack I would be up for signing Townes to my new label, Poppy. We shook hands on the deal."[4]

Clement and Malloy booked Van Zandt into Owen Bradley's "Quonset Hut" studio in Nashville early in the fall of 1968. The recording, supervised by Malloy and produced by Clement, with Eggers keeping a close watch and offering constant advice, took four or five weeks, off and on. As Van Zandt told it, the studio environment was strictly controlled. "I was literally brought here, sat on a stool, and told to play the song," he said. "I was just kind of awestricken and had all these great players around me, and so I just played and they played whatever Jack wanted. I really didn't have that much to do with it other than just sitting there and playing. They still weren't sure in which direction to record me; it's kind of toward country, but a little kind of underground country. 'Underground' was a term being used a lot then."

Townes also recalled that, for much of the recording, his guitar was out of tune.

By Christmas, the album, titled *For the Sake of the Song*, after one of the record's best songs, was ready for release. The cover artwork was a colorful, somewhat delicate Milton Glaser watercolor. Glaser's work—which included such well-known images as the rainbow-haired Bob Dylan silhouette on the poster inside the *Bob Dylan's Greatest Hits* album—radiated class and brought an instant prestige to the whole package. Mickey Newbury wrote the liner notes with a comparable degree of class:

"Townes Van Zandt, the man," Newbury wrote. "*He'll* be remembered. They'll talk about what he was thinking while his footsteps rang in his ears as he walked down the empty winter Denver streets. What he learned in that basement by lending a compassionate ear to a man who was more than just a janitor. What he heard in those songs, ringing off the black walls of back rooms in Austin and Oklahoma City. What he got out of swapping old stories in a shack outside of Houston with an old man, who has become a legend to blues lovers all over the world." He went on to observe that "the tools of a writer are truths. And truth is knowledge. And knowledge is love. And a writer like Townes writes songs not only of love between man and woman, but between man and man. And man and God."[5]

The production ("over-production, I would say," Clement laughs today) of *For the Sake of the Song* reflects Clement and Malloy's uncertainty over how to pigeonhole Van Zandt's music, as well as their implicit belief that the songs needed to be bolstered with modern production techniques. In their uncertainty, they fell back on some of the clichés of the time: swelling, echo-laden vocal choruses; trilling harpsichords; dramatic percussion arrangements; lush organ chords; elaborate decorative guitar figures; and a general tendency toward the baroque rock style that was then in vogue. Van Zandt's delicate acoustic guitar playing is virtually buried under such devices, and his voice sounds somewhat distant and uncertain, lost in reverb and filtering. For the most part, though, the songs themselves are strong.

Years later, Van Zandt said of "For the Sake of the Song," "This is an old favorite song of mine. This has been a true blue friend through the blue moons." It remained one of his most strikingly beautiful melodies, with a distinctly south-of-the-border flavor, and lyrically it shows a rapidly achieved advance over a song such as "Tower Song." Townes' lines fall into a simple rhyme scheme, but they also smoothly fall into sentences that wrap from line to line, a technique he would continue to develop. He is again addressing his lover, and again there is a conflict of values, but here he is much more generous and understanding of his partner's point of view than he was in "Tower Song." "Who do I think that I am to decide that she's wrong," he sings, as if in answer to his earlier piety. But there's nothing he can do to help the situation between them now; the nature of their personalities will forever keep them apart. "All that she offers me are her chains," he says; "I got to refuse."

Another song that Van Zandt kept in his repertoire throughout his career is "Tecumseh Valley," a lovely story song very much in

the folk ballad tradition, about a simple country girl who is ruined by life in town. For his first recording of the song, Townes
was pressured into an unpleasant compromise regarding the lyrics. The lines "She turned to whorin' out on the streets/With all
the lust inside her" were changed to "She turned to walkin' down
the road/From all the hate inside her," much to Van Zandt's dismay. He recalled that the word "whorin'" "just horrified everybody; [it] couldn't possibly be said on a record." But if that was
the game, Townes figured, he would play it. For now.

"I was a kid," Townes said just two years later; "a stone freak from
Texas. I wasn't too happy with what they did with the album." [6]

The song "Quick Silver Daydreams of Maria" is a curiosity
of Dylanesque psychedelia that the ponderous production ren-
dered even more curious, and the same can be said of some of
the record's other songs. "Waitin' Around to Die" suffers from
ill-conceived production choices but still is one of the record's
strongest songs, along with the title song and "Tecumseh Valley." The less said about youthful indiscretions like "The Velvet
Voices" and "All Your Young Servants," the better. On the whole,
though, Townes' first album showed promise for the artist.

With the recording in the bag, Van Zandt's business affairs
now progressed—or regressed, depending on the point of view—
rapidly. As Newbury recalls:

"We all had a meeting over at the old Andrew Jackson Hotel—
Jack Clement, myself, the guy that was in partnership with Jack
at that time [Jim Malloy], and Townes. The only person that
knew that I had Townes' management contract—and I don't
even know how he found out—was Kevin Eggers. And because
Kevin wanted Townes' management contract, he made a statement to Townes that I didn't care anything about Townes.... So
he offered me a hundred thousand dollars for Townes' contract.
And I turned it down, and I tore the contract up in front of
Townes. I first got on the phone and called Jay, and said, 'Jay,
this is what's going on.' I didn't tell him about the money offer,
but I just said, 'I would like to be able to give Townes' contract

back. If we don't do it, he's going to sign with this crook, and I don't want him to do that.' But he did it anyway."

Many years later, Newbury still felt the sting. "We never discussed it," he says. "I never discussed business or his career with him after that. It was the only way to remain friends."

It is purely a matter of speculation now to try to divine the reasons for Van Zandt deciding to go with Kevin Eggers and the tiny Poppy label. According to Newbury, though, the reason was simple: the street-smart New Yorker, Eggers, conned the eager young artist—who happened to have a strong hedonistic streak—with talk of "how we're going to go out there and set the world on fire." "'We're not with the establishment,'" Newbury recalls, was the thrust of the argument; "'we're not going to let these big guys roll over us; we're going to do our own thing. We're going to travel all over the world and we're going to have a lot of fun. We're going to have a lot of women and a lot of booze and a lot of fun.' I know exactly what he told him," Newbury says.

Things did not work out quite the way Van Zandt might have hoped; at least not at first. "Townes had signed the contract with Poppy," Fran recollects. "Everything looked great. He was supposed to get a big signing bonus, but he never got it. Well, there was a little bonus, but not much. Then the record came out, and nothing really came of it. He was on the road playing clubs more, because no real money was coming from the record contract. And the record didn't sell, because they didn't market it."

Townes told an interviewer years later that when the album came out, "The underground station in Houston would play cuts off it from time to time because my mother would just constantly phone in a request. She would try to disguise her voice. 'Could you please play that Townes Van Zandt song?' 'Yes, Mrs. Van Zandt, we'll play it as soon as we can get to it.'"

"One good thing about it was that I think for the first time he started realizing he might really have talent," Fran says. "You know, people everywhere were starting to say nice things about him. And, God, he was writing beautiful songs."

Townes and Fran had separated at the beginning of 1968, as Fran returned to Houston and Townes stayed out on the road in Oklahoma and north-central Texas, but within a couple of months they got back together, both determined to give it another shot. That summer, Fran announced that she was pregnant. "We were really excited about it," Fran says. "Then, everything kind of started unraveling." It was primarily the financial strains that worried Townes, she recalls. "He started feeling like a failure, like he was letting me down, and then like he was trapped.... So ... the rest of that pregnancy wasn't very good. We moved from the apartment that I had while we were separated, into a roach-infested, horrible place, on Blue Bonnet. We scrubbed it down and made it nice and stayed there a couple of months. Then I found a really neat little house, and he kind of liked that."

Fran's pregnancy ushered in a period of intense stress in the marriage, even as she and Townes looked forward to the baby and made plans for their future together. "With Shell, if you were pregnant at that time, you had to quit," Fran remembers. "So I tried to hide it for as long as possible, because he didn't have insurance, and I didn't have insurance, and we had no money to pay for it. I wound up having a bad first part of the pregnancy and the doctor put me to bed for two months. I was just barely three months' pregnant, and I had to quit.... this, I think, hurt him more than anything: first that his record contract sort of fell through, or showed no promise, and then that I didn't have a job and I was pregnant."

Townes' and Fran's son, John Townes Van Zandt II, called J.T., was born about six weeks early, coming as a surprise in the early hours of April 11, 1969. Fran had been to the doctor the day before and was pronounced well and right on schedule. She and Townes went out that night to a family party, celebrating Townes' brother Bill's engagement. "It was over at one of the cousins' houses," Fran remembers. "They really had fixed a great dinner, and it was really fun. It was one of the old family kind of parties. We went home and went to bed, and about two o'clock in the morning I woke up and ... I had gone into labor. I didn't want to wake [Townes] up, so I kept thinking, this will go away, this will go away."

Finally, at about six o'clock in the morning, Fran woke Townes up. "He jumped out of bed. He got so excited, he couldn't find the keys. Then he couldn't find the car. Then he jumped in the car and realized he had forgotten my bag, so he ran back. It was just like a cartoon. He drove out in the street—we lived in West University then, which was right beside the medical center—and he couldn't remember the way to the hospital. We got in there and I had the baby about two hours after I got to the hospital. [Townes] had a party that night at the house, which I didn't find out about until later."

With the birth of his son—a handsome baby with classic Van Zandt features, dark and angular—Townes manifested an increased reluctance to partake of a family life. He had decided firmly that he wanted to stay out on the road and play the folk clubs and coffee houses around the circuit, living simply. For now, he continued to pursue his artistic desires by writing steadily throughout the domestic turmoil. As Fran recalls, "If I Needed You" was one of the songs that took shape in this rocky period. "When Townes wrote 'If I Needed You,' he sang it to me, and I thought it was the most beautiful song he'd ever written," Fran says. "I couldn't even speak when I heard it…. I always felt like it was my song."

If Townes wrote, or wrote part of, "If I Needed You" at this early date, he was to keep it mostly to himself for a while longer, and he was later to invent a colorful alternate story of the song's inception.

For two or three months after the baby was born, things held together. "Then the pressures came back," according to Fran. It was at this point that Townes started dealing with the new pressures by turning to new substances. For the first time, he started shooting heroin. Even though he already was keeping odd hours and eccentric company, and again (or still) drinking steadily, the change in his lifestyle was drastic. Fran caught on quickly, and she became worried. "After J.T. was born, the one thing that made me not able to tolerate his lifestyle was that I just didn't want it around our baby," Fran says. "I would come home and he would have drugs in the house with the baby right there. At that point I started to have a different focus. I told him I would not tolerate it. I couldn't live that way. That really started the final split.... I never actually saw anything but pot at first, but I started finding out that he was going way off the deep end. I would get phone calls late at night to come get him, and I would have to go get somebody to take care of the baby and then go find Townes. He would be in some just God-awful places. Then I knew. I didn't know *exactly* what it was that he was doing at first, but I knew it wasn't just pot.... He needed more help than I knew what to do. It was one of those things: 'how do you love him best?'"

Townes and Fran soon agreed that they could no longer stay together. Even if Townes' daily drinking and his blossoming heroin habit hadn't made family life impossible, the increasing presence of other women in his life had made the marriage untenable for Fran. One of the women Townes was seeing during the months after J.T. was born was a quiet, dark-haired girl named Bianca, a native of Corpus Christi who had just dropped out of high school in Houston. "He was just strikingly handsome; very dark and brooding," Bianca says. "It's funny, I didn't even know at first that he was a singer and songwriter; he didn't tell me, somebody else told me, and somebody else told me that he was married and recently separated and everything. I was only fifteen or sixteen when we met. I looked older and I told everybody I was twenty-two, so it wasn't *exactly* like Townes was sleeping with a fifteen-year-old, although he was; he just didn't know." Whatever Townes knew or didn't know at this point, he did seem to accept that his marriage was over, and he took up with other women freely.[7]

The breakup of the marriage, according to Fran, "was not one of those things where one of us got angry and said we were going to leave the other one. It just gradually happened. Then, there was nothing else to do." This was the end of Townes' experiment with "respectable" family life. It wouldn't be his last attempt to settle into such a life, but it would set the pattern for his future attempts.

Ultimately, according to Bob Myrick, "Drinking and playing guitar was Townes' number one thing, and Fran was not. I guess for a while there everybody figured that it would all work out, and that Townes would be a good guy. Townes actually joked about that. He showed me some pictures of their wedding and pictures of him back then when he had really short hair, and he laughed and said, 'This is my good-guy days.'"

"Fran was his rock," according to Mickey Newbury. "If they had stayed together, Townes' life would have gone in a different direction, and he would have been a different person, and he still would have been a great writer. But I don't think Fran could stand the lifestyle."

That summer, Van Zandt was far away from Fran and the baby, in Malibu, California, where Kevin Eggers had brought Jack Clement and Jim Malloy to record his second Poppy album, *Our Mother the Mountain*. "Kevin Eggers wanted us to go to Hollywood to do it," Jack Clement recalls, "because he thought it was hipper, and that the people out there might get into his music more than people here [in Nashville]. [Eggers] was trying to take it in a little more of an esoteric direction than I would have." Bob Myrick accompanied Townes, staying with him, Eggers, and Clement in a large beach house at Malibu Pier, partying every night and working in the studio every day for three months. "We used a few different studios," Clement says, "and we worked pretty hard. Kevin sort of tried to control things, and he got his way very often, just by pushing for it, really pushing, even with some of the more off-the-wall stuff, but we got pretty much what we wanted on [the recording]."

Clement and Eggers assembled an impressive group of studio musicians for the sessions, including guitarist James Burton, drummers John Clauder and Donald Frost, and Charlie McCoy on bass, guitar, harmonica, and keyboards, among a dozen or so other first-rate musicians.

"Don Randi, the keyboard player, was really the big guy in the studio," Myrick recalls. "He'd look at the song, and he'd have the arrangement in five minutes. This guy was an amazing musician. We'd go in, and Jack and Jim would do their things, getting the production stuff all set up, and then Randi would point at somebody and the harp would come in, then this guy would come in, then that one, and they had the arrangement. It was very professional.... They dubbed all those strings in later, so I didn't hear all that."

From the first notes of the second album, it's clear that a more focused vision is at work than existed on the first album. The tracks feature well-integrated string arrangements, understated flute and harmonica, simple and crisply textured acoustic guitars, some well-placed autoharp, and generally a more subtle, less self-conscious approach than that that mars the earlier effort. The songs on the album are a mix of older material, like the ballad "St. John the Gambler"; love songs written for Fran, such as the opener, "Be Here to Love Me"—a fine example of the recorded arrangement complementing, not distracting from, the song itself—"Like a Summer Thursday," "Second Lover's Song," and "She Came and She Touched Me," all somewhat melancholy songs cataloging Townes' feelings as he and Fran grew apart; and some fine newer material.

As with the first album, this release took its title from one of the record's best songs, one that Townes had been holding onto for at least a couple of years. "Our Mother the Mountain" is a beautiful, dark, minor-key ballad in the style that Townes had been cultivating of songs that seemed as though they could be Elizabethan folk ballads ("a lady in waiting she stands 'neath my window"; "no trace of my true love is there to be found"; and the refrain "singing tur-alur-ali-o") but that were clearly of an entirely modern mindset. The arrangement—just acoustic guitars; a heavy, deep, bass; subtle strings; and a bass flute—is an understated success. "Tecumseh Valley" (which Townes re-recorded for this album, with the original lyrics intact and with a more sympathetic arrangement) was one of the earliest of these faux folk ballads, and "St. John the Gambler" is another, although both are simpler and more literal than the dark poetry of "Our Mother the Mountain." Lines such as "her skin fits her tightly" and "her eyes turn to poison/and her hair turns to splinters/and her flesh turns to brine" mark the modern influences, if not of Dylan then of some of the modern poets that Townes had been reading since his school days. But the achievement represented in "Our Mother the Mountain" is Van Zandt's own pure melding of his form—the song's musical structure and mood—with his content—the dark, mysterious, surrealistic atmosphere of the lyrics: the song as pure dream.

More in the vein of a nightmare than a dream, and darker still than "Our Mother the Mountain," is "Kathleen." Townes' friend Chito—with whom he shared not only the experience of the onset of bipolar disorder but also of treatment at Galveston—harkens to "Kathleen" as the embodiment of the dark depths of manic-depression. He asks rhetorically, "You don't know Kathleen, do you? Well, I know her, and Townes sure knew her. She's real, and when you go down to see her, you're really going down."

"Maybe I'll go insane," Townes sings, "I got to stop the pain/ Or maybe I'll go down and see Kathleen." One of the most pure and plain-spoken of the songs on the album, another darkly minor-key rumination, "Kathleen" turns around what would become one of Townes' dominant themes: nature. And it is clear that nature is leading Townes to the depths. "The moon is come to lead me to her door," he sings; "The waves, they take my hand/Soon I'm gonna see my sweet Kathleen." "You don't want to go," Chito observed, "but on the other hand you *do* want to go. You *have* to go, and there's comfort in that."

In "Snake Mountain Blues" Townes again occupies the timeless persona of the balladeer. Again working in a minor key, briskly this time, he is dwelling on the inevitable early death of the drunken poet, on the inability of his "yellow-haired woman" to appreciate him, and on the notion that, once he dies, she will move on with hardly a thought of him. Another ballad, far more sentimental, "My Proud Mountains" also focuses on the life and death of a rambling poet. The song is one of a series of Colorado songs (like the earlier "Colorado Bound"), where Colorado is the fondly remembered home to which our hero will return to die.

Townes seemed relatively happy and energetic during the period encompassing the recording sessions. "I liked the coast," Townes said later; "they laid this car on me. I'd get up every morning and cruise up and down the coast highway with the radio playin' loud classical music."[8] There was a small contingent of young women in Malibu who fell in with the group, and the Texas troubadour seemed intent to make the most of it. Nights were spent partying, drinking, getting high, and entertaining the guests and one another. While Townes had his darker moments, they passed quickly in the compressed rush of events surrounding the album project. He felt slightly more involved in the recording process than he had been for his first album, according to Clement; although "in no way did he seem inclined to exercise any control," he felt at least more a part of the "creative team."

As a sidelight, Myrick remembers Townes' playful yet competitive nature emerging in a game that he continued to play for the rest of his life. "Kevin and Townes were really close friends then," Myrick says, "but they used to play a game that would get Kevin absolutely irate." The game was known as "the slap game" and "Townes played it a lot," Myrick says, "and he played it with everybody. The guy slapping you puts his hands on his waist, and you put your hands out in front together, like you were praying, only you're pointing them directly at the person. And the person hitting can flinch, and pretend, but cannot move his hands off his waist unless he comes through with the full swing. But Townes was so quick, he'd just beat the shit out of everybody. He had such quick reactions when he was young, and even into his thirties and forties. Townes could slap you four or five times before you could even move! And Kevin was especially slow. Townes would beat the outside of his hands until they were damn near black and blue! It was a game, but it was kind of a weird, sadistic game. And it was a game that Townes never lost."

Van Zandt and Myrick hitchhiked from Malibu back to Houston later that summer when the recording sessions were completed, a journey not without its memorable moments. Somewhere between Los Angeles and Lubbock, Myrick remembers, "we got picked up by this black family, and they had like eighteen kids, and there's us, two guys and a guitar, and we could hardly fit in the car. And they were just really good folks. Of course, I was not used to that, at all. I was a little apprehensive. We were long-haired hippies. And we went to this little black bar, a real dive, somewhere between Lubbock and Houston. It was real small, it had no name, there was just an old screen door and a little bar set-up. But Townes just loved that; that's exactly what he preferred."

Another hitchhiking tale, also from the stretch of highway between Lubbock and Houston, is told by Joe Ely, who in 1969 was a young musician following in the tradition of fellow Lubbock native Buddy Holly, struggling to find his own voice. As Ely tells the story, he picked up a hitchhiker in Lubbock one day who was headed for Houston. They didn't talk much, but when Ely let the hitchhiker out, he reached into his duffle bag, which contained not clothing but record albums, and presented Ely with one of the records. The hitchhiker turned out to be Townes Van Zandt, and the album was Van Zandt's brand new release, *Our Mother the Mountain*. Ely listened to it, then listened to it some more with his friend Jimmie Dale Gilmore, and they decided that they too wanted to write and perform songs like that.

Before Poppy released *Our Mother the Mountain* in the fall of 1969, Van Zandt visited Kevin Eggers at Eggers' home in New York City, where Eggers had booked Townes for a series of gigs at some of the clubs in Greenwich Village, including Gerde's Folk City, where the young Bob Dylan had gotten his first big-city break.[9] "I first came here [to New York] after the folk thing was dead," Townes said later; "So they called me country-folk.... Who knows?"[10] The shows were lightly promoted, but Van Zandt's striking songwriting skill and dry, masterfully understated performances were well received by the Village folk crowd, and Townes became known as someone to pay attention to.

Townes returned to Texas, always glad to be back home after a stay in New York City. He played small gigs at the familiar clubs in and around Houston and drifted briefly from friend to friend, on "the couch circuit," as he and his friends called it. Later he played shows in Austin with his friend Cado Parrish Studdard and some other on-again, off-again musicians, calling the impromptu group the Delta Mama Boys, in honor of a then-favorite illicit high, Robitussin DM cough syrup, which they called Delta Mama. One of the few songs on which Townes ever collaborated with a co-writer was written with Studdard, and it later became the title song for the album *Delta Momma Blues*.

"I've never written with anybody," Van Zandt said in an interview, "because I just can't." He explained that his songs emerged at times of isolation, "like, when I'm in upstate New York in a motel room and it's freezing out and I don't know anybody and the gig's not been going very good and I haven't seen anybody I even know for weeks ... a song will come out."

Townes recalled this period in Austin and the origins of the Delta Mama phenomenon. "I was a house act in this club in Austin, one of the other guys was the manager of the club, the other guy of the trio was a good friend of mine. I would do my show and then, during the intermission, we'd do one. [We'd] Just kid around, play some Woody Guthrie songs, this that and the other. We wrote a couple of songs, but the only one that's ever been recorded was 'Delta Mama Blues.' That was our theme song; real light. It was about ... the time I was playing in Oklahoma City [and] I met these two guys that was in the army, stationed at Fort Sill, Oklahoma. Every time they got out on leave at the weekend they armed themselves with a jug of Robitussin-DM cough syrup. Some kind of dextromethorphan hydrochloride drug-store high, you know what I mean? Anyhow they called it 'delta mama,' and I wrote 'Delta Mama Blues.'" He concluded that, at least, "I just never have tried to write anything real *serious* with anybody."[11]

Back in Houston, Van Zandt's friend Rex Bell had been working at a VA hospital and continuing to play music at the Jester and Sand Mountain, sometimes opening for Van Zandt, and all the while trying to save the money necessary to open his own club. By the spring of 1969, Bell and a partner from his Navy days had saved enough to buy a place, a club called the Old Quarter.

"I think we had thirteen-hundred dollars between the two of us, myself and Cecil Slayton, who was my first partner, before Dale [Soffar]," Bell recalls. "The Old Quarter was at Austin and Congress, downtown Houston. It was just an old dive, and it was already called the Old Quarter; the Old Quarter was a ship … and the sign was already hung on the building. So we figured, what the hell?"[12] The building itself had once housed the Yellow Cab Club, a notorious speakeasy during Prohibition. In a written reminiscence, Texas singer–songwriter Vince Bell recalled that the Old Quarter was also "in earshot of the nightly howling from the Harris County Women's Jail," and described the place as "a run-down two-story stucco blockhouse of a building with iron bars across broken, cloudy windows. The 10-foot barn-wood front doors could not be locked without a chain and a stout broom handle on the order of a two by four."[13]

Van Zandt started playing at the Old Quarter in the summer of 1969. Fran, who was still seeing quite a bit of Townes at this time, remembers well the early days of the club. "The Old Quarter was in the part of Market Square where during the days all the street people hung out, then, about eight or nine o'clock at night the college kids and professionals would all come swooping down and pour into this old dirty bar and it would become the yuppie place. And Townes had both crowds. Both crowds loved him."

The fledgling club had some brief difficulty with Houston folk-scene matriarch "Ma" Carrick, but that didn't last long. "I would have the same acts that she had, except I had beer and you could smoke joints on the roof," recalls Bell. "It didn't take long to get all the hippies over there. At first, she tried blackballing anybody who would play at my club, until Townes played over there. Once Townes played over there, and Don Sanders and Guy Clark, that was it. She accepted it, and she still had a good club for a long time." As Vince Bell summed it up, Sand Mountain "served cherry Cokes with whipped cream on top. So it was no place for us budding writer types to drown our sorrows."[14] Dale Soffar, another native of Texas City, quickly joined Rex Bell at the Old Quarter when Slayton dropped out. "We stole a lot of the Sand Mountain crowd because we had drinks. The scene shifted over from there to the Old Quarter."[15]

Fran tells a story from the period just before J.T. was born that is typical of a pattern Townes would follow for many years. "Townes befriended a street guy down there at the Old Quarter," Fran recalls. "He brought this guy home. I remember waking up in the middle of the night because this guy was coughing. It sounded like he had TB or something … he turned out to be a great guy, and this guy loved Townes…. Townes couldn't sleep thinking about him being out on the street."

Meanwhile, that fall of 1969, Kevin Eggers was making things happen back in New York City. He managed to book Townes on an east-coast college tour featuring an unlikely pairing with Philadelphia rock band Mandrake Memorial, another Poppy act. Eggers billed the tour as sponsored by "The Poppy Foundation in Cooperation with College Radio," although it is possible, as some have said, that Eggers was the "Poppy Foundation" and the beneficiary of whatever profit the tour was to make. Milton Glaser was again contracted to do artwork and created a distinctive series of colorful, poppy-themed posters promoting both the label and the tour.

The high point of the tour, for symbolic reasons if nothing else, was a booking at Carnegie Hall on November 26. With a short set of songs punctuated by his own droll humor, the fairly obscure Van Zandt followed the fairly well-known political comedian Dick Gregory (also recording for Poppy at the time), and preceded the virtually unknown-outside-of-Philadelphia Mandrake Memorial. Townes was somewhat nervous and tentative, and he was received politely for the most part, although near the end of the set a round of applause arose when he announced that he was about to play his last song.

He opens provocatively with the facetious "KKK Blues," telling the audience, to their nervous chuckles, that he had considered opening with his talking blues about Thunderbird wine but decided to do the one about the KKK because he figured "there were more bigots here than winos." He is briefly heckled by someone yelling for him to enunciate better, but he proceeds to make his way through a nine-song set smoothly and steadily, in good voice and with crisp guitar playing. The recording of the show reveals that he's captured the audience's attention after a few songs, and they listen quietly to the understated set. Townes is clearly not a typical folk singer. He spends four minutes of his allotted time telling an elaborate joke about a martini-drinking nun, which he recounts to the puzzled crowd with good-humored authority to fairly good effect. In introducing "Talking Thunderbird Blues," he reveals his newly discovered favorite way to drink Thunderbird wine, which is to pour a little out of the bottle and mix in some grapefruit juice, which he calls a "shake-'em-up." His performances of "Second Lover's Song" and "Tecumseh Valley" are particularly strong and well received, but it is the two new songs he performs, the as-yet-unrecorded "Rake" and then "Lungs," that are the most gripping. These songs show the development of Townes' writing over the past year or so, and they remain among his best work.[16]

Van Zandt never made much of his Carnegie Hall appearance, rarely referring to it through the rest of his life, and this is one way to gauge what the appearance must have meant to him. Carnegie Hall was an establishment goal, but not a goal for a wandering folk singer. He told friends that he had refused to appear on the *Ed Sullivan Show* for these reasons; it is not too much of a leap to assume that Carnegie Hall meant little to Townes.[17]

## 8

# Don't You Take It Too Bad

OWARD THE END OF THE year, during a trip to Oklahoma City to play some coffee-house gigs with Guy Clark, Townes and Guy met a woman who was to become a major part of both of their lives.

"Townes claims that he was the one that introduced me and Guy," Susanna Clark recalls, "but I think Townes met my sister first somehow. I met Guy and Townes both exactly at the same time.... I was living with my sister. And apparently they had become friends with my sister.... I walked in and they were both sitting on the couch. And boy, did they look bedraggled. I introduced myself, and the first thing I did was offer Guy a vitamin pill. They both had hair down past their shoulders, and skinny as rails, both of them. My easel was set up in the living room, where they were sitting, and I was painting a painting. Townes was just still very, very quiet. And I was painting away and trying to kind of chat with them, and I said, 'I just don't know what to do with this foreground. I just don't know how to bring it forward. I just don't know what to do.' And Guy said, 'You know what to do.' And I thought to myself, 'Well, I can't drop my artistic hanky in front of him, because he ain't going for it.' And he got up and started showing me these things to do. So I really liked Guy because he knew about painting.[1]

"When I met Townes," Susanna Clark says, "he had decided to leave home and decided not to call home for help for any reason whatsoever, and to be completely self-sufficient. And, by hook or by crook, he did it, even though we were all starving to death."

Shortly afterward, Susanna's sister died unexpectedly, and Susanna decided to move to Houston with Guy. "Townes came over practically every day in Houston, whenever he was in town," Susanna recalls. "I remember one time that there were a lot of people down there I didn't know. And Townes came up to me. He recognized my forlorn-ness; I had just lost my sister and I was quite lost.... Townes came over to me and put his arms around me, and then held me by both shoulders and stood back and looked at me, and he said, 'If Guy loves you, I love you.' And for the first time I felt welcome and I knew I had a friend for life. And he stuck to his word. No matter what happened, he was always there for me."

On January 16, 1970, Townes and Fran made their split final with a divorce. Together, they went to the courthouse in Houston, filed the paperwork, then drove back to the house. "Townes said something interesting to me when we finally got the divorce," Fran recalls. "We were coming home from getting the divorce, and we were still friends. It wasn't an angry thing. And he said, 'I may have been physically unfaithful to you, but you were mentally unfaithful to me.' I'll never forget that. I said, 'You're just trying to make me feel bad.' But after I started thinking about it, I realized he was probably right, in a way. I always had a guilt complex over not sticking with him, feeling like I let him down. It's that mother–protection thing. And he really went off the deep end for a while after that."[2]

According to Townes' friend Bianca, "After he broke up with his wife, it was a steady downhill."[3] He continued to drink heavily, and more and more he supplemented the drinking by ingesting a wide variety of drugs, including heroin, persistently. He was engaging in edgy, dangerous behavior, and according to friends, his treatment of others, particularly of women, started to grow increasingly abusive. "When he was drinking, he'd needle people mercilessly," one friend recalls. "He would just go after somebody, and he'd smell blood, and he wouldn't let up, sometimes until the poor guy—or, yes, the poor girl—was in tears."[4]

That spring, Van Zandt continued to drift around Houston, wandering occasionally to Austin and sometimes as far as Dallas and Oklahoma City, playing the folk clubs and coffee houses, partying and crashing with friends, and writing songs. For a period, he moved into an apartment with his friend Darryl Harris. "It was a big place with lots of people," Harris remembers. "Truxillo Arms, we called it," he says. "The street was Truxillo, between Caroline and San Jacinto, on Burnett, just south of the downtown district." Harris describes the Truxillo Arms as "a great hippie dump. We'd get a bottle of wine and go up in this apartment and smoke joints and play the guitar.... It was a big party." Townes was seeing a girl he'd met in Austin named Dana Kinney. "There were always lots of girls after Townes, but Dana was special," Harris says. "They kind of looked alike; they both had that dark presence. She was very much the hippie queen; the 'dark angel,' she called herself."

Van Zandt wrote throughout this period under some degree of pressure for the first time, with the knowledge that he needed new material for the album he was already scheduled to record. This time it was back to Nashville for the recording, again at Owen Bradley's "Barn," where Jim Malloy would take over the production helm. Jack Clement was working on a very successful recording run with Charley Pride; "Charley was selling millions of records," Clement recalls, "and I just kind of bowed out of recording Townes. I got disgusted with Kevin too," Clement adds. "He was pushy about the music, and the production, which I felt that I knew more about than he did, and I think he really put it to Townes. He just never did what he said he was going to do. I don't think he ever paid [Townes] what he should have paid him. I basically tried to like the guy, and I think he probably had good intentions at some point, but he was just a fuck-up; that's what it is."[5]

Indeed, while Townes was to remain loyal to Eggers for years to come—or at the very least indifferent to the problems Eggers created or allowed with regard to his career—Eggers was from the earliest period forward to be followed consistently by accusations of business indiscretions, oversights, and downright wrong-doing, whether through malfeasance or misfeasance, and he never escaped the cloud of these accusations. For now, though, Kevin Eggers was in charge, and the business at hand was to get another Townes Van Zandt record on the shelves and to put the artist out on the road to support it.

So Eggers set out to work with Malloy on producing the third album. They agreed that the production of not just the first, but also the second record had been somewhat overdone, and that a more sparse approach would be in order. String arrangements were replaced by simpler arrangements of more standard folk instruments. One of Van Zandt's goals was to re-record some of the other songs he felt had been particularly mishandled on the first album, and some of the first tracks they laid down in Nashville were retakes of some of Townes' oldest and most favored songs: "For the Sake of the Song" and "Waitin' Around to Die." He also chose to re-record "I'll Be There in the Morning," this time as "I'll Be Here in the Morning," again with a stronger, more direct arrangement of acoustic guitars, standup bass, and harmonica. Just as he had re-recorded "Tecumseh Valley" more to his satisfaction on his second album, so he now hoped to record definitive versions of these strong songs, now more enlightened about recording techniques and production values. He also chose to record a more stripped down, intimate version of "Quick Silver Daydreams of Maria," now styled as "(Quicksilver Daydreams of) Maria," both because he hadn't been completely satisfied with the first recording and because he didn't have quite enough high-caliber new material to fill the record.

In fact, though, the songs he had assembled over the course of the previous few tumultuous months included some of his finest work. A case in point is "Lungs," with the opening lines "Won't you lend your lungs to me?/Mine are collapsing/Plant my feet and bitterly breathe/up the time that's passing." The song continues over an insistent bass-drum beat and minor-key strum, with a strong dobro accompaniment: "Breath I'll take and breath I'll give/pray the day ain't poison/Stand among the ones that live/in lonely indecision." There is a relentless quality to the progression of the verses; nature is invoked but there seems to be a power growing that is outpacing nature, an apocalyptic power, all couched, as Townes prefers, in a language of dreams. In this case, there is also a religious element, with invocations of the devil, of salvation, and of Jesus, an "only son," with "love his only concept." Townes is treading in new territory, and the maturity of his songwriting powers is clearly ready to support his ideas.

"Columbine" is another Colorado song, referring to Colorado by reference to the state flower and, as always, to nature. "Don't You Take It Too Bad" represents another leap forward in Van Zandt's songwriting prowess. The conversationally direct progression of verses seems effortless, punctuated with beautiful, intangible images like "how soft the time flies/past your window at night." He performed this song for his entire career.

The recording of the album, which was eponymously titled—an attempt both to keep the artist front and center and to draw the attention of an audience of those many who had still never heard the first two albums, or heard of the artist at all—was accomplished smoothly and quickly, and Van Zandt was as satisfied as he had been with any of his previous recorded work. The album cover was another Milton Glaser design, featuring a simple Sol Mednick photograph of Van Zandt seated at an old table in an antiquated-looking kitchen, booted feet crossed, his head resting in his hand, elbow on the table, eyes closed, cigarette in an ashtray, a bust of Shakespeare in the ironwork above the oven, pots and pans and implements hanging from the ceiling.

Townes celebrated his twenty-sixth birthday in March, hitch-hiked to Long Beach, California, to visit Guy and Susanna for a few weeks, then went back on the road in support of the new record.

During this period, Eggers was booking Van Zandt through an informal network known as the Bitter End circuit, after the famous New York City folk club, through which the booking originated. The venues were college coffee houses all over the country. According to guitarist Mickey White, who frequented the circuit, it was a relatively lucrative, steady arrangement for folk artists, lasting from around 1968 until it trailed off around 1972.

> The artist would either go up there [to the Bitter End] and audition or submit an audition tape or their records, then all these student leaders from the student centers from colleges all over the country would look through the selection or call up and say, "who can you get for us this week?" and that kind of thing. And you'd work five nights a week. It was great for folk singers. There wasn't a whole lot of money in it, but it was government money, it was guaranteed. You'd get your little VIP card for the lunchrooms at the college there, you'd stay in a dorm room or in a VIP guest house, and you'd play there for five nights, in the same spot, which was pretty cool. The idea was that you'd come in on Tuesday night, especially if you were an unknown, and by Saturday night, you'd have kind of built up your crowd. Then you'd do the big gig on Saturday night to a packed house, then go down the street and do it at the next joint.
>
> Plus the other thing was, like for Townes and a lot of people that really benefited from that, when you got close to a city, you could go into the clubs in that city and play there. So once the Bitter End circuit folded, you'd already built up your market in these areas, so you could go back, go into Chicago and Minneapolis and all these places that you'd played, and you'd already have a crowd that knew you.[6]

It was during these tours that Van Zandt worked at honing his performing craft, and at the same time living out what had become his ideal existence: the life on the road, the life of the wandering folk singer. And colleges provided fertile, easy grounds on which to meet women, another pursuit from which Townes gained much enjoyment and which came easily to him. He never had to seek out female companionship; on the contrary, he was now enjoying the kind of star treatment that he had always dreamed of, since seeing his sister's girlfriends' reactions to Elvis Presley on television. When he played on his home turf—the clubs of Houston—his reception tended to be grand and exalted.

The young Houston folk singer and guitarist Mickey White had started playing at the Old Quarter in the summer of 1970, which is when he met Van Zandt. Rex Bell knew that White had a fondness and an affinity for the finger-picking guitar style, so he suggested that White check out Townes, who was by this time an accomplished finger-picker. White recalls that, when Van Zandt was coming to Houston, the expectations were great at the Old Quarter. "Townes would call up and say, 'Hey Dale, or Rex, I'm leaving Montgomery, West Virginia, or wherever, and I'll be there in two nights. Can I book a gig?' So Dale would immediately put the word out, '*Townes is coming*,' like the Messiah or something. And whoever was booked on that night—and it might well have been me—was immediately fired."

White remembers clearly the first time he heard Van Zandt play that summer. "I walked in," he recalls, "and Townes was sitting up there on the little stool ... in his white pants and his kind of square-toed boots, singing these tunes. I think it was probably two or three songs into the ones that I heard when he played 'You Are Not Needed Now,' and that was the one that really blew me away. He had a couple of other new ones, and most of the stuff that I was hearing, I was hearing for the first time, including 'Who Do You Love?' which also really blew me away. I'd never seen anything like that, that slappin' guitar thing that he did with his finger picks.... I've never seen anybody do that lick like Townes."

White was attracted by Van Zandt's understated sense of showmanship as well as by the artistry of his songs and the skill of his playing. "Townes was playing a five-nighter at the Potpourri Coffeehouse, which is now the Cactus Café, in Austin. It was one of those Bitter End circuit gigs, so he opened up on Tuesday night and played through until Saturday night. Well, I went there on his opening night, and man, I'll tell you what.... I thought I was impressed at the Old Quarter, but when I saw him in a packed house, in a much bigger venue with a better sound system, better lighting, and all that kind of stuff, and with Townes standing up ... it was just really something. Townes, when he was standing up for all those gigs, he was kind of long and lanky and lean, and he had this little slouch, this Hank Williams kind of slouch that he used, with his guitar slung fairly low, and he was impressive. He could get up in a venue ... with between a hundred and two hundred people, and he was without equal. If it got a little bigger than that, he'd tend to, in my opinion, kind of lose it." And as the gigs did get bigger, White says, Townes grew more interested in working with supporting musicians.

Van Zandt had worked with sidemen occasionally when he grew tired of being on the road alone. Rex Bell, who had been playing bass with Lightnin' Hopkins off and on, was enlisted to play bass in support of Townes on many gigs during this period. "He took me with him just because he liked me, really," Bell says. "He didn't really need a bass player.... Most of the time we were not touring, but playing gigs and coming back, playing gigs and coming back, and Townes would take off and go to New York for a few weeks and come back and we'd play some gigs.... Then there were three or four tours that I was involved in ... where we went out and stayed together for months at a time. For one of them it was almost a year. Townes and I did two tours together, just he and I, and Mickey did a couple of big tours. We played the entire east coast; I remember we played

New York City College and the Pratt Institute, and we went all through North Carolina. We played a lot of college gigs. Townes was really locked into that college circuit, and that's where the big money was back then, better than the clubs."[7]

The college audiences loved Townes. "He was a star everywhere we went," Bell goes on. "We sold out lots of shows and the girls lined up like it was Elvis. Everywhere he went, it was a packed house, and not one person talked. He had a way of politely taking a room over with his intensity and with his comedy. He was so funny. And it was natural. Townes was one of those people, he opened his mouth and he got your attention."

As part of the promotion for *Townes Van Zandt*, Townes did guest spots on radio stations, including one late in October on DJ Bob Fass' show on the pioneering underground station WBAI-FM in New York City. The Fass show was fairly representative of the FM radio appearances Townes made during this period. The format gave Townes a comfortable hour-long setting in which to play and chat quietly with DJs like the laid-back Fass, one of the classic FM voices of the seventies, and that was time enough to settle into a comfortable pace reminiscent of an evening playing and talking in someone's living room, which suited Townes. He brought some friends to the studio for the show, including his current girlfriend from Houston, Gretchen Mueller, and he was mellow and relaxed. Among the songs he performed were covers of Lightnin' Hopkins' "Hello Central," Jimmie Rodgers' "Hobo Bill's Last Ride," Stonewall Jackson's "'Cause You're Mine," the Carter Family's "Engine One-Forty-Three" (which he was soon to record under the title "FFV"), and the traditional "Farther Along." He unveiled some of his own new songs as well, including one called "No Deal," which he introduced as "a true story."[8]

Susanna Clark remembers Townes writing "No Deal" the same weekend that Guy wrote "L.A. Freeway." She and Guy and Townes were returning in Guy's Volkswagen bus from a camping trip in the California hills; Guy was driving with Susanna next to him and Townes sitting in the back. "There was no seat in the back," she remembers, "and Townes was kind of squatted down and ... he just all of a sudden said, 'What do you think about this?'; and he goes [singing] 'No deal, you can't sell that stuff to me' ... and he went on. He had written the whole song.... It was just amazing. And we just went, 'God!'"

On the Fass radio show, Townes also gave an early performance of a song he'd written a couple of weeks before: "You Are Not Needed Now." While he did not mention it this night on the radio, he did mention consistently when he played the song later that he had written it "for Janis Joplin," on the occasion of her untimely death earlier that month. Mickey White recalled the setting and the story of the song:

> [Townes and Joplin] had met years before in Houston. Of course, the song's more about other things, but it was prompted by her death. "Allison laid an egg on me" is a cool story. Townes was just hounded to the ends of earth by groupies, right? "Whispering women, how sweet did they seem? Kneelin' for me to command." No truer words were ever spoken.... But there was this one girl, a college girl, Allison, and she took this little eggshell and cut out one side of it and put a little scene, like a winter scene or something like that, that she had hand-crafted with toothpicks and stuff like that, inside this eggshell, and she gave it to Townes as a gift. It was in Montgomery, West Virginia, doing one of those college gigs, and it was there he heard about Janis Joplin. I stayed in the same dorm, between the "blankets made of wool," with the "trains going by every half an hour." These tracks went right through the middle of town, and the little campus dorms were right next to them.

With Kevin Eggers based in New York City, and with Townes now reasonably well established in the New York folk scene, it was decided that the next album would be recorded there, at Century Sound Studios, with an experienced producer named Ron Frangipane producing as well as doing arrangements. Townes had been out playing regularly for months and had a handful of strong new songs, most of them well road-tested, as well as some older songs he now wanted to record for the first time. The time seemed right to get the record done while there was still some buzz about the previous record, and so that it could be on the shelves in time for Christmas.

For whatever reasons, Van Zandt had put off recording some of his earliest compositions, including songs as significant as "Tower Song" and as relatively inconsequential as "Turnstyled, Junkpiled," until these New York sessions in 1970. He also decided to record his old "theme song" collaboration with Cado Parrish Studdard from Austin, the tongue-in-cheek "Delta Mama Blues," then decided to name the album after that song (although the album title was *Delta Momma Blues*, while the song retained the "mama" spelling). At the last minute, the old Carter Family song "Engine One-Forty-Three" that Townes had performed for years under the alternate title "FFV," was added to the recording list, which, with the handful of new songs he had ready, filled out the album nicely.

"Brand New Companion" drew directly on Lightnin' Hopkins' influence, with Townes playing smooth, clean blues licks in a classic twelve-bar framework behind a well-crafted, slightly surrealistic lyric ("She cools me with her breathin'/Chases away those howlin' bottles of wine"). Townes' mastery of this form of Texas blues is evident in such lines as "She's got arms just like two rattlesnakes/Legs just like a willow in the breeze," and his performance is languid and comfortable, perhaps the most difficult part of pulling off a tribute to an accomplished mentor such as Hopkins.

In the three songs that close the album, Townes demonstrates another huge leap in his songwriting. In "Where I Lead Me," "Rake," and, especially, "Nothin'," he goes places no songwriter had gone before, and he achieves not just a new honesty and depth of vision, but an accomplished vocabulary with which to express that vision. "These are the precious things," he sings in "Nothin'"; these are dark songs, coming from a deep, dark place within the artist, that take the listener to that place purely through the strength of images created with an inspired amalgam of language and sound. At this point in the development of Van Zandt's craft, he seems to have achieved a sustained visionary mastery that he had only previously accomplished in hit-and-miss moments.

"Where I Lead Me" has a driving beat that Townes accurately described as a "stomp," and the lyrics blast through the dual worlds of darkness and light that Townes has inhabited so long. He makes it clear immediately that the dual worlds will not merge, that they can only be bridged by an effort of will, if at all. And Townes personifies this effort as a daily struggle between the dual sides of his own nature: "The boys upstairs are gettin' hungry," he says; "You can shout in the wind about how it will be/Or you can clench your fist, shake your head/And head to the country." He is almost clinical: When it looks like "you're not movin,'" he says, you need to "keep it loose/don't get excited/It'll pass before long." He's clear about how the two sides see one another: "Ask the boys down in the gutter/Now they won't lie 'cause you don't matter," he says. He knows where he belongs, and he tells himself what he has no doubt told himself many times before: "Roll down your sleeves, pick up your money/And carry yourself home."

"Rake" addresses the duality, and the possibility of merging its two aspects, in a more fantastic context, personified here by the classic duality of the sun and the moon. The title character thrives in the night and curses the day, expressing the feeling of many sufferers of manic-depressive illness, except here the darkness is not depression, but life-infused mania, casting the rake into a vampire-like existence, while day "would beat me back down," rendering him hardly able to stand. The rake's self-awareness is sharp throughout. In the last verse, however, he gets a surprise when "my laughter turned 'round, eyes blazing and said/ 'My friend, we're holding a wedding.'" Through some transmutation—like medication—the night and the day become bound together, and the sharp joys of the life of the night are turned into pain. "Now the dark air is like fire on my skin/And even the moonlight is blinding." A more vivid rendering of the manic-depressive state is hard to come by in modern verse.

"Nothin'" is a peak in Van Zandt's artistic expression, one of his most starkly honest songs and one of the greatest poetic expressions of stark depression. "I didn't really come up with it," Townes once said of "Nothin'"; "it came up with me." According to Townes, he wrote the song immediately after he had finished reading *The Last Temptation of Christ* by Nikos Kazantzakis. "I was in upstate New York, and I'd been reading that book and I finished it. Wow. And I put it down and picked up the guitar and I wrote that song, all at once." The song is serious, and it is sad, but it reveals a self-knowledge and depth of hard-gained wisdom that make it ultimately a statement of strength in the face of the crushing depths of depression. In fact, the song seems to inhabit a world beyond depression, a realm of pure abstraction, or of "nothing."

When Townes sings "I stood there like a block of stone," with simple, finger-picked guitar accompaniment, in a brooding minor key, "Knowin' all that I had to know/And nothin' more/And man, that's nothin'," it's clear that we're being taken someplace unusual, someplace where we'll have to drop our preconceptions and follow our guide closely, because we won't want to risk getting lost. "Being born is going blind/And bowing down a thousand times/To echoes strung on pure temptation"—this takes us outside the everyday experience of life and leaves us wondering how much further we can go; "Sorrow and solitude/ These are the precious things/And the only words that are worth remembering"—this tells us something we didn't know, and aren't sure we want to know, or are ready to know. The song leaves us with what seems like the memory of a vivid experience, and with a knowledge and understanding of something we might have known but couldn't have expressed, and perhaps with a new way of looking at the world. We're exhilarated, possibly somewhat frightened, and exhausted.

Van Zandt himself was exhausted after the sessions, and like always after a long stay in New York, he was glad to get back to

Texas, where he returned to the bosom of his friends in Houston and took up again an unrestricted courtship of his heroin habit. In New York, while he was working, there were a number of factors controlling his heroin use. Back home, those restrictions disappeared, and he had the time, the money, and the access to indulge himself fully. It was during this period, from toward the end of 1970 well into 1971, that Townes sank further into this indulgence than he ever had before.

It very nearly killed him.

*Delta Momma Blues* was released in time for Christmas. Van Zandt visited his mother and the family at home for the holidays, bringing copies of the new album, and Fran and the baby were central in the family festivities. While Townes' relationship with Fran and the baby was loving, even tender—when he saw them, which was rare—it was strained. To Fran, Townes' behavior was noticeably distant and erratic that Christmas. She knew the cause, but she felt that Dorothy and the rest of the family had no idea that Townes was using heroin regularly.

By early spring, Townes was settling into another of his periodic semi-permanent domestic arrangements, again at the place known as Truxillo, in an apartment with Rex Bell, Mickey White, and a friend called Bear. Townes had met a Houston girl named Leslie Jo Richards at the Old Quarter, and she too was a steady presence at the apartment. Darryl Harris and his brother, known as Smiley, lived nearby, and Leslie Jo was friends with them as well. Mickey White remembers her as effervescent and positive, happy and outgoing, a "real, natural woman," White says. "We were always the first ones up in the morning, drinking coffee, and we spent a lot of time talking. Townes was on and off the road in the spring and early summer of 1971, and we became pretty good friends then. She was sweet, and still she tended to not put up with any bullshit from Townes. But he was extremely fond of her, and she of him."

Richards told White something about Townes that struck him. "I had just learned 'Don't You Take It Too Bad,'" White remembers. "And I played it for her, and she said, 'you know, you play that really good. Townes, he gets really frustrated sometimes about his guitar playing.' She said that one time he was trying something on guitar, and he stopped and looked at his hands and said 'I just can't get 'em to do what I want 'em to do; I can't get 'em to play what I hear.'"

That summer, Van Zandt returned to California to record his next album, his fifth, this time in Los Angeles. Jim Malloy was sharing production credit with Kevin Eggers. Kevin and his wife, Annie, had made the trip and were enjoying the California summer with Townes, and Guy and Susanna Clark were living in nearby Long Beach, so Townes had plenty of company and was enjoying an upbeat, productive period. The recording sessions had been going well for a few weeks, and Townes would often drive down to Long Beach to visit the Clarks. "One night," Susanna remembers, "Guy and I had gone to the movies, and we came back, and all the lights were on and there was a Dolly Parton record playing, her first album. And Townes was there, waiting for us. He had broken in and climbed through the window and set himself down and had been playing that record over and over and over and over again the entire time that we were at the movies."

Van Zandt soon invited Leslie Jo to join them in California, and she hitchhiked from Houston to L.A. immediately. Susanna Clark recalls that Townes was overjoyed when Leslie Jo arrived and moved into the comfortable condominium that Eggers had acquired as a base of operations.

One night not long after Leslie Jo's arrival, Guy and Susanna got a phone call from Townes. "He called from L.A.," Susanna recounts, "and he said, 'Would you come and see me?' And we said, 'Sure.' So we drove in, and he said, 'I didn't want to tell you over the phone, but Leslie was killed. She was murdered.' And we just said, 'Oh, God,' and we all spent the evening weeping and weeping and weeping. Townes was really distraught; he couldn't drive down there, he could hardly speak."

Leslie Jo had been at the studio with Townes late one after-noon. When Townes realized he had left something at home that he now needed, Leslie Jo volunteered to go back and get it. As was her custom, and as was very common at the time, she set out hitchhiking. She was picked up by a man who took her onto a back road, stabbed her more than twenty times, then dumped her in a ditch. She was bleeding profusely, but still alive, and was able to crawl a considerable distance to a nearby house, where she started screaming for help as best she could. A woman came to the door, saw Leslie Jo dying before her eyes, and immedi-ately went to call for an ambulance and the police. When she returned to the front door, Leslie Jo was dead.

Townes immediately blamed himself for Leslie Jo's death, and he was never to escape this self-accusation as long as he lived. He soon began to idealize and mythologize his relation-ship with Leslie Jo in song, transmuting his sorrow, even as he pushed through the final weeks of recording in Los Angeles that summer. "What better way to mourn than to sing?" Susanna Clark says.

Townes returned to Texas, exhausted and deeply depressed. For a couple of months, he lived in an area called Pasadena, southeast of Houston, "down on the ship channel," says Mickey White. "It's a real industrial area; the petrochemical industry. 'The air is greener in Pasadena.' [Townes] was living with this drug dealer and his wife, and I'm not sure exactly how the ar-rangement went down, but I know that Townes was really in love with her. At that point in time, he got really, really strung out. They had the highest quality dope, and he had as much as he could get his hands on. And the thing is, he continued to write songs. In fact, 'Two Girls' was written during that period. 'Two lonesome dudes on an ugly horse' is about two guys look-ing to cop. The ugly horse, of course, is heroin."

During this time, Townes remained in touch with Fran. Fran recalls, "This is when he was giving so much of his stuff away, just giving everything away; his record collection and all kinds of stuff. He had an incredible record collection." Fran delicately but firmly tried to overcome Townes' strained reluctance to visit J.T., who would be three years old soon. Not only could J.T. possibly give Townes a renewed sense of self-worth and responsibility, but J.T. needed a father. She recalls that J.T. often included an "imaginary father" in his games. "This imaginary father was incredible," she says. "When J.T. would swing he would sit on the side of the swing and say he was saving room for his father to sit with him." Townes usually offered a reason not to come visit; when he reluctantly would agree to come, he would never manage to firm up an actual time. He was still distraught over Leslie Jo's death, and this period of depression was being both temporarily relieved and ultimately exacerbated by his heroin use.

Eventually, that fall, he did call and arrange a time to come by the house and spend the afternoon with J.T. That afternoon, Fran had a dark feeling. "I always had this intuition," Fran says; "I could always feel when Townes was really in trouble. J.T. knew that his dad was supposed to be coming that day, and he was just sitting with his hands folded waiting for him. Well, Townes didn't come, and he didn't come, and he still didn't come.... Townes was supposed to be at my house at three. I started calling around, and I tried to call over at Dotsie's, at his mom's, to see if I could get hold of him there. I didn't get an answer, didn't get an answer, then somebody finally answered the phone and said 'he can't come to the phone right now, and we're leaving.' And that *really* worried me."

She waited at home by the phone until late that night, when she got a call from one of the Van Zandts, who told her that Townes had been rushed to University Hospital. "They said 'he's overdosed and we don't think he's going to make it, but he's calling for you,'" Fran says. "He had overdosed on heroin. He overdosed in his mom's house. She was out of town and he went and stayed there."

Townes was staying at his mother's place and some friends had brought over some particularly potent heroin. Pushing the limits, Townes shot up more than anyone else and overdosed, turning blue, his eyes rolling back in his head. One of his friends called an ambulance, and they decided to wait with Townes until the last minute before the ambulance came before leaving the scene. Someone answered the phone when it rang, which turned out to be Fran's call, then they decided to split right away. Some of them had seen ODs before; Townes was breathing when they left, and the ambulance couldn't be far away. They gambled that it would arrive soon and that their friend would have some of his nine lives left.

Fran arrived at the hospital in the middle of the night, and they took her to Townes. "Immediately, I was scared really badly," she recalls, "because they'd knocked his teeth out at the hospital. They told me he was DOA, and they knocked his teeth out trying to get the tubes out of him. His heart had stopped. He was dead." A couple of friends remember that somehow, one of the emergency room attendants, a young intern, recognized Townes on the gurney and led the successful effort to revive him. At any rate, he had regained consciousness and called for Fran. When she arrived, the doctor told her to keep Townes from drifting off by holding his hand and talking to him. "They said, 'just keep talking to him.' So I talked to him all night long," she remembers. "He was breathing irregularly, and I was just talking real sweet and telling him how much I loved him, and saying 'you just can't die.' Then I'd get real angry at him and say, 'you're not gonna leave this legacy for our son.' Oh, it was horrible."

Shortly after dawn, Townes' condition stabilized. "They said 'he's going to be okay, he's made it,'" Fran recalls. "They made sure there was no brain damage, and he woke up and knew who I was, and he was okay. He was in the hospital for several days, but he came back out of it."

The family, Fran recalls, were horrified. "His mother loved him so much; they were so much alike," she says. "Bill has this great sense that some would say Townes was her favorite, but Bill thinks that his mom just knew that Townes needed her the most. That's the kind of love that family had; all of us knew that. We had always thought his mom was kind of a dependent woman, dependent on her husband, but it turned out she had incredible strength and independence." With this incident, Townes withdrew further from his family, in part because he saw clearly the pain he was inflicting on his mother. This was bad, even for him, and he knew he had to keep his family—including Fran and J.T.—away from this part of his life. He joked about it with some of his friends, though. Bob Myrick visited Townes and was giving him a serious chewing out about the dangerous situation he was placing himself in. "Townes just looked at me with a real funny smirk and he said, 'Well, it's not my drug of choice.'"[9]

"Living was painful to Townes," Fran says reflectively, tenderly. "There was too much suffering in the world. Townes just didn't know how to live in this world. I personally always believed that he had a chemical imbalance, that if we could have ever found the right diet or the right pill or the right something, he could have been okay. It would come on so suddenly, it was like there would just be neurons flying off balance that would drive him to some other place. Because when he was good, he was just incredible. He was one of the kindest, gentlest, smartest, most compassionate people you could ever know. I think that's why I hated drugs so much, because I watched what it did to him. But I couldn't understand why he was so dependent on it. It was more than alcoholism. It was something else. It was like something just couldn't fire right in his body."

# 9

# Highway Kind

THE NEW ALBUM, CALLED *High, Low and In Between,* was released in the fall of 1971. It was a heady time in popular music, seeing the release of a seemingly endless slew of great records such as the Rolling Stones' *Sticky Fingers, Who's Next,* Rod Stewart's *Every Picture Tells a Story, Led Zepplin IV,* Van Morrison's *Tupelo Honey,* and the Allman Brothers Band's *Live at the Fillmore East.* Still spinning on many turntables from the previous year were the swansongs of the Beatles (*Let It Be*) and Janis Joplin (*Pearl*). Recent work from singer–songwriters included Joni Mitchell's *Blue,* Leonard Cohen's *Songs of Love & Hate,* John Prine's first album, and Neil Young's *After the Gold Rush.* All in all, a formidable field.

*High, Low and In Between* explored a vein that ran through many of the prominent recordings of the day and that was the inevitable result of a generation coming of age. A seriousness of purpose had been coalescing among so-called "pop" artists and musicians that signaled the end of the innocence of the sixties. Significantly, many of these artists were reaching their thirtieth birthdays. Townes had turned twenty-seven that spring. By fall he must have felt that he was more than ready to close out this particularly hard year, and the new record reflected this.

The arrangements are low-key, complementing the lyrics in an intelligent, understated way, and the Jim Molloy/Kevin Eggers production is nearly transparent, the best of any of Van Zandt's recordings up to this point (and as good as nearly any that followed). In its quiet way, *High, Low and In Between* is one of Townes' most artistically successful records. The opening cut, the knock-off gospel number "Two Hands" ("I got one heart/I'm gonna fill it up with Jesus"), sets a bright mood. "You Are Not Needed Now" certainly suggests something harder to penetrate, but the song has a gentle quality. Some of the songs that follow also have a light, welcoming mood. The wistful "Greensboro Woman" is Townes' speech to a North Carolina girl about being faithful to his woman back in Texas. "Standin'" and "No Deal" are similarly straightforward and relatively light ("No Deal," in fact, is hilarious). "When He Offers His Hand" is a somewhat better faux-gospel song than "Two Hands." "Blue Ridge Mountains" is an exuberant country–folk workout. But the album's remaining songs leave a particularly strong impression and, examined as a batch produced over a short period, show Van Zandt at a high crest of his writing powers.

Prominent among these is "Mr. Mudd and Mr. Gold," a sublime, tongue-twisting account of a cosmic five-card-stud poker game. "I have songs of every degree, from pure craftsmanship to inspiration," Van Zandt told an interviewer.[1] "Of all my songs, 'Mr. Mudd and Mr. Gold' was closest to just coming out of the blue," he said. Townes was in South Carolina during a small circuit tour, and late one night, as he sat in the kitchen with his guitar, the song suddenly came to him. "It felt like my right arm was going to drop off," he claimed, from writing so quickly. After three and a half hours of writing, with crumpled pieces of yellow legal paper all around him on the kitchen floor, "it came to its own natural conclusion," according to Townes. He reread the lyrics in the morning and changed only "a couple of things." The album recording is tight and the performance is clean; the song stood out in Van Zandt's repertoire throughout his career.

The album's title piece is one of Van Zandt's most beautiful poems, touching on some of his familiar themes with a refined touch, focused but relaxed, with an effortlessness that belies the precision craftwork that he put into his best songs. "High, Low and In Between" develops the mythology of the traveling poet: "There is the highway/and the homemade lovin' kind/The highway's mine." The poet philosophizes about his own condition; he asks what he could leave behind after "flyin' lightning fast and all alone"; his answer is humble but is also a perfect example of the poetry that will in fact be his legacy: "Only a trace, my friend/spirit of motion born/and direction grown."

But the real "meat" of the album—and of this entire period of Van Zandt's writing—is in two of Townes' strongest songs, "To Live's to Fly" and "Highway Kind." "To Live's to Fly" is written with one foot in the material world and the other in a world beyond. Townes makes one of his most exuberant declarations, not exactly of love, but of devotion, then shares some of the wisdom he has acquired in life, of life, with his lover, "soft as glass," and his friends as he prepares to depart life. The language is gentle, lulling, as is the music, the chords delicate, almost lilting, with full resolution. Here is some of Van Zandt's most beautiful imagery, expressing a grand, cosmic vision simultaneously with a tender, romantic invitation: "we got the sky to talk about/and the earth to lie upon." And the lessons of life, too, are gentle, "like rain on a conga drum." The message of "To Live's to Fly" is hopeful: "To live is to fly/low and high/so shake the dust off of your wings/and the sleep out of your eyes."

From "To Live's to Fly" to "Highway Kind" is a short step. A line such as "where you been is good and gone/all you keep is the getting there" in "To Live's To Fly" becomes more concrete in "Highway Kind": "My days, they are the highway kind/they only come to leave/but the leavin' I don't mind/it's the comin' that I crave."

"Highway Kind"—darker, more inevitably set in its minor key—is another piece seemingly written from the mountain top, where primal forces are represented metaphorically as features of the landscape, the place where the inner man is reflected in the outer world, and where the inner and the outer worlds are shown to be one. This duality is reflected in the dual points of view taken in the song's verses, leaping from the heavenly to the earthly.

The road—the highway—is one of Van Zandt's favorite metaphors, one that he used repeatedly, always treating the road as though it were a natural, not a man-made, feature. "Highway Kind" is Townes' expression of his place in the universe, the familiar and highly imperfect place that he has accepted as his destiny. The song's real subject is the Tao, the true way, where darkness and light share a dependent relationship. It's easy to picture a weary traveler as he looks from the window of a car speeding to another gig in another town, feeling his destiny, seeing it literally in front of him, the stripes on the road flying toward him like lightning bolts, only to flash past in the blink of an eye, and then more of the same. And that's what the traveler has come to crave, not only accepting his destiny, but relishing it. Or does he?

In lines such as "Pour the sun upon the ground/stand to throw a shadow/watch it grow into a night/and fill the spinnin' sky," Townes is writing like Van Gogh painted, with technically discrete parts, whether a word or a line, a broad brushstroke or a tiny point, all united in a flashing expression of a universal point of view, filling the cosmos. The protagonist is a reverse Prometheus; he stands, and the shadow he casts, in the light of the sun he himself has poured upon the ground, turns into the very night itself, filling the "spinnin' sky."

But where does adopting this universal point of view get him? The answer in the following verses is bleak, as he grins a grin not of bitterness, but certainly of grim irony. There are small pleasures—summers in the mountains, for example—but, ultimately, the knowledge of the void is all-encompassing. How can he care about day-to-day life while staring into the void? He hovers tantalizingly close, asking where we'd be if we were to "follow the circle down," with the answer implicit: the void. And then the final cosmic joke: "You're the only one I want now/I never heard your name/Let's hope we meet some day/if we don't it's all the same."

This droll acceptance of the sad fate of never finding a true "soul mate" in life adds a darkly amusing cap to the song. Perhaps knowing that he has yet to discover that true soul mate allows this pilgrim freedom to explore "the ones between," though always mindful of his quest. He is, at any rate, accepting, but unsatisfied. "Highway Kind" is an amazing document of Townes' philosophy of existence as he approached his thirtieth birthday.

In the fall of 1971, Van Zandt was playing a stand at the Old Quarter in Houston when some out-of-town guests dropped in to see him. The Allman Brothers Band, then at the peak of their musical powers, had played the Houston Coliseum that night, and Duane Allman had heard that Townes was playing the Old Quarter. "They came down just to hang out with Townes," Rex Bell remembers. "They played all night, and Townes played. We locked the door and smoked joints and played until four in the morning."[2]

"Duane, in particular, wanted to come down and hear him and meet him," Mickey White remembers. "It was pretty late, it was like one o'clock and he'd done his two sets. He was kind of hedging a little bit about whether he'd do one more. There were plenty of people there still. And Duane pulled out a little vial and said, 'well, maybe this … '. So Townes did up a little snort, and he went up there and did really one of the best sets I've ever heard him play. Back in those days—man, he was always good, but back in those days, he was great."[3]

After the set, the musicians went upstairs. "We were up there smoking some substances when the joint was closing down," White continues, "and … somebody ripped off all the money…. So Dale was going, 'God….' He said, 'oh man, I don't have the money to cover it. I don't have any money to buy beer and wine for next week, man.' So Duane said, 'well, look, don't advertise it too much or it'll be nuts, but kind of put the word out, and we'll come down tomorrow night and play a little bit.' So they came down; it was Duane, Dickey Betts, Berry Oakley, and Jai Johanny Johanson. Gregg wasn't there, but nevertheless it was really, really cool. They played like two two-hour sets. And Townes and Duane really dug each other, and they started hanging out, doing various illicit activities.... And sure enough, just a few weeks after all that, Duane died on the motorcycle."

"Oh man, it was something," Dale Soffar adds. "I remember them doing 'Stormy Monday.' Very, very touching. It was something else, I'll tell you that."[4]

Van Zandt was staying with Kevin Eggers and his wife Annie in their New York City apartment when Guy Clark reached him on the phone in January 1972 and asked Townes to serve as best man at his upcoming wedding to Susanna in Nashville. Guy and Susanna had lived together for eight months in Houston, then for eight months in Long Beach, California. Guy then landed a song publishing deal, and as Susanna recalls, "They asked him whether he wanted to go to L.A., New York, or Nashville. So, we came to Nashville. And we decided to get married. Guy asked Townes to be best man, and we decided to take Mickey Newbury's houseboat for a nice ride down the Cumberland River, to a small town in Tennessee. And we got off at the courthouse, went in, got married, then got back on the houseboat. Mickey and Susan, his wife, baked us a wedding cake on the boat.... Townes came down to be the best man in the wedding, and he stayed for eight months. At first I thought it was kind of strange, but then I just sat back and watched and learned. We were like a family."[5]

Susanna describes their home in East Nashville as "this cheap, little house, with no air conditioning, no television set, no furniture. And the furniture that we had, the guy at the publishing company had given to us. And we had found Townes an old mattress in back of the Safeway there and drug it in."

Townes was on the circuit in support of *High, Low and In Between*, and was in and out of town, and he was also writing songs for the follow-up record, the sessions for which were already planned to commence at Bradley's in Nashville. Jack Clement was returning to the production helm for the first time since *Our Mother the Mountain*, and he had lined up Nashville veteran Chuck Cochran to handle the arrangements. Townes had a handful of songs ready early, and he continued to write up to the beginning of the sessions, despite a somewhat hyperactive environment. "It was pretty wild around there all the time," says Susanna Clark. "Townes would bring home people that he had met in cabs on the way in from the airport, sometimes people he had met on the airplane, and sometimes people he had found in bars. I remember one time he came in wearing this shirt that was huge.... It was a red, see-through nylon shirt. And I said, 'What happened?' And he said, 'Well, I met this guy that weighs about 400 pounds, and we were gambling, and he lost his shirt to me.' And sure enough, following, lumbering in after him, was this 400-pound guy with a pair of overalls on and no shirt." Women were prominent among Van Zandt's many visitors. "There were just *all kinds* of women," Susanna continues. "I'd wake up in the morning and there would be blondes under the couch."

Susanna Clark vividly recalls a morning that has since become part of Van Zandt's legend. "Townes had just been in New York," Susanna remembers, "and we picked him up at the airport. And he came walking down the concourse, and both of his pockets were going 'flip, flip, flip' here, and 'flip, flip, flip' there, and 'flip, flip, flip' here, and 'chh, chh, chh' there, and we couldn't understand what was flopping under his coat. And when we got in the car, he pulled out these two parakeets, Loop and Lil. He had smuggled them on the airplane. He called them his road birds, because they traveled well; his road 'keets."

As for the morning in question, "We would all get up every morning," Susanna says, "and Loop and Lil would do aerobatics for us.... Anyway, that morning, Guy and I were already up at the kitchen table. We did have a kitchen table, and that's where we spent all of our time. And Townes woke up and came in, and said, 'I just dreamed a song, music and everything. See what you think.' And he picked up the guitar and completely sang 'If I Needed You.' He said, 'what do you all think?' We were just amazed."

Townes many times told audiences and interviewers the same story of how "If I Needed You" came to him whole in a dream. One night, he says, he dreams he's a traveling folk singer, singing before a small audience in a club. The song he's singing is "If I Needed You." He wakes up and finds that he remembers the song perfectly. He turns on the light, grabs a pencil and his notepad, and writes down the words. The music, he thinks, is so simple and clear that he'll have no trouble remembering it. He turns out the light and goes back to sleep. He wakes up and plays the song fully formed.

The story is a classic, perfectly illustrating the subconscious nature of the writer's muse, a tenet to which Van Zandt always adhered. "I don't figure out what I want to say then work out how I'm going to say it," he told an interviewer. "All of a sudden there it is, it pops into your brain. Then you step back and decide about it. You block out everything else that comes along.... The subconscious must be writing songs all the time. I've heard a lot of songwriters express the same feeling, that that song came from elsewhere. It came through me."[6] One such songwriter was the great Mississippi bluesman Booker T. "Bukka" White, who called some of his songs "sky songs" to acknowledge the way that they came to him with no conscious effort on his part. Bob Dylan has made similar comments about his songwriting. "I don't really write my songs," Dylan said, "I just write them down."[7]

Townes told the "dream" story of the origin of the song for the rest of his life, and both Susanna and Guy Clark recall the incident the same way. Yet, considering this story brings up certain questions. To recall Townes' former wife Fran's recollection that "If I Needed You" originated a few years earlier, presented to her perhaps in an unfinished state, is to call Townes' dream story immediately into question.

Townes' young friend Bianca, back in Houston, recalls another origin of the song. "I was at the Old Quarter," Bianca recalls, "and Townes called and asked to speak to me, and asked
me if I would fly to Nashville if he sent me a ticket.... And when
I went to get the ticket to get on the plane, [I discovered] he had
sent it to me as Bianca Van Zandt. And so I figured that I was
going to go there and marry him. He got Susanna to pick me up
at the airport there, and that's what she told me too.... We went
back to the house, and Townes had just gotten a royalty check
for like five-hundred bucks or something [from Buffy Sainte-
Marie's recording of 'Mister Can't You See']. He went and got a
fiddle out of the pawn, which, of course, everybody was saying
to him, whatever you do, don't do that. Because he played the
worst fiddle of anybody in the world.... After I got there and
we hung around and he got the fiddle out of the pawnshop,
we were drinking, of course, and that's when he played me 'If I
Needed You,' then finished writing it. He played the first part of
'If I Needed You,' and he said, 'now that you're here with me, I
can finish the song.' And he sat down in front of me and wrote
the last verse."[8]

Roughly three years had passed since Fran had heard Townes
play an early version of the song to her, according to Fran's
recollection; Townes had yet to record the song, although he
would do so within a few weeks of Bianca's visit to Nashville.
Bianca also recalls it as a song Townes had started some time
before, and then just finished in her presence. So, a plausible
conclusion might be that Townes indeed finished the song to
his satisfaction there in Nashville, and played it for Bianca that
day; then, shortly thereafter, he awoke one fine morning and
presented it with his "dream" story to Guy and Susanna.

Much later, Kevin Eggers would claim that Townes had written "If I Needed You" in Eggers' New York home. And Townes
would embellish the story of dreaming "If I Needed You" by
saying that he had the flu at the time and the codeine cough
syrup he was taking caused him to dream vivid dreams, including the one in question. Whatever the case might be concerning

the origin of the song, it would become one of the jewels of his body of work.

As for Bianca's part, she recalls that she and Townes went out drinking in the Nashville bars that night. "He really wanted to spend this money," she says. "It was burning a hole in his pants.... But later, he picked up this woman, this barfly, in some bar, and he ended up taking her home. We all just got staggering drunk, but I felt that he knew what he was doing. The next morning, everybody was really hung over, and nobody knew what to say.... That evening I got packed up and they took me to the airport, and I got on the plane.... But I was really pissed about it."

Bianca moved to California shortly after leaving Nashville, but she and Townes would cross paths again.

Much like the folk music scene that had formed around the Lomaxes in Houston in the early sixties—a scene the young Guy Clark had absorbed studiously—a growing community of itinerant Texas musicians soon began to form in Nashville, with the Clarks as their nucleus. An early refugee was Richard Dobson, a songwriter from Houston who had been working on oil rigs in the Gulf of Mexico and decided to pursue his dream and give Nashville a shot. As Dobson remembers, "Nashville at that time was kind of a wide-open town. A songwriter could get into any office in town just by knocking on the door, pretty much."[9]

Another figure in this burgeoning scene was an extremely tall, lanky standup bass player named Skinny Dennis Sanchez, with whom Guy had played in a bluegrass group in Long Beach, and who had followed Guy to Nashville six months after the Clarks had left the west coast. Van Zandt recalled the scene in a 1977 interview: "Guy had this house in Nashville next to Mickey Newbury, and I used to stay there, and Dennis, Richard Dobson, Rex Bell, and Mickey White from Houston, and David Olney, who showed up from North Carolina.... It got so intense one day that Guy just nailed himself in his room to get away from everybody. He used big 16-[penny] nails and later had to climb out through the window because he couldn't get the door un-nailed."[10]

———•◆•———

Van Zandt dropped in and out of the Nashville scene as he continued to go on the road for three or four weeks at a time throughout 1972. He also continued to stay in close touch with his friends back in Houston, and he traveled back and forth between Tennessee and Texas often. It had not escaped him that some of the old crowd were not doing so well, and that heroin was taking its toll. As Mickey White recalls, "That fall [of 1972], I was getting really strung out. Townes had kind of got out of town. The song 'White Freightliner Blues,' which says, 'It's bad news from Houston, half my friends are dying,' was about us being still stuck there. Me and Rex, 'half my friends are dying,' that's what that's about." Townes told him about the growing musical community in Nashville, the positive energy among the songwriters and musicians there, and it didn't take much more to convince White to leave what seemed to be a decaying scene in Texas and come to Tennessee.

"I had bought this little piece of shit car," White remembers, "and I sold it to my dealer for enough money for a plane ticket to Nashville and a half a paper. So I did it up and got on the airplane, and I ended up in Nashville, fall of seventy-two. And Townes was exactly right. That energy was back. All the energy that was going on with the pickin' and everything in Houston a couple years before had been regenerated up there." Like the others, White started playing for tips at Bishop's American Pub, a songwriters' hangout on West End Avenue, not far from Guy and Susanna's house, where Richard Dobson had landed a job tending bar. In fact, White recalls, "except for Bishop's, there wasn't anything in Nashville. I mean, there were no gigs in Nashville. Everybody was up there for the same thing, myself included; I went up there to try to be a songwriter."

In fairly short order after arriving in Nashville, White kicked his heroin habit. "It was great," he says. "I pulled up. And Townes went through the same pattern. The drug of choice changed from heroin to Jack Daniels Black." It was an improvement over his recent darker days in Houston, but as White was quick to see, "my alcoholism started really kicking in, and Townes'. For him, that is when drinking became far and away number one." That is not to say that Van Zandt did not return to heroin as soon as he had the opportunity; only that he was able to place his habit on a back burner. Until then, the whiskey flowed like water wherever musicians were playing.

During this period, Townes wrote a song that he would claim was among his favorites of all his songs, but that he would never perform after it was recorded. He wrote "Snow Don't Fall" for Leslie Jo, who had been killed the previous summer. On a snowy day in Kentucky, he quietly shaped his tribute, which he later said was "about the purest song, melodically and lyrically, that I've written." He also complained that he had "recorded it perfectly and then they changed it around."[11]

In March, Van Zandt went back to Texas, visited a new girlfriend, Donna Gay, in Houston, and played an event outside of Austin called the First Dripping Springs Reunion. Conceived as a sort of country & western Woodstock, the outdoor concert is now remembered as the fountainhead of the "Outlaw" movement in country music. Among others on the bill were Waylon Jennings, Billy Joe Shaver, and Willie Nelson, who had recently returned to Texas after his years in Nashville. The next Dripping Springs Reunion the following year would be the first annual Willie Nelson 4th of July Picnic, an event that would continue for more than two decades. "It was a great idea," Nelson recalled, "so I stole or picked up on their ideas. They had it in March and the weather was cool and kind of windy, so I moved it to the 4th of July when it would be hot. I figured that with all the marijuana and the beer, it would cool everybody out. So that was the first 4th of July picnic."[12]

That summer, Townes did something he'd been aching to do: he returned to the Rocky Mountains in Colorado, this time to Aspen, where he visited his old college friend Bob Myrick and where a friend named Bronco Newcombe ran a horse stables. Newcombe had spent the winter in Nashville, writing songs and hanging out with the Clarks and their circle, and Skinny

———•◦•———

Dennis had accepted his offer to work at the stables that summer. Townes showed up in Aspen shortly after, and after visiting with various friends he planned to head into the wilderness on horseback. "I ended up kind of living up on the hill above the stables with Dennis in a tent, taking care of the horses," Van Zandt recalled later. Sanchez accompanied Van Zandt on horseback into the backcountry a few times that summer, and Townes remembered him as a natural outdoorsman, "hunkering down over the fire flipping flapjacks and eggs, looking like he came right off the range...."[13]

At the end of the summer, after about a month in Colorado, Townes returned to Nashville. He was seeing a dark-haired woman named Gloria, a publicist from New York who was living in Nashville and who, according to Richard Dobson, was "madly in love" with Townes. Dobson recounted a drive from Nashville to Austin that September with Townes and Gloria. Townes had brought along his recently acquired fiddle and spent the entire trip trying to play "Farewell Tiawatha." "His fiddling was painful to the ears but he was clearly enjoying himself," Dobson says. "Gloria was not so amused." The unhappy traveling companions wound up at a friend's house in Austin, where they slept on the floor. The next morning, Gloria, furious that Townes had refused to get a hotel room, took a cab to the airport and flew back to Nashville.[14]

Van Zandt played a series of gigs in Austin and was back in Nashville by October, but returned to Texas more than once before the end of the year. He was in Texas when he got word that Skinny Dennis Sanchez had died in October. "He died onstage playing bass," Townes later recounted. "Though he knew he had this bad heart disease he kept playing bass and drinking, a little cocaine every so often, weed and cigarettes."[15] Guy Clark later immortalized Sanchez in his song "L.A. Freeway": "Here's to you old Skinny Dennis/The only one I think I will miss."

The album that Van Zandt had been working on in Nashville over the course of those months was finally released at the end of the year with the title *The Late, Great Townes Van Zandt*.

"I think the title was a joke of Kevin Eggers'," Townes later said. "A lot of my friends saw it at the music store and tried to call my mother. She didn't believe it was me on the back cover. When she and my aunt went to buy it in Houston they had this argument with the hippy in the store. She said it wasn't Townes Van Zandt, he said it was, and she said 'I should know, I'm his mother!'"[16]

As far as Mrs. Van Zandt was concerned, it's very likely that her son's new album title represented a possibility that had been too close to becoming a reality for her to appreciate the joke.

Even at the time of its release in late 1972, the story of *The Late, Great Townes Van Zandt* was the story of "Pancho and Lefty," which was to become Townes' best known, most successful song, and "If I Needed You," which was to become his second-most successful song. Other songs on the album were strong, particularly Townes' homages to family life, "No Lonesome Tune," and to Leslie Jo Richards, "Snow Don't Fall." His covers of Hank Williams' "Honky Tonkin'," Guy Clark's "Don't Let the Sunshine Fool You," and, finally the old country chestnut—the first song Townes learned on the guitar—"Fraulein," are pleasant recordings, as is the wonderful collaboration with Susanna Clark, "Heavenly Houseboat Blues." The other songs on the album are less impressive. But "Pancho and Lefty" left an immediate impression, which was reflected in FM radio play very shortly after the record's release.

"I'm not sure how 'Pancho and Lefty' came about," Townes once mused, "but all of a sudden it was there and I was beginning to write it down. I remember thinking at the time I was writing it that it wasn't Pancho Villa. It was the first song I'd ever written with any reference to Mexico because I haven't spent a lot of time there. A lot of people from Texas are real close to it and associated with it, while I've lived in Colorado and the mountains."[17]

Townes was on the road in Texas with his friends Daniel Donut and Gretchen Mueller; he recalled sitting down in a motel room outside of Dallas for the express purpose of writing a song. By evening, he had written "Pancho and Lefty." "It came to me pretty fast," he later said. "It was an afternoon." He played the song at his gig that night. As he later recounted, the Dallas songwriter B.W. Stevenson was "one of the three or four people in the crowd," and Townes spoke to him after his set. He recalls Stevenson telling him of the new song, "Boy, that's gonna be a beautiful song, but it's not quite finished." He says, "So I went home that night and wrote the last verse."[18]

However, at least one friend recalls that Townes had started working on "Pancho and Lefty" at the time of his overdose and hospitalization in Houston a year earlier. "I'm almost sure that he wrote 'Pancho and Lefty' right in the hospital," Dale Soffar said later. "When he came out of the hospital, he came over and sang that song." Soffar and others close to Townes believed that the song was closely related to his overdose and near-death experience, and that the story's two protagonists are Townes' expression of the two sides of his personality. Townes said, "I think of it in a lot of different ways."[19] Indeed, the masterstroke of the song is its willful ambiguity and mystery. Of all of Van Zandt's songs, it is the one most open to interpretation, and the one most rewarding in this openness. However, a look at the song's structure is revealing.

The first verse stands apart from the rest of the song as a prologue, a statement that ties the story that follows to the teller on a personal level. And it's clear who the storyteller is: it's Townes, speaking to himself, and barely recognizing himself: "Now you wear your skin like iron/And your breath's as hard as kerosene." He's losing himself, or losing the side of himself that his mother would recognize. The presence of the mother in "Pancho and Lefty" reinforces the closeness that Townes felt toward his mother. The line "You weren't your mama's only boy/But her favorite one, it seems" reflects a sentiment that Townes' family was familiar with. Townes and his mother were very much alike, and Townes' brother, Bill, had always believed that Townes was his mother's favorite. The inevitable transformation that haunted Townes' life with Fran—the "bad" Townes taking over from the "good" Townes—was becoming reality, "as you sank into your dreams," he sings. In the rest of the song, those dreams come to life as a wistful fantasy of bandits and federales, betrayal and regret, the story firmly based in this dichotomy, which he seemed to be experiencing clearly and in stark relief.

As for the recording of "Pancho and Lefty," Townes was not pleased that the Spanish trumpet part had been placed so far down in the mix. "It's one of those things," he said, resigned.[20]

Early in 1973, while "Pancho and Lefty" was finding still wider airplay on FM radio, Poppy Records filed for bankruptcy and ceased operations. When the dust settled, United Artists owned the label's assets but would not be issuing records under the Poppy imprint any time soon. Kevin Eggers' accounts of the details of the transaction are less than revealing, but it is clear that money changed hands. Eggers landed on his feet and decided to lie low. Meanwhile, Townes Van Zandt was without a record label. He headed for Texas that spring.

After making the rounds in Houston, Van Zandt played a string of gigs around Texas. Peggy Underwood, a young lawyer in Austin, remembers meeting Townes at a gig at the Saxon Pub there. "He was with a girl named Donna Gay, a real pretty girl from Houston. They were arguing, and it got bad, and at one point he had Donna Gay down with a knife at her throat in the kitchen of the Saxon Pub. Later, he started talking to me, and we went outside, and next thing I knew he ripped my shirt off. And then he went home with me. I don't know why, he just did. He told Donna Gay to head back to Houston, and he moved in with me."[21]

Life in Austin took a similar course to life in Houston. "He pretty much drank all the time, and shot heroin as much as he could," according to Peggy Underwood. "He'd shoot up cocaine too. This was the first time I ever saw anybody shoot up drugs. He and [a friend] were shooting up bourbon and Coca Cola. Bourbon and Coca Cola. Somebody said they'd seem him shoot up vodka before. He would talk to his mother, he would get on the phone and call his mother and cry and cry and cry. He'd talk for an hour or two, talk to her and cry, and I'm sure she was crying on the other end too. His mother told him he had to be the man of the family and he wasn't capable of being the man of any family."

Peggy remembers Townes being depressed continuously during this time, with no periods of mania. "I was with him on his twenty-ninth birthday, and he thought he was going to die because Hank Williams died when he was twenty-nine. We were hanging out with Jerry Jeff Walker and Murphy, his wife, at their house, and they were talking about Hank and all that 'Hank Williams syndrome' crap, that you have to die young and leave a good-looking corpse and all that. I laughed about it, it was so ridiculous, but Townes was obviously taking it seriously."

That Van Zandt was more than capable of good performances during this period of depression and inebriation is clear from the recordings made at the Old Quarter in Houston that July. After a fire in the club early that year, Rex Bell had left the business to Dale Soffar and joined his fellow Texans in Nashville "to try the singer-songwriter thing." Soffar rebuilt the club and kept it going with mostly the same audiences and artists who had frequented it for years, including Townes, who continued to play there regularly.

Earl Willis was a chemical engineer with a love of music and ties to the recording business through his friendship with Jack Clement; he was also a regular at the Old Quarter and friend of Townes. Willis had developed an idea for Townes' next album. He believed that Townes never came across as well on his records as he did in front of a live audience, and that he should record live.

"Townes and I talked about it a lot," Willis recalls. "This was not too long after he had written a whole batch of fresh new songs. There weren't a lot of live albums then, and we decided that he should try to sell Kevin on doing a live album." With Poppy in bankruptcy, Eggers was not free to pursue the idea, but Willis decided he would buy some recording equipment and record Townes himself. "I was ready to get a new tape deck anyway," Willis remembers, "so I told Townes, for my part of it, that I had seen this 3340 Teac, which was one of the first four-track recorders that was halfway portable. It wasn't really that portable, it was heavy, and I had to carry it."[22]

Armed with the Teac and Electrovoice 635A low-impedence microphones, they chose the Old Quarter as the natural location for the recording, and Soffar booked Townes for a Thursday through Saturday-night stand in July, "so that we'd have a night to kind of work it out and a couple of nights where we could pick the best stuff," according to Willis. Van Zandt promised to take the recording seriously, "and he did," says Willis. "He stayed reasonably sober and relaxed and was enjoying himself, but he still had that edge of performing; not just playing, but being aware of the recording. He did it. He played every song he ever did, and we recorded them all. We had several cuts of some songs. For some of the new ones, we wanted to be sure we got a good one."

The Thursday night recording turned out to be unusable because of the prominence of the sound of the rumbling air conditioners. "This was July, and oh man, it was hot," Willis says. "With the air conditioners running it was hot at the Old Quarter; with them off, it was *really* hot. The second night, Townes decided to change strings between sets because he was sweating on them so much. But we recorded two sets Friday and two sets Saturday, so we had four sets, and we cut out a seven-and-a-half IPS sample and sent it to Kevin. Then I didn't hear anything...."

Willis sent a copy of the finished tape to Eggers along with a letter detailing the technical specifications of the recording and making suggestions as to the final mastering. Originally, Willis had experimented with dubbing in a bass guitar track on one cut, "Darcy Farrow," with Dusty Hill laying down the track in Willis's Houston apartment, but in the end he decided not to use that cut. "Nothing should be added," Willis wrote to Eggers in the transmittal letter. "Discarding the first night's tape due to noise," he wrote, "seventy-five recordings were made of forty-four different selections. Sixty of the recordings seem to be as good technically and artistically as those on the tape copy." He recommended to Eggers that the same Teac 3340 on which the original recording and copying was done be taken to Nashville and used to play the tapes into the board at Jack Clement's studio so that no quality would be lost because of any misalignment of the machines. After the tracks were mastered onto a sixteen-track machine, adjustments to tone, equalization, and centering were made, but nothing else was done to the original recordings.

Eggers decided early on that he wanted Townes to record another regular studio album, and that he was not going to use the Old Quarter recordings. It wasn't until 1976 that Willis heard from Eggers again. "I had moved up to Ohio, working at a chemical plant, and Kevin tracked me down there and asked me if I would be interested in trying to put together an album out of the tapes. I said I had to stay where I was, but if I could do it there, I could do it.... And he said, 'see what you can come up with and I'll pay for the tape and studio time.'"

Willis found a small studio in Lima, Ohio, called Northwest Recording Studio. Benny Young was the engineer. "I had all these fifteen and a half IPS quarter-track tapes, and they had the capability to play them.... What we did was we spliced where we needed to. There was a lot of extraneous noise; somebody would drop a beer mug or stuff like that that would ruin your continuity, so we dropped out that kind of stuff. Mostly, we picked the best cut of a song from the three or four we had, then used that. The album, the original album, was a double record. When I set it up, it wasn't gonna be a double, but we got real good cuts," Willis says.

Among the songs that were recorded but did not make it onto the eventual double album were Van Zandt's own "Silver Ships of Andillar," "St. John the Gambler," "Columbine," and "If I Was Washington"; The Rolling Stones' "Dead Flowers"; Hank Williams' "(I Heard That) Lonesome Whistle Blow"; Dylan's "Little Willie the Gambler"; Jimmie Rodgers' "Waitin' for a Train"; "Darcy Farrow"; and Townes' old "Dream Spider."

Of the performance overall, Willis believes that "it's Townes at his best. He had a lot of great performances, but this is one where he finally had it all together. He was straight, tending to business, and singing. The place was packed, and more than that, it was packed with people who were used to hanging out there.... Basically, like they say, when Townes played, it was like he was playing for friends."

"It was a stellar performance, actually," recalled Dale Soffar. "It was bright and sober. In the early days, Townes didn't have a lot of problems. He had his problems but he was open to the fullest, and he was bright and alive and whatever happened, happened.... I can listen to that CD, and I'm at the club. The buses going by and the way the room sounds.... It is a great memorial to that club."

Musicians would usually play the Old Quarter "for the door." According to Soffar, "The door was usually a dollar, two dollars, something like that. Not much. And they'd make maybe a hundred and twenty-five bucks, something like that. And we'd pass the pan around." Instead of the traditional passing of the hat, the Old Quarter utilized a beat-up hospital bedpan. In the six years the Old Quarter was open, not only did young folk and country artists such as Guy Clark, Rodney Crowell, Lucinda Williams, Eric Taylor, Nanci Griffith, Richard Dobson, Vince Bell, and Steve Earle accept offerings from that bedpan, but so did Lightnin' Hopkins, Mance Lipscomb, Big Walter Jenkins, Juke Boy Bonner, and other established black artists who at that time were not commonly seen in predominantly white clubs. Hopkins in particular had a close relationship with the club, appearing regularly for years.

"Dusty Hill was playing bass with me, back before ZZ Top," Rex Bell recalls. "And Dusty's brother Rocky was playing with Lightnin'. Well, when Dusty got more famous with ZZ Top, Rocky had his chance too, because he was a writer and player, and he actually groomed me and said 'I can get you this job playing with Lightnin'.' So I bought all of Lightnin's records and I started playing, and then he slowly slipped me into some gigs with Lightnin'. And after I played a few gigs with Lightnin' I started hiring him at the Old Quarter."

One of the new songs recorded that night at the Old Quarter was "Rex's Blues," written for Rex Bell. With the simplicity of a nursery rhyme, the five chorus-less verses lead the listener through the heights and depths of a man's life, from birth to death, through darkness and light, and give us a concise, complete picture of the man, with all his faults and in all his glory. This all transpires in twenty short lines, sung over an achingly simple structure of two alternating chords, with a beautiful, simple melody line finger-picked from the chords like lush, round grapes picked from the vine.

Shortly after the Old Quarter recording was made, Townes played a guest spot on Don Sanders' radio show on KPFT in Houston, and while hanging around in the lobby during a break, he met a striking young strawberry-blonde girl who was doing volunteer work at the station. She was an experienced horsewoman and had been riding and jumping in shows since she was a child. Townes mentioned his recent excursion on horseback in the Colorado mountains, and the conversation became animated as they explored their mutual interest in horses. The girl was Cindy Morgan.

"I was fifteen, fixing to turn sixteen," Cindy recalls. "It was a big deal because I had to talk my mom into letting me leave school, leave with this man. Mama was very good about it, actually. At that point, we were talking about me dropping out of school, that maybe a month before I turned sixteen and I could drop out if I wanted to. She had remarried and lived with my stepfather, and I didn't like him, so I wasn't living at home, I had my own apartment in town. But I was a youngster. By the time he finally found out how old I was, I think I was sixteen, but I was fifteen when we met."[23]

Later that summer, Townes took Cindy back to Colorado with him.

# 10

# White Freightliner Blues

TOWNES' FRIEND CHITO RECALLS FIRST meeting Townes in Colorado in the early seventies:

We're sitting in this bar in downtown Aspen, and I'm drunker than shit, and Bob brings over this guy. And this guy has big old patches of hair missing out of his head, because he'd gotten a haircut from a bunch of cowboys. And they used sheep shears. I mean, if he was a real cowboy, that would have never happened. So Bob says, "Hey, Chito, this is Townes Van Zandt." I was totally not impressed. But that's how I met Townes.

Townes wanted to be a cowboy in Montana and sing his songs around the campfire.... But he never was a cowboy, he didn't know shit about horses, and he never fuckin' went up more than a week into the mountains, ever, if that. Jesus Christ, do they have a liquor store up there? The only way I would go up in the mountains with him would be that we had enough goddamn booze, and how long would that last? Think about it.[1]

For years, to maintain a sense of balance and perspective, and to escape—or at least quiet—some of his more pressing demons, Townes had sought and found comfort in the mountains of Colorado. Townes would base himself with one of a network of his Colorado friends, including Bob Myrick near Aspen, Chito near Boulder, and others in Crested Butte and elsewhere. "Generally," Mickey White says, "his records would be released in the fall, and he'd come down from the mountains and start touring to support the album."[2]

Bob Myrick rode into the backcountry around Aspen with Townes a number of times, occasionally accompanied by one or another of Townes' old girlfriends from his Colorado days. Myrick remembers the Maroon Bells region as one of Townes' favorites. The two peaks of the Maroon Bells rising above the Maroon Creek valley are among the most famous sights in Colorado, and some of the trails around the Bells are notoriously challenging rides. A Park Service trail sign refers to "The Deadly Bells" and offers a warning against loose, unstable rock that "kills without warning." The Bells earned this "deadly" reputation in 1965, when a series of accidents took the lives of eight hikers, and it was surely this reputation that attracted Townes as much as the scenic beauty of the region.[3]

That summer of 1973, Townes' companion was the fifteen-year-old Cindy Sue Morgan, a far more accomplished horseback rider than Townes, but no match for his other proclivities. The two stayed with a friend of Townes', then set up camp in the woods outside of Crested Butte. "We rode from Crested Butte to Aspen," Cindy recalls. "If you drive it, it's like a hundred and fifty miles around, but as the crow flies over the mountains, it's just twenty-five miles. And it's very beautiful country."[4]

In Cindy's expert estimation, Townes was a moderately skilled horseman. "He knew how to saddle up the horses and pack them. He got them all packed up good." But Cindy soon understood what Townes was doing. "I was so young back then, I didn't realize what an alcoholic I was dealing with," she says. "It was kind of a godsend to get him up in the mountains, where there's not a liquor store handy. He would have his vodka or whiskey or whatever he was drinking at the time, but he'd moderate himself pretty well, because he only had so much."

As Earl Willis recollects, the purpose of Townes' trips to the mountains was to dry out from his heroin habit as well as from alcohol. Willis says, "His way of kicking the habit was to go cold turkey, which he did a number of times. He'd go out in the mountains to clean up his act. He had a half interest in a horse out in Colorado, and he'd go and load that horse up with supplies and ride out into the mountains. He'd come back straight, then turn around and go back to Houston and start all over."[5] The heavier his use was at a given time, the longer he would try to stay out in the backcountry when summer came. "First it would be a couple-weeks' run out there, then he'd have to come back," according to Mickey White. "Two weeks is enough to make you feel pretty shitty once you get away from it. And then, the next time he'd come back, if he had a little more time in Houston, the doses would get a little bigger, and next trip he'd try a three-week run. So finally, about the time we were all finishing that epic of the Houston experience, he was strung out."

After his first trip to Colorado with Cindy, Townes indeed stuck with his pattern and returned to Houston and to his habits. Mickey White says, "Even before he'd go play a gig, he would go score. And he would shoot up, then he'd go play." White had a sober approach to the music business, as well as a desire to see Townes' career move forward. Around this time, he began taking on some booking and management duties for Townes, and it was due to this intervention that Townes was still playing a full schedule of club and college shows, including his first appearance at the new Kerrville Folk Festival in Kerrville, Texas, and a wintertime trip back to Minnesota for shows at the University of Minnesota in Minneapolis. Townes' musicianship was not affected by his heroin use to nearly the degree it was by his drinking, and he had actually learned to moderate his intake when he was on the road.

After another series of gigs in Houston, Townes took Cindy and Mickey to Austin. It was during this visit that Townes first learned Cindy's age. "I made the mistake of telling Mickey," Cindy remembers, "and Mickey instantly beelined it to Townes— 'Townes, you know your girlfriend's only fifteen?' But he was fine with it. We weren't separating. We were joined. It was one of those relationships where you never leave each other's sides for five or six years."

Cindy turned sixteen in January 1974, and Townes celebrated his thirtieth birthday two months later. He spent the next months working the circuit: colleges, clubs, and coffeehouses. He had a developed a small batch of new songs, and he was able to refine them quickly on the road. He spent a few weeks in New York City, playing some club dates and staying with Kevin Eggers, who was simultaneously trying to set up a new record company and making arrangements to record Townes' next album. *The Late, Great Townes Van Zandt* was selling fairly well and was still getting FM radio airplay, and Eggers knew that there had to be a followup. He knew that Townes' career couldn't survive being put on hold while he settled his business affairs. He and Townes came up with a list of songs for inclusion on the upcoming record, and Eggers finagled and soon finalized plans for recording with Jack Clement in Nashville.

Eggers accompanied Townes to Nashville for the sessions at Clement's studio, Jack's Tracks. Townes got along well with Cowboy Jack, but Clement continued to consider Eggers a nuisance in the studio. Overall, the recording went fairly smoothly, thanks to the solid working relationship between Townes and Clement, straightforward arrangements, a good crew of professional musicians, and strong songs.

Some of the songs they recorded had been in Townes' repertoire for some time, such as "Rex's Blues," "No Place to Fall," and "White Freightliner Blues." Others demonstrated advances into new territory for Townes. "Buckskin Stallion Blues," beautifully enigmatic, with a meandering melody, is in an almost childlike realm of pure song, with meaning sublimated to a flow of dreamlike feelings; "The Snake Song" is one of Townes' most vivid pieces of imagistic writing; "Pueblo Waltz" is a languorous love song that offers the familiar-sounding, soft speculation "Maybe we'll move to Tennessee/Leave these Texas blues behind/See Susanna and Guy."

Another song that Townes had been performing for some months—and would keep in his stage sets almost continuously for the rest of his life—was "Loretta." A joyous barroom song addressed to a perfect dream of a barroom girl, "long and lazy, blonde and free," the piece shows Townes at his most insouciant. Loretta tells him lies that he "loves to believe," she spends his money "like waterfalls," but she asks of him only what he is glad to give: "Darling, put your guitar on/Have a little shot of booze/Play a blue and wailing song." What more could a barroom troubadour want?

The album was going under the working title *Seven Come Eleven*, and unfortunately, by the time recording was wrapping up, the project had the feeling of a crapshoot gone bad.[6] As part of his finagling, Kevin Eggers had arranged to delay paying any recording studio fees until after the sessions were complete, and Jack Clement had fronted Eggers more than $6,000. The sessions ended, and it was immediately clear that the project had hit a major roadblock when Eggers revealed that he couldn't come up with the money. Clement insisted on being paid before he would turn the tapes over to Eggers. "We cut that record in my studio," Clement recalls, "and Kevin never paid the studio bill. So I kept the tapes—for years. And he never did pay me."[7] Years later, John Lomax III (who was to take over Townes' management within a couple of years) said of the record, "It would have been a major piece in the puzzle and made the whole picture easier to understand."[8]

Resigned and glad to escape the pressures of the Nashville sessions and the attendant business worries, Townes returned to Texas for a "mini-tour" with Mickey White that included a

second trip to the Kerrville Folk Festival and, on a bill with Taj
Mahal, a benefit for the ailing bluesman Mance Lipscomb at
the new Armadillo World Headquarters in Austin, which was
to become the headquarters of the nascent "cosmic cowboy"
movement. Later that summer, Townes and Cindy returned to
Colorado, and that Christmas he took her to meet his family at
the home of his sister, Donna, and her husband, Ron, in Mobile,
Alabama. The visit was pleasant, polite, and low key. Townes'
mother seemed to like Cindy, whom Donna remembers as
"pretty" and "shy." Everyone realized that she was considerably
younger than Townes, but Cindy recalls that, "like everybody
else, I'm sure they thought I was twenty-three or twenty-four,
not sixteen or seventeen."

A series of coincidences and whims led Van Zandt, Mickey
White, and Rex Bell to the idea of a winter tour of the Rocky
Mountains. White and Bell had been accompanying Townes at
gigs off and on, and Mickey had been growing more intent on
booking a proper group tour. Rex came up with a name for the
group: the Hemmer Ridge Mountain Boys. "It was just a joke
name," Bell recalls, "but it stuck because we didn't have time to
think of anything else."[9]
   White began to look into booking some gigs in resort towns in
Colorado and Wyoming. Both Townes and Mickey were well acquainted with the pleasures of these mountain towns, which included plentiful top-quality drugs, party-hungry young women,
and high-stakes gambling. When Townes' and Rex's friend
Johnny Guess showed up with a newly purchased used motor home called the Blue Unit, Townes immediately convinced
Johnny to come with them on the tour, with the Blue Unit as
their mode of transport. By the end of December, with a handful
of shows booked at lodges and barrooms from the Grand Tetons
down to Aspen, Townes, Cindy, Mickey, Rex, and Johnny had
set out north from Texas in the Blue Unit. After a stop for a gig
in Chicago, they headed for Jackson Hole, Wyoming. Rex's girlfriend, Mary Baldwin, flew to Denver and drove to join the crew

in Jackson Hole in time for the first gig of the Rocky Mountains tour, a two-week stand at the Mangy Moose Lodge at the Teton Village ski resort starting on New Year's Day 1975.

Also flying in was Richard Dobson, whom Townes had invited along to play some guest sets. Dobson was to tape-record hours of conversation, partying, and playing and take copious notes which he would later work up into a memoir, *The Gulf Coast Boys*. The book provides an engaging first-hand look at the goings on inside and outside the Blue Unit, and strongly suggests that the actual act of getting up in front of an audience and playing the gig for a few hours each night was taking a back seat to the drinking, drug taking, and general mayhem that occupied most of the participants' waking hours.[10]

Tales of whiskey, cocaine, and LSD indulgence during the Mangy Moose gig—not to mention the covert heroin use by Townes, Mickey, Rex, and Mary—and the raucous gambling, drunken skiing, and freewheeling carousing, were followed by a speed- and booze-fueled drive down the Rockies to Denver. Most of the money that "the boys" earned from their first two weeks was gone already, and they continued to spend what they had on liquor, pot, and other immediate necessities.

Townes was protective of Cindy when it came to heroin; he made it clear that he did not want her to try it. "I'd given up trying to keep up with them drinking when I ended up puking my guts out in front of the Silver Dollar Saloon down on Westheimer in Houston," Cindy says. "I was getting into bars and no one was questioning my age, but at that point I wasn't drinking. After a while, I figured out what was happening with the heroin, and I started wanting to see what that was all about. He'd tell people, 'Don't you dare ever give Cindy any smack.' But finally, Rex's girlfriend Mary gave me some."

After a couple of shows at the Oxford Hotel in Denver—one of which included an impromptu fiddle solo by Townes that culminated in him smashing the fiddle in front of a small, puzzled crowd—the troupe headed for Crested Butte. As Dobson wrote in *The Gulf Coast Boys*, "Excess for its own sake had achieved a momentum all its own." He describes Townes as "by turns droll, maudlin, lugubrious, gentle, caring, vicious" and recalls that sometimes "toward the dawn hour, listening over muted snores, I could hear the faint sound as he unscrewed the bottle, followed by the chink and flare of his Zippo lighter, holding the night together while the others slumbered on."[11]

The final gigs of the Rocky Mountains tour were at the Pioneer Inn in Nederland, Colorado, which the Blue Unit reached only after a harrowing trip through the mountains in a snowstorm. Richard Dobson had met a woman named Mickey Sweet (whom he called Maggie in his book), who with her dog, Dumpster, joined the crew for the trip back to Texas. "We were really excited to be getting back to Texas," Mickey White recalls. "I think one of the things that really frustrated both Townes and myself is that we were putting forth this effort to keep it going, to keep Townes out there in an overall business strategy, and nobody else—the money, the powers that be—nobody was paying any attention to us at all."

By 1975, the Houston scene had died and the Nashville scene was withering, but the music scene in Austin was flowering. Townes and Cindy had returned to Texas from another trip to the Colorado mountains early that summer with a dog named Geraldine, a mixed shepherd–husky who would remain their companion for some years to come. "Somebody's mother had her and gave her to us," Cindy remembers. "She was a big dog, but she was very dainty. You could tell that she was used to being in the house with a little old lady. You know, for being a big dog, her tail didn't go out of whack and knock over lamps and all that." In September, Townes taped a performance for the *Austin City Limits* TV show, then decided to accept his friend John Storbot's offer to live in his trailer in Clarksville, on the west side of Austin, while he was out of town.

Clarksville was originally established as a community for ex-slaves shortly after the Civil War, and it remained an "outsiders" community. Many Clarksville residents picked cotton or farmed.

The city of Austin had at one time attempted to push the black population to the east side of town, and had pressured blacks in communities such as Clarksville to move by curtailing services. Clarksville residents still used kerosene lamps and outhouses well into the 1950s and '60s, and the community remained isolated. In 1968, residents unsuccessfully protested a plan to build a highway along the Missouri Pacific Railroad, on the western edge of Clarksville. The completed MoPac Expressway split Clarksville in two, and dozens of homes were relocated.[12]

According to Mickey White, "The streets weren't paved. You'd go up Westlyn and take a left on 12th and down and you were just literally in another world. The black people and the white people lived right across the street from one another, they got along, and there was no bullshit."

As Cindy sums up the scene: "Clarksville was basically a place where we were all on heroin, all shooting." Peggy Underwood remembers accompanying Townes to Austin's East Side to buy heroin. "I thought it was exciting to go to the East Side with him to score, which, now that I look back on it, I wonder how I could have been so stupid. It got real scary, but that's the way he liked it."[13]

Most of Townes' contingent in Clarksville came and went, but the group included Cindy, Rex and Mary, Mickey, Chito—whom Townes had convinced to move back to Texas—and his girlfriend Mary Ann, Darryl Harris and his brother Smiley, Phyllis Ivy and Phyllis Peoples, two old friends from Houston named Suzy Terrell and Linda Miller, a friend named Kathy Tennel, and occasionally Richard Dobson, Peggy Underwood, and a few others. The group felt comfortable in Clarksville: Townes was pleased to be living a spartan existence in the barely furnished trailer—which they called Goat Hill—with some chickens to look after; the liquor store was around the corner, and the pharmacy sold syringes and codeine cough syrup. "One time, Phyllis Peoples went to get her codeine cough syrup and crashed her car into the front plate-glass window of the North Loop Pharmacy,"

Underwood remembers. "They didn't do anything to her; she just walked in and got her codeine cough syrup."

Notwithstanding cars crashing through plate-glass windows, the white hippies found themselves able to live somewhat anonymously in Clarksville, and they were occasionally able to bond with their black neighbors. Mary Ann and Chito lived in an apartment across the street from seventy-nine-year-old Seymour Washington, a lifelong blacksmith whom everyone called Uncle Seymour, just up the street from Townes' and Cindy's trailer. Linda Miller lived in an old house across the street from the trailer, and next door to Uncle Seymour was a friendly, older black woman named Rosie. "Uncle Seymour was kind of like our patron," says Underwood. Washington's small house and yard became something of a neighborhood gathering place, and his simple hospitality toward and empathy with his young white friends quickly grew into a bond. Mickey White recalls that some of the older black neighbors felt uncomfortable about Uncle Seymour "because all the whites hung out at his house, and there was grumbling here and there about that."

It so happened that the two women from Houston, Suzy Terrell and Linda Miller, were both former girlfriends of Townes. Furthermore, the two women happened to have in common the experience of having Townes live with them for some months, then go away on tour for a month or two, then, on his return, ignore them—not call, not speak to them, just leave them "cold turkey." Mary Ann recalls that most of Townes' girlfriends left *him*, *he* didn't leave *them*, but these two were among the few whom *he* had left, and left cruelly. Yet here they were in Clarksville. Suzy was considerably younger than Townes, had lied about her age and become a stripper in Houston, and had developed a serious heroin habit. One night in Clarksville, Suzy finally confronted Townes. Mary Ann recalls: "Suzy was real drunk and came home about one or so in the morning. Everybody was out on the porch talking, and she went over there—and this was a good two or three years after it happened—and she said, 'Townes, I want to ask you something.' He said, 'what?' And she said, 'Why'd you do that to me, why'd you just totally ignore me when you came back in town?' And he had a classic answer. He said, 'Because I was falling in love with you.' But it was a destructive relationship. They were both hell-bent on destruction."[14]

The story of Linda Miller is more tragic. "She was totally devoted, committed, in love with Townes," Mary Ann remembers. She was taking a bus every day to a methadone clinic across town. One day, coming back from the clinic, she fell from the bus and was injured. As Mary Ann recollects, "They gave her a whole big bottle of Percodan—synthetic morphine—and she went back to her house in Clarksville and started taking those pills. She was seen wandering around the neighborhood naked, and a couple of days later she was dead."

Mary Ann is one of a number of Townes' friends with a vivid recollection of the contrast between the two apparent sides of Townes' personality. "Townes was hilarious, quick-witted, charming, a one-hundred percent woman charmer and all of that," she says. "But as I told the movie people that came here, he could be really mean-spirited when he was drunk or on codeine."

In October 1976, Townes and Cindy attended the Country Music Association convention in Nashville along with Guy and Susanna Clark. Townes was drinking heavily all evening, and toward the end of the program, he went up on stage with Guy, Waylon Jennings, Jerry Jeff Walker, and others for a large-group singing finale. Townes decided to try to stand on his head, repeatedly falling and trying again, crashing into equipment, instruments, and other people on the stage. "I woke up with a hangover and went into hiding from all my friends for a week or two. Guy practically disowned me," a writer quoted Townes as saying after the incident, adding that Guy must have "come to the conclusion that I'm from the wrong side of the tracks."[15] In fact, Guy was not indulgent of this kind of behavior, and he and Susanna were steering clear of Townes, although Townes and Susanna continued a close friendship by phone.

It was during this period that Townes reached a point where it became crystal clear to those around him that a dangerous pathology was at play in his life. Townes told a writer about the incident shortly after it occurred, describing how he and Rex Bell, in a fit of "alcoholic derangement," had been climbing through dumpsters and covering themselves with filth, then going to bars and clubs where they were acquainted with the managers and demanding money for pints of vodka, threatening simply to hang around in their disgusting condition if they didn't comply. Early in the morning after a night of this extreme behavior, someone found Townes unconscious in one of the dumpsters and called an ambulance. "The next thing I knew," Townes told the writer, "I was lying on a stretcher in a hospital with a bottle of, like, pure Valium running into my arm." [16]

In fact, Townes was taken to Brackenridge Hospital in downtown Austin.[17] He was admitted to the alcohol and drug abuse treatment ward, where he went through only ten days of a forty-five-day detoxification and rehabilitation program before checking himself out, although not before being placed on a lithium regimen. It is common for people with bipolar disorder to reject lithium, or any other drug that smoothes over the highs and lows of their condition, and Townes had been no exception since he was originally placed on medication at the hospital in Galveston more than ten years before. When he left Brackenridge, Cindy took on the responsibility of trying to keep him on his regimen.

The film *Heartworn Highways* would immortalize a rosier side of the Clarksville experience.[18] The novice director, James Szalapski, had originally approached John Lomax III for advice on who he might include in a documentary on the "new wave" of country music coming out of Nashville. Lomax suggested that Szalapski could focus on the Nashville-based Texans associated with Guy Clark. Part of the premise that emerged from the film was that these new country artists had as strong a connection to family, simple living, and, apparently, strong drink as the traditional country artists did, and that these things were reflected in their music. That December, Szalapski and his film crew showed up in Clarksville looking for Townes. As Townes recalled, "They wanted to have a barbecue in Clarksville ... because Uncle Seymour's barbecues were kind of famous." The cold weather prevented a barbecue, but the crew set up to shoot Townes playing in Uncle Seymour's tiny house. "There are all those arc lights coming through his little windows," Townes remembered; "Seymour said it's the only time his house has ever been warm in December."[19]

On the first day of shooting (which appears as the second of Townes' sequences in the film), with Phyllis Ivy[20] washing dishes in the background and Uncle Seymour sitting by the kitchen pantry next to Townes, Townes interviews Seymour for the film crew ("Unc, you had a birthday lately didn't you, on July twelfth, and you were ... thirty six?" Townes grins at Seymour. "I was seventy-nine," Seymour says. "Born in 1896."). Townes talks with Seymour about his career as a blacksmith and Seymour talks about horses and horseshoeing and blacksmith philosophy, then indulges his propensity for preaching. He leans toward Townes, looking directly at him.

"People condemn whiskey, but they have no right to," Washington says. Townes smiles. "Because when God created the heaven and earth, He created all things, and He also created barley, and rye, and if He didn't think those things were good for man, He wouldn't have let them grow." This gets a whoop from the assembled hippies off-camera, and Townes gives a hearty "Amen!," grinning.

"He also created cattle of the fields, and birds of the air, and food for us to subsist on," Seymour continues. He's looking right at Townes, gesturing with his hands. "But He didn't mean for us to eat so much of it that it's detrimental to us, or will make us sick." Townes looks straight ahead, smiling, his cowboy hat pushed back on his head. "And the same thing applies to whiskey, or beer, or anything you drink." Townes looks down at the floor; Seymour continues preaching directly to him with a gentle insistence. "You don't have to drink a barrel of whiskey because you see a barrel sitting there." He is emphatic. The camera zooms in closer. "You drink a little bit of it and then stop, and ask God to give you the knowledge to do that."

Townes begins to play a song on the guitar, finger-picking the opening bars of "Waitin' Around to Die." Seymour listens attentively, hears the refrain, and leans over to Phyllis. She says something, reassuring him, and he listens more closely. Phyllis sways gently to the music, eyes closed, cigarette burning. Seymour, right beside her, is gazing intently, nodding his head as he listens. The camera is on Seymour now; he is listening intently, seemingly full of understanding. He nods his head; "That's right," he mouths silently. He looks grim. "A friend said he knew where some easy money was," Townes sings. "We robbed a man and brother did we fly."

Seymour's eyes are red, filling with tears now. He has a look of dead seriousness, of grief, on his face. "They told her they'd take care of me/They drug me back to Tennessee/And it's two long years of waitin' around to die."

At this, the tears fall from Seymour's eyes, down the lines of his world-weary face. He wipes them away with the palm of his hand; Phyllis puts her hand on his shoulder and leans over and says something to him, then she wraps her hands around his and holds them. Townes goes on with the song, singing, as always, with his eyes closed. Seymour Washington shakes his head sadly at the last lines of the song, and the tears stream down his cheeks as the final minor chord fades into the air.

The next day, the crew shot footage outdoors, including a sequence where Townes stages a "fall" down a "giant rabbit hole" in the yard behind Goat Hill. "This whole thing occurred ... starting on the Sunday after Mickey White and Rex Bell and I had had a real successful gig at Castle Creek, a club on Lavaca," Townes said. "So by the time Sunday came, we were into the celebrating."

Cindy recalls that the shooting of the film was interfering with their heroin shooting: "I remember us trying to do a dodging act with some of those people who filmed that, because we were doing heroin then and we didn't really want them to know, so we were dodging them. Finally these people had us cornered, and I said to Townes, 'Why don't you just let them come over?'"

*Heartworn Highways*—which wasn't released until 1977—is revealing in a number of ways. As far as Townes Van Zandt is concerned, the film shows clearly that he was far and away the most charismatic of the musicians he was associated with, including Guy Clark, Rodney Crowell, Steve Young, Steve Earle, Charlie Daniels, and David Allen Coe, among others. Clark—who has roughly the same amount of screen time as Van Zandt—is shown to be a craftsman (literally, in a sequence showing him repairing a guitar), serious and workmanlike, and it is evident that his songs are carefully written and effectively performed. He is clearly the center of the somewhat motley gathering of songwriters surrounding him. But Townes shines with a naked energy and makes an immediate, direct connection with everyone around him, whether he's performing or just clowning around. And he eclipses all competition musically with "Waitin' Around to Die" and "Pancho and Lefty."[21]

Cindy has a less-than-sanguine summary of the Clarksville period:

> It's a good thing I was fourteen years younger than him, because I ended up really kind of babysitting ... you kind of start to realize what you're dealing with, living with an alcoholic.
>
> There was one time I remember—and this really kind of sums it up—I had fallen and sprained my ankle. I was on crutches, and Smiley and Darryl came over, and they had some real good heroin. We'd all been drinking, and they told Townes, "don't do your regular dosage." Well, he balls up his regular dosage anyway and shoots it on up. Next thing I know, he's out—he's turning blue. I'm on crutches, but I've got Darryl and Smiley and all these experienced druggies, and they all know to start shooting him up with salt water. And I have to deal with this.... Those people doing that movie wanted me to talk about that in the movie, too, and I just didn't really want to. You see your husband OD in front of

your own eyes, you know, it's not really something
that you want the whole world to know.

Peggy Underwood offered a rosier reminiscence: "Everything
was fun then because we were young and, I don't know, we
would just do whatever Townes did. It was just a lot of fun, a lot
of craziness."

John Lomax III moved from Texas to Tennessee in 1973. He
knew most of the Texas singer–songwriters in Nashville, including Guy Clark and Townes, and he rented an apartment outside
of town, not far from Old Hickory Lake, where Guy and Susanna
held court. "I realized I wanted to be in the music business,"
Lomax says, "and I had built up enough credibility by writing
about music for three or four little underground papers. I had
a couple of things in *Creem*. I came up here [to Nashville] because I had gone to New York and L.A. and I couldn't stand the
thought of living there." Lomax had originally come to Nashville with Texas guitarist Rocky Hill, brother of Dusty Hill of ZZ
Top, for a recording session. Lomax recalls, "He was really into
the symbolism, the parallels between Leadbelly and my grandfather and him and me."

Lomax liked Nashville, and he got a job as a publicist with
Jack Clement's Jack Music Incorporated. He worked at JMI for
the next few years, absorbing as much knowledge of the music
business as he could, and continuing to write. "I was beginning
to understand that what I wanted to do in the music business
was be a manager. I think I was born probably with some sort
of genetic ability to tell if something's really really good or if it's
only average, some sort of sense, because the family's had it for
all these years."

Based on what he had learned of the situation, Lomax blamed
Kevin Eggers for what he saw to be the stagnant state of Van
Zandt's career. "Kevin was totally inept at being able to function
in any way other than to get some records into the pipeline, col-
lect the money, and keep it," Lomax says. "So I decided, I'll be

his manager, and I'll just tell everybody that this is the world's greatest songwriter, and we'll ride off into the sunset and count our money. What could be easier?"

Townes and Lomax agreed to proceed with this new management plan. It is easy to imagine that Townes might have felt the same kind of fascination with the symbolism of being under the wing of a Lomax as Rocky Hill had felt, particularly given Townes' grounding in the Houston folk and blues scene that the senior Lomax had mentored in the sixties. So now, for openers, Townes agreed that Lomax would place an ad in the classified section of *Rolling Stone* magazine: "AMERICA'S GREATEST songwriter, Townes van Zandt Fan Club, News, pictures, rumors, lies. Box 12542, Nashville, TN 37212."

"I got something like 150 letters," Lomax says. "And they were all amazingly literate. By this time, I had worked as a record company publicist for some years, in the country business, with Don Williams, Charley Pride, the Stonemans, and all these people that Jack worked with.... So I was used to getting fan mail. But these were like the Rhodes scholars of fan mail: eloquently written letters talking about Townes' music in great detail; saying how he'd saved their life, by listening to one of his songs." Lomax started mailing out "just write-ups on what was happening," he says, "and I'd throw an itinerary in there and send it out."

This early publicity effort was an encouraging experience, but Lomax knew that he had other issues to address. Most immediately, he knew he had to get Townes out on the road more regularly. He hired Bobby Cudd, an agent out of South Carolina with good connections, who took Townes on and quickly booked some dates. "He started getting Townes back on the folk circuit and broadening the base a little bit," says Lomax. "You could go play almost anywhere if you had a record out in the shops and a bit of a rep, which Townes had developed in spite of Kevin and despite any effort ever being made to systematically do something, because of the sheer brilliance of the work and the word of mouth that would ensue from somebody that was that good."

———•◆•———

The next step was to work on landing a new recording contract. "I knew we had to get a real record deal, because by then I
was going, 'Wait a minute, aren't we supposed to be getting publishing statements and royalty statements?' I started realizing the
shell game that was going on. There was simply no accounting."
Lomax became determined to get to the bottom of Townes' financial dealings with Poppy Records and with Kevin Eggers.

The final step was going to require a bigger leap, a more momentous commitment. Lomax believed that, in order to move
his career forward, Townes would have to move to Nashville.
Townes had already considered the possibility. He had been relatively rootless and drifting for long enough; Clarksville was no
longer a viable option; he had "kind of decided" that Cindy
"should have some kind of home base instead of couches and
suitcases." So Townes and Cindy moved to Nashville late in the
summer of 1976, "to get my songs heard and recorded by other
artists," Townes said.[22]

# 11

## Dollar Bill Blues

T HE ACTUAL GENESIS OF TOWNES' decision to move to Nashville came during his last trip to the Rocky Mountains. Out in the wilderness for a week-long ride, he and Cindy made a serious, sober assessment of his career. Townes knew that, artistically, things were stagnating for him. He felt that he had some responsibility to try to resuscitate his muse and revive his career, to get back to the buzz of writing and recording new material, and of connecting with his audience on the road. He and Cindy decided that a move to Music City would give Townes the best chance of getting things going again. He also wanted Cindy to be comfortable. He always tended to spend his gig money on the road, but royalty payments from recordings were a dependable, renewable source of income, and he realized that "to have money coming in the mail box is a real treat."[1] This is exactly what his new manager, John Lomax, was telling him as well.

Townes and Cindy agreed that they didn't want to live in the city proper, but would look for a place in the country not far from town. The "place in the country" was something that Guy and Susanna Clark and many of Townes' other musician friends in Nashville had sought for years and not found, and they realized that they might not succeed in this quest. Mickey Newbury and the Clarks had small houses on Old Hickory Lake just east of Nashville, but anything viable farther out had proved elusive. In a stroke of good fortune, however, within a week of arriving in Tennessee, through a friend of Steve Earle's named Bobby Walker, Townes and Cindy found a cabin in Franklin, about twenty miles south of the city. "We found this eight-hundred acre place for thirty dollars a month," Townes said at the time.[2] "We have electricity and running water, sometimes, but no insulation." An old friend of Townes', Michael Ewah, who was half Eskimo and half American Indian, soon moved into the cabin across the creek, as a "co-caretaker" of the property.

As Cindy recalls, "The place was on back there in the woods, and they grew tobacco on the farm, so the big tobacco barn that they hang that stuff in was between the two houses, and there was a little creek kind of through the center of it all. And there was an old rock wall that was originally the county border." Standing on a pleasant, grassy rise in a stand of trees, with a small barn and some dilapidated outbuildings, the house itself was a rough wooden shack with a metal roof. "There was two bedrooms and then one long kitchen in back of the bedrooms, and the front porch was about the length of both bedrooms," Cindy remembers. At first, when Townes had gigs, Cindy spent a lot of time alone at the house, but it wasn't long before she got to know a woman who owned a horse farm just down the road. Eventually, the woman hired Cindy to work with her horses a few days a week.[3]

Through Guy Clark, Townes and Michael Ewah had known each other at Bronco Newcombe's stables in Aspen, and they had explored the backcountry on horseback together in the Rockies a number of times. At the farm, they were able to continue their outdoor rambles. "Townes and Mike would hunt off that property," Cindy says. "Mike would go out in the back ponds up there. Turtles, big turtles, come out of them back ponds, and Mike would catch them and make turtle soup. And Geraldine killed skunks. But Mike was really a hunter, living off the land." Ewah also did volunteer work for the Humane Society, rehabilitating hawks that had been injured. Cindy recalls, "he had to ... kill the little chipmunks that are up there in Tennessee for food for the hawk while it was cage-ridden. Finally, when it was able to come out of the cage, he would keep it on his hand and get it to where he'd send it to tree when he'd see a chipmunk." As a reminder of their precarious financial condition, Cindy says, "I remember the three of us cutting up a lot of trees off that land and selling them for firewood for spending money."

The most notable feature of the property was that it was located on the site of a Civil War battlefield. The Battle of Franklin, one of the bloodiest, most savage battles of the war, took place on a bitter cold November 30, 1864, in the woods and hills surrounding the creek and the adjoining Harpeth River. "If you walked back to the end of that property, you could see the Civil War redoubts on top of those hills, from the Battle of Franklin," Cindy recalls. Townes was already keenly interested in American history, and he was fascinated by this intimate proximity to past events. He took time to read up on the history of the battles of Franklin and Nashville, and particularly on the flamboyant Texan John Bell Hood, the Confederate general who commanded the Army of Tennessee at these battles.[4]

Meanwhile, John Lomax was at work. "We started to get Townes out on the road again, mostly by himself at this point," Lomax says. "I would go out a little bit, but not much, because managers really don't belong on the road. But I was trying to get a record deal. I believed I had to get Townes away from Kevin and had to get him with a record company. And it was hard, because Townes didn't know about business at all. He was sort of trying at this point, but really he just wanted to be the troubadour, the mythic figure."[5]

Van Zandt returned to Houston in June for a three-night stand on a bill with Hoyt Axton at Liberty Hall, promoted by Lomax as "The Return of the Hemmer Ridge Mountain Boys." Townes was glad to have the boisterous support of Mickey White and Rex Bell, and was glad to be playing his old home town again. According to Lomax, "I knew Bob Claypool would give me a bunch of ink with the *Post* and he did a big feature. We got him on the radio, on one of the hip stations where he came on and played live, and we actually got a TV spot—'The prodigal son returns home, three nights at Liberty Hall.'"

With his ear to the ground, and after a few unsuccessful attempts at deals, Lomax heard that Kevin Eggers was working again with Earl Willis's live recordings of Townes at the Old Quarter, and that Willis had edited and mixed the tapes in preparation for a release. "Kevin got some more money from somewhere," Lomax says, "and suddenly he got Tomato going." Tomato Records was a United Artists-backed revival of Eggers' concept for Poppy Records, which was to feature an eclectic array of artists. Townes was willing to give Eggers another chance. Lomax and Eggers talked about how they might work together to do three things. The first was to release the Old Quarter recordings, with liner notes by Lomax. Next, Lomax was intent on re-releasing all of Townes' old Poppy albums, which were now out of print and very difficult to find. Then, for the final stroke, Townes would record a new album, which they would release, of new songs, to which they, along with Townes, would jointly hold the publishing. Coinciding with these releases would be a publicity blitz that included a special limited publication of a songbook of lyrics and sheet music for a handful of Townes' songs, along with photos, critical testimonials, and a specially commissioned biographical essay. "Then we go to the labels and say, here's this great artist, you can probably acquire all his stuff from this scoundrel for dirt and give him an override, and you've got this momentum, and you've got the next Dylan," recollects Lomax. Lomax didn't particularly like Eggers, but he felt that his utility to this business plan was unavoidable.

"Then I started asking Kevin questions about financial statements, things like that; 'What's the deal on the publishing, anyway?'" Lomax says. "I wanted to have a publishing company, me and Townes. I was going to go after every single song and get 'em all back to Townes. I would run it, and we would each own half, and we'd live happily every after. I was supposed to be the publisher for all the songs on the album we wanted to make, which was *Flyin' Shoes*. And I couldn't get a straight answer on anything from Kevin."

The first of Townes' and Cindy's two winters in the cabin in Franklin was long and very cold. "We stayed pretty warm with the coal stove and the wood fireplace," Cindy says, "but it was bitter out there. We had a pump that ran running water through a hose, and it froze up. We'd go to Lomax's house and bring back five gallons of water to brush our teeth and wash and make coffee with." As Townes told an interviewer that spring, "for a month or two eighty percent of my energy went into wood. I had dreams of wood at night."[6]

By the spring of 1977, the couple settled into a routine at the cabin that had both a positive and a negative impact on Townes. After the episode that required his hospitalization in Austin two years before (and another brief hospitalization in Nashville shortly after the move), he was back on his lithium prescription, and his bipolar disorder was relatively in check.[7] He was happy living a quiet life in the country, chopping wood, mending fences, building a cattle guard for his driveway, watching the cows and horses on the surrounding properties, fishing, and just watching the weather change. But, while he and John Lomax were going forward with their plan to advance his career, and he was still playing gigs, he was not writing much, and he was drinking more and more. Heroin was not readily available to Townes in Tennessee, but, through Michael Ewah, he had an occasional supply of Dilaudid, which Townes would inject, maintaining his narcotic self-medication habit. And, while cocaine was in vogue around the Nashville scene during this time and was not unknown to Townes and Cindy and their acquaintances, alcohol was still the drug of choice, and Townes fell quickly to indulging his familiar fancy.

"He had a daily schedule," Cindy says. "At seven a.m., he'd wake up, and the first thing he'd do was call Susanna. He'd unplug the phone the rest of the day, but, by God, he'd wake up and call Susanna first. Then he'd put his glasses on and sit there and read quietly until nine-thirty, and he'd be at the liquor store at ten on the nose and get his first jug of the day. But as soon as he'd take that first drink, the glasses would come off and he'd be a different person. He'd be mean, sometimes, or just crazy. It was like Dr. Jekyll and Mr. Hyde." It fell to Cindy to make sure that Townes was taking his lithium and vitamins every day, but there was little she could do to keep Townes sober.[8]

John Lomax realized that first winter that Townes' drinking was going to be a problem. "I didn't say, hey, you got a problem.... I didn't feel like it was my right to run somebody's personal life.... He wasn't missing dates. He never missed a date. But when I say I was Townes' manager, I like to put quote marks around it. I managed to keep him out of jail, I managed to get him to shows, but he was an unmanageable person, even then."

"I was outside on the porch, probably smoking a joint or something," Cindy recalls, "and Townes and Michael were shooting dice inside. Next thing I know, I hear, 'Hey baby.' And I look around, and he's got blood coming out of his mouth. And Mike Ewah comes out from behind him, a big old smile on his face, and I can't believe what I'm seeing. He'd gotten Townes' gold tooth out with a little pair of pliers. They were gambling and Townes bet his gold tooth. And Mike got the tooth.... I was pissed."

On a few of the tours that Bobby Cudd booked around this time, the singer–songwriter David Olney opened for Townes. Olney remembers, "Cindy traveled with us. She was just unbelievably good-looking, with fiery red hair, very devoted to Townes. And, traveling with them in the car, it was her and him in the front seat and me in the back seat, and I might as well have been in the trunk."

Olney recalls a gig in Little Rock where the entire audience consisted of a half-dozen people. "I was gonna open for him," Olney
says. "And before the show we were talking to these people who
had driven all the way from Texas. Then I went on and it turned
out that they were the only people in the place. I did my set, then,
as Townes was getting ready to play … these five or six people
who had driven all the way from Texas got in a fight, a fistfight,
and were all thrown out of the place." Olney and Townes were
stunned. Townes laughed. "There goes my audience!"[9]

That spring, Van Zandt hit the road for a nationwide tour with
a newly recruited team of side men. Guy Clark suggested to
Townes that he might like to try out a veteran guitarist who
had worked with him, Danny "Ruester" Rowland. Rowland had
worked with a number of musicians and songwriters, including
the prolific Nashville songwriter Billy Edd Wheeler (who wrote
"Jackson" for Johnny Cash and June Carter, among other songs)
and was a seasoned instrumentalist with a sensitive ear. Along
with Rowland came bassist Jimmie Gray, who had played guitar
in Waylon Jennings' original band the Waylors in the sixties,[10]
and fiddle player Owen Cody, who had toured with Billy Joe
Shaver and recorded with Freddy Fender and Rod Bernard for
Huey Meaux's Crazy Cajun label in Beaumont, Texas. Professionals all, the trio played some gigs with Townes late in 1976
and was road-tested and ready to tour by the spring of 1977.
    Also landing in Nashville around this time was Kevin Eggers'
younger brother, Harold. Harold Eggers had knocked around in
Austin on the fringes of the music scene and had come to Nashville to find some more solid work in the music business. Harold
had met Townes years before, as a teenager, at gatherings hosted
by Kevin. When they reconnected, Townes, no doubt taking
counsel from Kevin, offered Harold a job as his road manager.
John Lomax concurred with this seemingly inevitable development—Townes needed somebody on the road to keep him out
of trouble, and he knew that wasn't going to be him—and Harold enthusiastically accepted the job. He would have a chance

to hone his skills during the upcoming tour, which was to begin shortly after Townes' thirty-third birthday.

By this time, too, Tomato Records was up and running with the long-delayed release of Earl Willis' live recordings of Van Zandt from the summer of 1973, a two-record set titled *Townes Van Zandt Live at the Old Quarter, Houston, Texas.* The package, designed by Milton Glaser around a shadowy black-and-white photograph of Townes, shirtless and wearing a straw cowboy hat, was an auspicious kickoff for Van Zandt on his new record label. The pristine recordings of the young Townes at what already could be seen as the peak of his powers would be cited as an example of his best work for years to come. At the last minute, Kevin Eggers changed his mind about using John Lomax's liner notes for the album and went with notes written by Willis instead. It could be argued that this move was a signal of Eggers' re-emerging ascendancy—and Lomax's growing marginalization—in Townes' business affairs. But, in any case, the release of the *Old Quarter* album was a significant step. Next, Townes hit the road.

After a few local shows in early April, Townes left Cindy in Franklin and flew with Harold Eggers, Danny Rowland, Jimmie Gray, and Owen Cody to Los Angeles for a week of gigs. The schedule was intensive: April took them from L.A. back to Nashville, then to two nights each at the Quiet Night in Chicago, Bunky's in Madison, Wisconsin, and the Blue River Café in Milwaukee; then it was on to Larry Joe's in Augusta, Georgia, Gilley's in Dayton, Ohio, and the Great Mideast Music Hall in Louisville, Kentucky. May saw the group at Michigan State University in East Lansing, in Long Island, in Boston, and at the Lone Star in New York City and the Cellar Door in Washington, D.C. Then it was back to Boston, then to St. Louis. Townes played solo at the Kerrville Folk Festival on May 26, then the group reunited in Nashville and flew back to California on the first of June. They played the Great American Music Hall in San Francisco, then headed up the coast to Seattle.

After a gig at the Euphoria Tavern in Portland, Oregon, Harold Eggers checked into a local hospital with a badly swollen knee, and the tour started catching up with the musicians. While visiting and arguing with Harold in the hospital, Townes took all the money they had made on the tour so far, which he carried around with him in cash, and he threw it out the window. Even at this early point in their relationship, Eggers had begun to fall into the role of caretaker for Townes, seeing that he made it to gigs, didn't drink too much, and didn't give all his money away. Harold would perfect this difficult role over the next twenty years.

A few more gigs got Townes and the group to the end of June, and they went home to rest up for a shorter second leg, which would begin in October. The dozen-odd stops included D.C., Boston, New York, and some of the other cities they had hit earlier, plus a few others. By the end of October they were home, exhausted but exhilarated from a long, successful run. The gigs had been well received, with good crowds in many of the venues, and the band had formed strong bonds among themselves.

Harold Eggers had been recording nearly every show from the soundboard and soon began to cull through the tapes for the best performances.[11] These recordings reveal Townes as a seasoned, comfortable performer. He sounds road-hardened. His voice has developed a mature, rough edge, and his singing is assured. The ensemble sound meshes perfectly—two acoustic guitars (Townes strumming rhythm or finger-picking, Ruester playing lead); subtle but solid electric bass guitar; and fluid, melodic, hillbilly–gypsy fiddle—and gives Townes' songs a clean, uncluttered showcasing they often lacked in their more elaborate studio recordings. The set lists included a core group of songs that Townes had performed since they were new, and that he would continue to perform for the rest of his life: "Pancho and Lefty" and "If I Needed You," of course, and "For the Sake of the Song," "Our Mother the Mountain," "To Live's to Fly," "Lungs," "Loretta," "No Place to Fall," "White Freightliner Blues," "Brand New Companion," "Tecumseh Valley," "Don't You Take It Too Bad," "Tower Song," "No Lonesome Tune," "Rex's Blues," "Rake," and "Waitin' Around to Die," among other old favorites, which all sounded fresh and new.

He also played a wide variety of covers, including the familiar Lightnin' Hopkins songs, such as "Short-Haired Woman Blues" and "My Starter Won't Start," plus classic folk and country numbers such as "The Coo-Coo," "Wabash Cannonball," "Cocaine Blues," "Jolie Blon," and, of course, "Fraulein." He featured an affecting, deadpan reading of the Rolling Stones' "Dead Flowers," a twist on Bruce Springsteen's "Racing in the Streets" (wherein Townes takes the point of view of the man who's ready to "just give up living/and start dying little by little, piece by piece"), and a tender rendition of Joe Ely's "Indian Cowboy." ("This is the only circus song I ever liked," Townes said onstage of "Indian Cowboy"; "I don't like zoo songs either.") A couple of lesser-known Bob Dylan songs—"Little Willie the Gambler" and "Man Gave Names to All the Animals"—found their way into the sets as well.

As he was performing, Townes deftly read his audience and made adjustments to his sets, as he always had, but on this tour he had such a broad array of material to choose from that the sets had a depth and a variety that they never had before. Townes and Jimmie Gray worked out some rudimentary vocal harmonies for a couple of songs, and Ruester and Cody spun off well-focused, melodic solos, intertwining intuitively with one another and with Townes' solid guitar work. According to Rowland, the band did not rehearse, but "we understood each others' competence and capabilities." And the group kept the performances fresh and interesting for themselves. "Each song was different every time it was played, depending on the circumstances," Rowland says.[12] For example, they might stretch "Brand New Companion" out into a swinging jam that merged smoothly with a ragtime-jazzy "Cocaine Blues," and Townes might decide to sing some of the verses of "Cocaine Blues" in French. Or Dylan's "Man Gave Names to All the Animals" could become a reggae romp, with Townes playing a bongo part on the back of his guitar and Ruester vamping and cavorting like a funky Django Reinhardt. The group was feeling comfortable enough, and having enough fun, to try almost anything.

As they made their way from town to town, the musicians became close; they exercised the same proclivities that Townes and other musicians on the road had always exercised—drinking, drugs, gambling, and women—but they managed to maintain a focus on their nightly performances that had been absent on some previous tours. The quality of the music was inspiring this focus, which in turn was driving the quality of the music. Enthusiastic reactions from their audiences reinforced the entire creative cycle. Things were going well on the road for Townes.

Things were going well professionally for a number of Townes' contemporaries in the mid-1970s. Mickey Newbury—who recorded a string of classic albums in the first half of the decade—had spearheaded a revolution in songwriting and recording that had ensured country-oriented artists the same kinds of artistic freedoms that rock artists had been enjoying. Artists who had only a few years before been considered outsiders in Nashville were experiencing an insider upwelling of their own, the "Outlaw" movement, led by Willie Nelson, Waylon Jennings, and Billie Joe Shaver, among other—primarily Texan—progenitors. In 1975, Nelson's home-grown-in-Texas *Red Headed Stranger* helped solidify the movement and shifted the center of country-music gravity away from Nashville and toward Austin.[13] Still, in Nashville, Kris Kristofferson had followed through the door opened by Newbury, and his success in the early seventies had blown the door off its hinges.

Guy Clark—who in the early seventies had a minor hit with Jerry Jeff Walker's recording of his song "L.A. Freeway"—finally recorded his own album for RCA in 1975. Rodney Crowell landed a publishing deal in the early seventies, then in 1975 he moved to Los Angeles to sing and play guitar in Emmylou Harris' band. Harris would record a number of Crowell's songs, including "Till I Gain Control Again," "Ain't Livin' Long Like This," and "Bluebird Wine." Harris' first album, *Pieces of the Sky*, was one of the top records of 1975. The following year, she had a number-one record with her cover of Buck Owens' "Together

Again" and won a Grammy for her second album, *Elite Hotel*. In 1977, this success rubbed off on Townes Van Zandt when Harris recorded "Pancho and Lefty" on her third album, *Luxury Liner*. Reviews of the album inevitably drew attention to Townes' song, and the song received healthy FM radio play. The stars seemed to be aligning.

While Townes was on the road that spring and fall and Kevin Eggers was working on re-issuing Townes' old Poppy albums on Tomato, Lomax was at work on *For the Sake of the Song*, a book of lyrics, sheet music, photographs, and essays on Townes that he had arranged to have published at the beginning of 1978 by Wings Press in Houston, a small publishing house run by Lomax's brother Joseph. Lomax felt that the book "would give us a way to promote Townes to a whole 'nother audience, the literary audience, the poetry audience, the libraries." Lomax wrote an essay, and he and Townes "spent quite a while choosing all the songs, and he wrote little blurbs about each one.[14] I tracked down the sheet music on all the songs and got the pictures together, some of which I took and some I just gathered up." He also commissioned a biographical essay by the writer Lola Scobey.

"Townes carries the terror and the sorrow of a sensitive man who has looked into the abyss and seen....the abyss," Scobey wrote. Her essay quotes an article by the writer Bill Hedgepeth— a friend of Townes'—who quoted Townes discussing his depression. Townes describes the torment and actual physical pain he experiences in his most severe bouts, and he mentions his recurring desire to chop off his hands. Scobey also quotes Townes summarizing his early life—including the claim that he "had a nice childhood and all that. I don't remember it, but that's what I've been told." She summarizes his career and notes his recent rave reviews in *Crawdaddy*, *Esquire*, and *Rolling Stone*, all the result of Emmylou Harris' recording of "Pancho and Lefty." She also mentions the other artists who have covered Townes' songs: Doc Watson's "If I Needed You," Robin and Linda Williams' "None But the Rain," and Steve Young's "No Place to Fall."

In discussing Townes' six Poppy albums, Scobey notes that the records have been "caught up in multifarious distribution deals" and that they have been "virtually unpromoted." Lomax echoes this in his Introduction, writing that Townes "has received no coherent management, advertising, booking or financial support during his career. His records have been pressed in limited quantities, sold, then never reissued." On a more personal level, Lomax writes that Townes "has alienated friends, exasperated promoters, and flabbergasted club owners with his sometimes eccentric behavior," but that there is an "eternal quality to his music and lyrics" such that "everyone I have ever introduced to his writing has emerged from the experience as a full-fledged convert....."[15]

By the end of 1977, Lomax was able to include in the songbook an impressive compilation of critics' quotes from publications from all over the country. An article in the December 1977 issue of the small British publication *Omaha Rainbow* mentions the songbook and notes that, thanks to John Lomax, Townes' "career is on the upsurge after years of bad luck," and speculates that "maybe Townes Van Zandt's time is at hand." In the same article, Townes mentions the fact that his previous record company "couldn't get their distribution together, and had zero promotion." But he goes on: "Getting that record out on Tomato [*Live at the Old Quarter*] meant to me that all the mire that the business end of my career got wedged into was finally evaporating. I was out of the chute on a brand new horse, right?" He says that, with the live album and the songs he's going to be recording soon for his new album, "something's got to give, and it ain't gonna be me."[16]

In mid-December of 1977, Townes signed 500 "limited-edition" hard-cover copies of *For the Sake of the Song* in two long sessions, 250 books a sitting.

Townes had been having a difficult time writing songs for the new album. His last batch of songs had come before the aborted *Seven Come Eleven* sessions in Nashville in 1974. Cindy says, "I remember him saying that he'd wake up nights and his hands

would just be burning. He'd shake his hands, like he was trying to shake something bad out of them." At Townes' request,
Cindy took him to a motel in downtown Nashville and dropped
him off to stay and write for a couple of days. "At that point,
he'd come up with part of 'Flyin' Shoes,'" Cindy recalls. "When
he came back, he'd finished it, and he played me the whole
song. It was really pretty."

Townes told Cindy that the song was inspired by hours of
gazing at the cold waters of the Harpeth River in the dead of
winter. Later he elaborated, saying the song was about the dying
thoughts of a soldier lying on a cold battlefield as the winter sun
descends. Whatever the subject and inspiration, "Flyin' Shoes"
is one of Townes' most beautiful, enigmatic songs, full of despair
and hope, somehow in the same breath. It was the first and is
probably the best of the small crop of songs he wrote while sitting beside the Harpeth, where he went regularly seeking inspiration and peace.

Besides the natural beauty of the spot, as Townes was well
aware, the Battle of Franklin had raged there. Townes' day-
dream of a wounded soldier inspired him to write the song.[17] It
is the dying soldier's voice speaking in the first verse, a kind of
dreamy despair immediately and happily tempered by no less
than the certain knowledge of eternity. The second verse takes
one of Townes' favorite themes, the seasons, and turns it into
the young soldier's last, brief, sentimental reflection that there
won't be another winter for him. The third verse seems to rise
into the skies with the moon and take the cosmic perspective
that Townes had by now mastered, with the "silver sails" of the
moon setting among the quiet hills.

In the end, besides "Flyin' Shoes," Townes brought few new
songs to Nashville for his new record, deciding instead for the
most part to re-record most of the material from *Seven Come Eleven*,
which, after all, remained unheard on record by the public.

Lomax credits Kevin Eggers with landing Chips Moman to
produce Townes' new record. The legendary Memphis producer
got his start at Stax studio, then in 1965 started his own record-

ing studio, American. Part of American's studio package was a top-notch house band that included guitarist Reggie Young, bassist Tommy Cogbill, keyboardists Spooner Oldham and Bobby Emmons, drummers Gene Chrisman and Eddy Anderson, and the young stringed-instrument wizard Randy Scruggs. American soon turned into a hit-making factory for various labels and various artists, including Wilson Pickett, Aretha Franklin, Dusty Springfield, and the Box Tops. Between November 1967 and January 1971, American produced some 120 *Billboard*-charted hits; during one week, there were twenty-eight records from American on the charts, all with the same musicians playing on them.[18] In 1969, Moman sealed his legend by overseeing Elvis Presley's career-reviving sessions at American, which produced "In the Ghetto," "Suspicious Minds," and other classic recordings. He had moved his operation to Atlanta for a while, then just recently to Nashville. Now, Chips and his boys were ready to work their magic on the music of Townes Van Zandt.

The sessions were about to get under way when Mike Ewah and Townes, both drunk, set out in Townes' pickup truck on the muddy road from the cabin, with Ewah driving. They hadn't gone far when the truck crashed into a tree. "Townes was in the passenger seat and got thrown into the dash," Cindy says. "Mike took the steering wheel in the sternum. But Townes got the worst of it." With Cindy's help they made it to the emergency room and found out that Townes had a broken right arm—with possible nerve damage—and needed stitches to close a gash on his cheek.

The accident did not change the scheduling for the sessions. Moman's feeling was that he had plenty of guitar players who could cover Townes' parts, so long as Townes could sing. Cindy says, "even once the bone healed, they said the damaged nerve would only come back an inch a month, all the way down his hands. It was right as we were just starting to do *Flyin' Shoes*, and he did not have the full function of his finger-picking."

Phillip Donnelly, Billy Earl McClelland, Randy Scruggs, and Moman himself covered the album's guitar duties admirably, and the entire ensemble sound that Moman and his band created in the studio brought a breath of fresh air to Townes' music. Moman deftly assembled a full-bore studio band sound, with layers of electric guitars, pedal steel guitars, mandolins, and harmonicas, underpinned with solid Memphis-style drums, percussion, and bass guitar, augmented by a small group of buoyant, soulful backup voices. The sessions were loose and fun—and were interrupted briefly by the birth of Moman's daughter—but the actual recording was taken care of expeditiously. Cindy spent time at the studio during the sessions and became friends with Chips and his crew, many of them sharing an interest in the popular recreational substances of the time. The results of the recording process were clearly positive, and everyone involved was pleased when they heard the final mixes of the album, which they agreed would be named *Flyin' Shoes*, after what everyone considered Townes' best new song.

The opening track, "Dollar Bill Blues," was another of Townes' more recent compositions, written after the move to Franklin. The song is styled essentially as a traditional drinking song, with a sea-chantey-ish "early in the morning" refrain, but with a somewhat sinister minor-key cast. Cindy shows up as a "red haired thing," whom the singer is going to buy a diamond ring—"early in the morning." For the subject matter of murder, thievery, gambling, and drinking, and no doubt particularly for the line "Mother was a golden girl/Slit her throat just to get her pearls," this was the one song of Townes' that his mother said she did not care for.[19]

"Snake Song"—one of the batch from *Seven Come Eleven*—is another particularly striking song—again set in a stark, minor-key atmosphere—that shows a new focus in Townes' writing. Again in the style of the traditional folk song, with a strong flat-picked bass line, the metaphor of the snake goes deeper and deeper, from the straightforward "You can't hold me/I'm too slippery" and "I got poison/I just might bite you" to the more abstract "Ain't no mercy in my smilin'/Only fangs and sweet beguiling," and to the stark, pure poetic imagery of "Solid hollow wrapped in hatred/Not a drop of venom wasted." "The Spider Song" is a more directly personal song, a song of the familiar struggle against the dark forces lurking inside the human psyche, and, through Townes' use of a very simple metaphor, one of his best songs addressing that struggle. "Pueblo Waltz" is a different kind of song altogether. The mood is soft, wistful, conjuring up a comfortable relationship between the singer and his green-eyed lover, all wrapped in a comfort that we, the listeners, all seem to be sharing as friends with Townes. The evocation of Susanna and Guy has an even more direct effect than the evocation of Loop and Lil in "If I Needed You," another instance of the listener being brought closer to the song through a kind of conspiratorial personal inclusion.

Two of Townes' finest songs from this period were recorded both for *Seven Come Eleven* and *Flyin' Shoes*: "Rex's Blues" and "Loretta." A comparison of the versions recorded for each of those two albums shows the similarities between the approach that had been taken to recording Townes throughout his career so far—that of Kevin Eggers and Jack Clement—and the approach taken by Chips Moman on *Flyin' Shoes*. While different in many details, the overall results were remarkably similar for both producers—except that *Flyin' Shoes* was successfully released to the public, while *Seven Come Eleven* would not be released until years later.

"Rex's Blues" fares well on both recordings. The first features acoustic guitars, a soft-plucked banjo, a loping string bass, brushed snare drum, and an insouciant vocal from Townes resting in the center of the mix. Halfway through the song, background voices chime in for half a chorus, then go away. There is some uncertainty as to what the banjo is meant to evoke, and what relation the background voices have, but on the whole it's a pleasant recording. Chips Moman's version begins with an acoustic guitar and a moody pedal steel, then falls easily into a country gait, set by a deft Memphis-style rhythm section. The groove is rhythmically complex, but flows, and the song builds gradually until the final repeat of the first verse. There is more of a sense of clarity and certainty in this recording than there is in the first version. The Moman version is better, but it's a close call. The two recordings of "Loretta" show more differences. The *Seven Come Eleven* take is upbeat, with a fiddle-driven Cajun feel that makes perfect sense for the song. The sound is bright and clean, but the background voices again seem out of place. Moman's take is slower, more thoughtful, with a moaning harmonica and stately strummed acoustic guitar. He also employs a background vocal ensemble, but sparingly and with more of a country feel, and well integrated as the song builds with steel guitar and organ, and the rhythm section again takes up the beat and lopes the song to its close.

It is interesting that "At My Window" and "Buckskin Stallion Blues" were both recorded for the *Seven* sessions but not used for *Flyin' Shoes*, and "Two Girls" and "White Freightliner Blues" (versions of which were also included on *Live at the Old Quarter*) were not included on *Flyin' Shoes*, but *Flyin' Shoes* does include a rather redundant version of Townes' cover of Bo Diddley's "Who Do You Love?" the definitive take of which was Townes' solo version on *Old Quarter*.

*Flyin' Shoes* was the end of the line for Lomax and Townes. There was in fact a new momentum building from the release of the live album, the impending re-release of the old albums, the songbook, the new record, the Emmylou Harris cover, and a batch of good national press. But Kevin Eggers had reasserted himself in Townes' life and business affairs, and Townes was inclined to give him the benefit of the doubt, as always, especially with the new Tomato label in the picture. According to Lomax, Eggers sensed that he—Lomax—was getting too close to uncovering the shady money trail related to Townes' previous recordings and publishing, and Eggers got nervous. "I was fixin' to find out who was stealing the money and where it was going," Lomax says.

Lomax understood that, to take care of the publishing business, "you just need to get somebody to administer it and make sure that you're getting paid. They make sure the money comes in, they take a cut, and we get the rest." Kevin Eggers now had brought Jack Clement's old friend and former Elvis Presley confidant Lamar Fike back into the picture and was pitching him to Townes as an excellent choice for a new manager. "Kevin talked about Lamar Fike, and Elvis' publishing, as a model. But the whole Elvis thing was that he lost out on so many great songs because they wouldn't give up the publishing. When you stop and think about what he could have done, with that kind of talent, if he'd had the sense to just get all these fucking parasites off of him." Lomax told Townes that he thought that Fike was "nothing more than Kevin's pawn."

But Townes trusted Eggers and went along with his plans. "I met with Kevin and Townes and they said, 'Well, Lamar's going to manage Townes, thanks very much. Give us a bill for what we owe you, and see you later.' Kevin would get Townes drunk and get him to sign. God knows I've never seen the documents, but he must have had him sign something at some point. Then I was ousted, which was a little bit after *Flyin' Shoes* came out, because it came out and Kevin had the publishing, not me." Lomax was angry, but resigned. "I managed to keep him going, I managed to get a bunch of records out again and really stir the pot and get him back in the public eye," he says. "I convinced a lot of people that this was an amazing talent. There was a lot of momentum. First of all, all the negative momentum was reversed, and the forward momentum built, and all these records came back out, and who knows if they would have ever come back out again if I hadn't been in there prodding."

Years later, Kevin Eggers also reflected on this period, starting by noting the dual nature of Townes' personality—a "brilliant and unique" side and "a side that was determined to degrade himself and everyone around him." A writer who interviewed Eggers for the *Austin Chronicle* writes, "Eggers says those demons kept driving Van Zandt back to him at Tomato when other labels weren't interested in signing him. He maintains that Van Zandt's reputation for poor sales figures and self-destruction led him to be written off as damaged goods by the music industry at large. In fact, Eggers says Van Zandt's mid-Seventies heroin habit was so bad that Van Zandt offered him the publishing rights to the songs on his first four albums for $20. 'I didn't do it and told him that if he sold [those rights] to anyone, we'd never talk again,' recounts Eggers."[20]

Despite the management turmoil, Townes was soon back on the road, with gigs booked by Fike. "It was Lamar that kind of at that point broke up the old ladies going on the road with the band," Cindy recalls. "He made me stay at home while Townes went off, and that was the end of our being joined at the hip, basically. We had done everything together, then you've got one manager that says, no, she can't go with you anymore." Cindy continued her work with local horses, but soon was heading into town and hanging out at bars, spending her sixty-dollars-a-week allowance drinking beer. She missed the daily closeness of the past nearly four years. They had their ups and downs, but she loved Townes and wanted to be with him.

After discussing the matter off and on for more than a year, after some gentle but firm prodding from his mother, and after having the requisite blood tests and obtaining the necessary license, on September 15, 1978, John Townes Van Zandt took Cindy Sue Morgan to the Williamson County Courthouse in Franklin, Tennessee, where they were married in a civil ceremony.

Townes invited Rex Bell up from Houston for the occasion, and Bell witnessed the brief, simple wedding. Danny Rowland loaned the couple a turquoise ring for Cindy to put on during the ceremony, but shortly after Townes reported the happy news to his mother, she presented Cindy with another ring. "His mother at that point saw that we had been together that long, and she was kind of pushing him to marry me," Cindy says. "So she was real happy, and she gave me the ring that Townes' daddy had given her. She told me that, back in 1944, when Townes was born, his daddy went and got this beautiful ring and brought it to her in the hospital as a maternity gift. It's my understanding that he paid thirty-five hundred dollars for it in 1944, so the ring has some value to it, I do know that." Cindy, wearing the ring a quarter-century later, describes it as "a beautiful six-point star sapphire set in platinum, with a flaw that gives it depth."

She describes their wedding day as "no different from any other day, because we'd already been together for three years."

"Out at the farm, we had an outhouse that could be spooky at night," Cindy remembers. "That was the only time in my life that I really felt the presence of something that I could not see. And I pretty well figured out that it was a Civil War person. He would stand in the kitchen at the back door towards the outhouse. And I'd go into the kitchen and I could just feel him. He was watching me. And when I pulled the truck out, there would be like this *sssshht* going across the road in the headlights. Like a transparent light. I always knew he'd be there. And I'm thinking it was probably one of those Civil War guys just checking me out, because I was this young, twenty-one, twenty-two-year-old girl, with a lot of kinetic energy, and I'd go back in the back yard and lay out there nude sometimes, sunbathing, and … you know.…"

One night, Townes and Cindy returned to the cabin after dark. "I felt something in that cabin, man," she says. "It wasn't in our bedroom or in the other bedroom, it was in the kitchen. Townes kept saying, 'no, no, no, no, it's nothing.' Then later, he was up by himself, reading. Evidently it was a fairly sober day, because he was there reading at night. But suddenly, the bookshelf pops out of the wall, and wham!—everything hits the floor. I had to just laugh when he told me. He paid attention to this guy after that."

Townes' son, J.T., was nine years old when he came to stay with his father and Cindy in Franklin in 1978. J.T. had seen his father only briefly and sporadically, whenever Townes visited him and Fran in Houston, and he was eager to get to know him better. Once he had arrived, though, J.T. says his father "did his best to scare me to death." Townes was confrontational, badgering

J.T. with unanswerable questions; he drank heavily and used drugs openly throughout the visit, which was "pretty grotesque, a frightening eye-opener to the lifestyle of a songwriter to a suburban Houston kid," according to J.T.[21]

On the second day of J.T.'s visit, he joined Townes and Michael Ewah in a nearby hollow as they drank from a bottle of vodka and took shots with a BB gun at a bird on a wire. J.T. offered to take a shot, and his first shot hit the bird squarely, bringing it down for Ewah's hawk to eat. "Townes was so proud," J.T. remembers. "Instead of me being this nuisance, I had earned my way into the circle." Later that day, J.T., "trying to ride out the good impression I had made on him earlier," heard a bird singing and casually asked Townes what kind of bird it was. Townes replied harshly, "That's a mourning dove, you little idiot! Don't you know you shot its fucking soul mate?" J.T. was hurt and startled by his father's intensity. "He was all saliva and veins, off the deep end," J.T. says. As Fran recalls, "J.T. called me in the middle of the night to get him out of there."

Townes spent most of 1979 on the road in support of *Flyin' Shoes*, while Cindy remained behind in Franklin. Townes' still-healing arm and diminished ability to play the guitar caused the 1979 tour to be remembered as the "broken arm tour," but Ruester, Gray, and Cody were a dependable support group, both musically and as friends. Townes' drinking was getting worse, but it was always worse at home than on the road. At one point that year, when he was home with Cindy, he instructed her to chain him to a tree in the yard so he would not be able to get any more booze. "I thought, 'well, okay, get ready to get yourself chained to the tree.' So he had a big old chain and a lock and I did it. I told him to give me the key, and I'll leave. And I left in his truck. Ooohhh, he was mad."

She left him with a half-pint of vodka and a can of orange crush. "I came back about four or five hours later, after he'd well finished his half-pint and had been sitting there for two hours," she recalls. "He was mad. He said, 'Give me the key.' I threw him the key to the chain to unlock himself and I ran. I went running down that driveway and down the creek and I hid up there in the woods. He came racing down the road in his truck, fishtailing sideways. It was scary."

Cindy tries to sum up their Nashville experience: "Townes was able to support himself with the gigs. I always had to take care of the money, to make sure he didn't just give it away, or gamble it away, and eventually I was having to babysit him, someone who was older than me. But he had lots of opportunities that he just didn't take. He could have pushed some of his songs. We were wanting Waylon Jennings and people like that to do maybe one of his songs, or Johnny Cash. But he'd say, 'If they want to do one of my songs, they can come see me.' He wasn't gonna go to them."

Townes offered his own summary to a contemporary writer, declaring that "The kinda songs I play—poem songs, story songs—are not what you'd call a particularly accepted mode of art these days. Then, too those people in Nashville consider me a weird recluse who they've heard of but who never comes to land. I'll come into town, like, five minutes and give 'em a tape and disappear. But still, most of those Nashville folks won't do a waltz. Won't do a ballad. Won't do things in a minor key. Nashville's just not geared for minor keys."[22]

*Townes Van Zandt.*

PHOTO BY JIM MCGUIRE, COURTESY OF NASHVILLEPORTRAITS.COM

*Townes performing, early 1972.*

COURTESY OF THE PHOTOGRAPHER, ANDREW STERLING.

*Townes and Fran's wedding, Houston, Texas, 1965. From left: Fran's parents, Fran, Townes, and Townes' parents, Dorothy Townes Van Zandt and Harris Williams Van Zandt.* Courtesy of Fran Lohr.

*Townes with Guy and Susanna Clark, Nashville, Tennessee, 1970s.*
Courtesy of Guy and Susanna Clark.

*Pickin' on the porch, Nashville, Tennessee, 1970s. From left: Townes, Susanna, Guy, and Daniel.*

PHOTOGRAPH BY AL CLAYTON, COURTESY OF GUY AND SUSANNA CLARK.

*Townes and Cindy, Houston, Texas, 1970s.*

COURTESY OF DANNY ROWLAND.

*Townes with Mickey White.*

Courtesy of Jet Whitt.

*On the road, late 1970s. From left: Danny "Ruester" Rowland, Townes, Owen Cody, and Jimmie Gray.*

COURTESY OF DANNY ROWLAND.

*Amigos, fellow songwriters: Richard Dobson and Blaze Foley, Nashville, Tennessee, 1980s.*

COURTESY OF LYSE MOORE.

*Townes, Jeanene, and Will Van Zandt, 1983.*

PHOTO BY JIM MCGUIRE, COURTESY OF NASHVILLEPORTRAITS.COM.

*Townes with Royann and Jim Calvin at the Old Quarter, Galveston, Texas, 1996.*

COURTESY OF ROYANN CALVIN.

*Claudia Winterer, Nashville, Tennessee, 1996.*

COURTESY OF ROYANN CALVIN.

*Father and son: Townes and J.T., back room, Cactus Café, Austin, Texas, 1996.*

COURTESY OF ROYANN CALVIN.

*Townes performing in Glasgow, Scotland, 1995.*

COURTESY OF THE PHOTOGRAPHER, GRAHAM STEWART.

*Backstage, Glasgow, Scotland, 1995.*

COURTESY OF THE PHOTOGRAPHER, GRAHAM STEWART.

*Townes with guitar and Bo Whitt paintings at Rex Bell's house near Galveston, Texas, 1996.*

COURTESY OF ROYANN CALVIN.

# 12

# Still Lookin' For You

S VAN ZANDT TOURED THE club circuit throughout 1979, he repeatedly circled back to his old stomping grounds in Houston and Austin, where he revived some old friendships and fell into some new business relationships. John Cheatham had been part of the Clarksville scene a few years before, and Townes often stayed at his house in north Austin when he was in town. At some point, they decided that it would be mutually advantageous for Cheatham—who had some funding and an entrepreneurial bent—to take on some management duties for Townes, at least as far as getting some bookings in Texas. Townes had grown distant from Lamar Fike, and from Kevin Eggers, often informally landing gigs on his own, especially in Texas. "I don't think he had a clue what to do," John Lomax says of Cheatham, "but the vibe was good and they went with it."[1]

Mickey White and Rex Bell had been playing gigs as the Hemmer Ridge Mountain Boys, and when Townes came to Texas they again accompanied him. The Hemmer Ridge Mountain Boys had increasingly become a novelty band, featuring comedy bits in their act and actually recording a single version of

"Up Against the Wall, Redneck Mother" sung in pig latin. In late 1979 and early 1980, White and Bell were glad to have Townes back and to have the chance to develop a more serious outlet for their music. "I was making a living playing with the Hemmer Ridge Mountain Boys," White recalls, "but I really felt that we'd shot our wad as far as having an opportunity to move up."

In what turned out to be the group's final project—and their most lasting—in early 1980, they worked with Louisiana singer Lucinda Williams on her second album. "She approached me and Rex and Mike, our drummer, about being her backup band," White says. "She had this whole slew of new songs, which became *Happy Woman Blues*." Mickey and Rex—and Townes— knew Lucinda from their days in Nashville, "from the big house with Rex and Rodney Crowell and Skinny Dennis and everybody," White says. "She had recorded an album for Folkways, doing all those traditional blues songs, then she moved into the songwriting thing, which I think she always wanted to do."

That spring, with uncertainty about Townes' future with his touring band, Danny Rowland had backed away from playing to return to school, so Townes asked Mickey White to accompany him and Jimmie Gray on a brief Texas tour. "Lo and behold," White says, "the old double guitars were clicking pretty good."[2]

In the early summer of 1980, John Cheatham offered White a long-term job with Townes on a "major tour" of New England and the Northeast, including New York City. In the past year, Townes had played some dates in Vermont booked by semi-professional promoter Ron McCloud, who had now called Cheatham about a four- to six-week tour package he was assembling for Townes. According to White, "Townes came down in the Colonel, his truck, which he and Ruester and Jimmie had traveled around in—the gray Chevy six-cylinder pickup with a camper on it. We played a couple more dates down in Texas, and then, me and Jimmie Gray drove the pickup up to Vermont.[3] Townes had some other kind of obligation, so he was going to fly up there and meet us." They met Townes at McCloud's house, along with Billy Joe Shaver, who was headlining the tour with Townes. "Townes was real enthusiastic about the whole thing," White says. "Cheatham was there, so we had some management, and we go up to Vermont and we end up at this beautiful 130-year-old farmhouse out there in the hills, kind of right in the center of Vermont. We were there two or three days in advance of the first gig, just ready to go."

The first gig of the tour was at a bar in an old house that had been converted to a bed-and-breakfast on the town square in the village of Royalton, Vermont. "There were maybe about a hundred and fifty people, about half full," White says. "It was certainly not a bust. Eddy Shaver was playing with Billy Joe … and it was really cool to see this kid that had become really good very fast." Shaver had known Townes and Mickey for some years, "so it was a great reunion," White recalls. The next stop was to be "the big gig" of the tour, the one "that was supposed to pay for this whole thing," according to White. McCloud had rented a small concert hall just over the border in New Hampshire with the intention of showcasing Townes and Shaver along with several local acts. "But there was no promotion, no nothing," White says. "We had this big hall, and Ron McCloud had put every penny he had into this gig, and nobody showed. I mean, maybe twenty people showed up. It was just a total, total bust."

October began to unfold in the New England hills, and the road-weary Texans took note of the changing leaves and of a disturbing trend. "We became more and more concerned about what was going on with this little tour, and we became more and more aware that we needed to play the next gig just to get the money to get out of there," White recalls. In the meantime, McCloud tried to sustain the group "by cashing hot checks all over the area to keep us in whiskey and food … very little food, lots of whiskey. It was starting to get like ten days between dates, and we were getting really, really drunk."

White co-wrote a song with Townes during this time called "Gone, Gone Blues." According to White, "We got into listening to Muddy Waters' *Hard Again* album, and I came up with this riff, which is basically the old blues riff, kind of based on 'Mannish Boy.' I wrote a couple of verses, then I went to Townes and I said, 'Hey Townes, let me show you this. Remember those verses you used to make up for "Come On in My Kitchen"?' We could never understand the words, and Townes had just made stuff up. I said, 'Do you mind if I use that, and we'll kind of co-write this song?' … And, on the spot, he just wrote the rest of the verses of the song. So we were doing some things. We were picking and trying to keep the best foot forward, but it deteriorated pretty fast."

Besides the gaps between jobs, the lack of income, and the bad checks, the group were becoming aware of a disturbing pattern, in which McCloud would announce just before a scheduled engagement that the gig had suddenly been canceled. "We became suspicious that these gigs weren't there in the first place," White says. "But then, lo and behold, the minute we got kind of antsy, one of them would come through." By far the most notable gig that came through during this stretch was an engagement at Gerde's Folk City in Greenwich Village, New York City.

"We all climbed into the Colonel and drove down to New York City," White remembers. "For me, man, this was it. Gerde's is where Bob Dylan played, Simon & Garfunkel, John Hammond, Phil Ochs, the whole crew. The joint was absolutely jammed." Rex Bell and his new wife showed up at the gig, as did friends from all over the country. Townes rose to the occasion. "Townes, man, he was just on fire," says White. "It was one of the best gigs I ever saw the guy play … really striking that perfect balance of having just enough whiskey to get loose and be very witty and spontaneous and not too drunk." In addition, it seemed to the musicians that they were playing to a deeply appreciative audience. White believes that Townes was feeding off of the energy of the crowd in a way he had only rarely seen. "As many times as I'd played with Townes, I'd never really been in awe of what he was doing while I was up there on stage with him, because I was usually so involved, making sure I was in tune and knowing what song we were playing next, kind of watching the crowd, feeling the pace. This time, I was just standing up there blown away by this guy."

Encouraged by the success of the Gerde's gigs, the musicians headed back to Vermont ready for a final round of New England shows. A late cancellation meant that there would be a week until the next gig, and, with Townes leading the parade, they all began drinking more heavily to fill the interim. Jimmie Gray became concerned that things would get out of hand, and he moved into another house nearby with some people he had met in town. Mickey White, who was still suffering through a recent breakup, started "stepping up" his drinking to an alarming degree. "Man, that's all we had to do," he says, "waiting for another gig to come along." As White recalls, "The leaves started going from all these brilliant colors to just falling off one by one.... Then, all of a sudden the cops are at the door looking for Ron McCloud for the hot checks that he'd been writing."

Townes and the group played gigs in Montpelier, then Burlington, then Green Mountain, which was the last show in New England before a final show at the Childe Harold in Washington, D.C. They headed for D.C. in the Colonel with just enough money to make it to the gig. White recalls, "So we walk into the Childe Harold, and the bartender sees Townes and says, 'Hey, Townes, how's it going, man? Good to see you. What are you guys doing here?' And Townes says, 'Well, we have a gig here tonight.' And the bartender says, 'No, we got somebody else booked.' They'd never heard anything about it at all." This was the final indignity inflicted by McCloud.

Dejected and tired, Jimmie Gray went home and Townes and Mickey went to Franklin, where Townes had left Cindy minding the cabin nearly a year earlier. He had spoken to her on the phone a few times in the first months after he left, never suggesting that he would not return, telling her that he was staying here or there, writing songs with one person or another, but always remaining vague. Meanwhile, through horse owners she knew in the Nashville area, Cindy had gotten an offer to go to Florida to train some horses. "I took off for Florida with the horses, and then I met a man down there from Montreal who was pretty wealthy. He eventually—after a dozen roses and dinners out and this, that, and the other—encouraged me to go to Montreal with him and look at some horses up there, which I did. We ended up buying two thoroughbreds for him, which I then trained, and another horse that I got going for him that jumped pretty good, jumped five feet, so I got him going on five-foot fences pretty solid. I really ended up liking this guy, too. He was okay." She wondered about Townes, but figured he would come back when he was ready; or, he wouldn't. "Townes and I never really broke up. He just never came home off the tour, and then I went and did my thing with the horses, and somebody snatched me up."[4]

When Townes and Mickey pulled up to the cabin, they knew that Cindy was gone. "He really loved Cindy," White says. "I think he still thought that maybe there was something salvageable there." Townes decided to stay for a few days and see what he could learn about Cindy's whereabouts. She had left Geraldine with Mike Ewah; most of her belongings, including clothes, a trove of photos and mementos, and some saddles and other riding gear, were still in the cabin. "I'll never forget, there was a jar of Ragu and one little thing of spaghetti, and we cooked that up and ate it," White recalls. "We went out and cut some wood, so we were staying kind of warm, and Townes had this little bitty TV, and we watched the Godfather saga. So we were kind of hanging in there. We had just a couple of bucks, and we kind of bummed here and there for a little whiskey. We'd drive into Franklin to get a pint in the morning."

At some point, Townes hooked up with some dealers from Nashville, staying at their house and indulging in his old heroin habit. "He was staying in the house and I was staying in the Colonel," White recalls. "I was getting a little pissed because I wasn't getting in on any of the goods, but I knew that it was going on. And after three or four days, maybe even a week or so of staying around this junkie house, Townes and I saw the benefit of getting away."

Back at the farm, on the Sunday before Thanksgiving, Townes and Mickey were visited by some locals that Townes knew. "These hillbilly guys came by," White says, "and they had some whiskey with them, and Townes ended up getting in an arm-wrestling match for another pint that they had. And he won. Townes was a great arm wrestler.... He understood the leverage, and he was really good at it. He could go in with guys that were much bigger than him and beat them handily. In fact, it was the only thing he was good at gambling on, arm wrestling."

With their options running out, Townes and Mickey were hoping for some good luck. "That afternoon, the phone rings—thankfully the phone hadn't been cut off—and it's Cheatham calling from Austin," White says. "He had just opened up a little folk club and ice cream shop called You Scream, I Scream. And he said he wanted Townes to come down and play his grand opening. So Townes said, 'yeah, sure.' Cheatham said he'd pay for Townes' ticket and Townes could go down to the airport and pick it up." At that point, Mickey, desperate, grabbed the phone away from Townes. "I said, 'Cheatham, if you don't pay for my ticket, I will crawl down there and wring your fucking neck.' He said, 'Okay, all right, you get a ticket too.' I would have been stuck with nothing, absolutely nothing. And of course, Cheatham had been the one that called me to offer me the job in the first place."

Townes phoned John Lomax, who picked up the two forlorn musicians and took them to the airport. "We left the Colonel there at the farm and blew into Austin," White recalls. "We showed up at You Scream, I Scream, and it had been well pro-moted, and the joint was packed, and we played really well. It was like we'd found a home. Townes and I clearly understood at that point in time that we had just moved to Austin, Texas."

Summing up his impressions of Townes' feelings about returning to Texas, Mickey White says, "He felt pushed out of Nashville; everything was totally bankrupt in Nashville, and the pull in Austin was that there were gigs there, and he got such a huge reception and everything. And of course Cheatham had a place for us to stay, a big house on the near north side." The Austin scene at that time was vibrant. "Guys like Butch Hancock and that whole 'Lubbock mafia' had invaded, Jimmy Dale Gilmore and all those guys," White says. Texas had recovered from the oil bust in the late seventies and was starting to benefit from rising oil prices, and a real estate boom was under way in Austin, generating a lot of construction jobs. "A lot of hippie carpenters were making really good money and going out and supporting these clubs," clubs like Antone's, Spellman's Lounge, the Austin Outhouse, Soap Creek Saloon, the Hole in the Wall, and many others.

Austin provided Townes with a stimulating variety of places to play, he was surrounded by friends, and he was living comfortably in Cheatham's large house. However, by all accounts, he was not writing, and he was drinking heavily. Peggy Underwood remembers: "Many times, he would show up at gigs too drunk to go on." Along with Cheatham, Underwood was also lining up gigs for Townes, which at that point was not a difficult task. The difficult part was seeing that Townes followed through. "I used to have to manage him," Underwood says, "and I would set these things up and get money in advance, and then he would show up and be too fucked up to perform." Not long after settling back in Austin, Townes took up with Conni Hancock, a striking, dark-haired singer and guitar player and a well-known member of her father Tommy Hancock's popular Supernatural Family Band. "He was being pretty straight when he started hanging out with Conni Hancock," Underwood recalls, "then he started hanging out with Blaze down at Spellman's."[5]

Blaze Foley was the name adopted by Michael David Fuller, who at this time was essentially an itinerant living on the streets on the fringes of Austin society. Foley grew up in West Texas singing in his family's gospel ensemble, the Fuller Family Gospel Singers.[6] As Peggy Underwood recalls, "Townes somehow met Blaze in New York, but Blaze had been hanging out in Houston some, and it's probably because of Townes that Blaze wound up showing up over here [in Austin]. Blaze was a street person. He'd live on the street, or on someone's couch if he was lucky. Blaze and this guy, Rich, used to have horrible fights, because they would both want the same couch." Foley had been writing songs and performing for the past year or so in Houston and Austin, and was known as much for his eccentric lifestyle and habits—such as decorating his clothing and belongings with duct tape—as for his music, although he was a sensitive writer with a rich baritone voice.[7] He shared with Townes a fondness not only for drinking, but for outrageous behavior while drinking, and he would share an orbit proximate to Townes' for most of the remainder of the decade.

On December 6, 1980, Van Zandt played one of the last shows at Armadillo World Headquarters, opening for Taj Mahal. "It was one of those things that helped solidify that we were in the right place, in Austin," Mickey White says. "It was really a terrific gig, with screaming, foot-stomping, encores."

Two nights after the Armadillo gig, on December 8, Mickey White was at Spellman's playing pool when a friend came in and told him that John Lennon had just been killed. "I remember looking up in disbelief, then looking back at the pool table and sinking the eight ball," White says.

The next day, a memorial gathering was held at Zilker Park. One of the attendees was a Corpus Christi native, a diminutive twenty-three-year-old brunette named Jeanene Munsell. Munsell was living in south Austin, where she had worked over the summer for a landscaping business and was currently collecting food stamps. She had previously worked as a "cocktail bunny" at Austin's White Rabbit disco, and had been living with a man associated with the White Rabbit, an establishment alleged to have Mafia connections. She had been mistreated, and she had gotten into some trouble with the law during this period. After more than three years of living with this man, she had recently "escaped" from him. It was a rough time for Munsell, but she was tough, and she was determined.[8]

At the memorial that day with her friend Gradi Sterling, Jeanene happened to see her ex-boyfriend with a woman in a mink coat ("at a John Lennon thing, wearing a mink coat! What the hell!"). Jeanene was suddenly inspired to want to meet the handsome guitar player that Gradi had recently told her about, whom she knew through John Cheatham. They left the gathering and went to You Scream, I Scream, where Gradi figured Townes was likely to be found. She told Jeanene they had imported beer, ice cream, and folk music. "I can't imagine a worse combination," Jeanene says. "I was a punk rocker. I was hanging out at the Continental Club … I was a wild thing. Folk music to me was like people dancing in matching costumes, you know, like yodeling or something. I didn't know what she was talking about, folk music."

At the club, Gradi spotted Townes sitting at a table with "four or five beautiful women all around him," and she pointed him out to Jeanene. "So I walk over," Jeanene recalls, "and here's this, like, drunk, greasy … it looked like he hadn't bathed in at least a week or two." Jeanene sat near Townes, and he soon approached her. According to Jeanene, he said to her, "Darlin', do ya gamble?" She allowed as how she did, because "I was liking him; he was charming me." Extremely drunk, Townes proceeded to play a game with her in which he dealt three cards, one of which was an ace, and "whoever gets the ace has to kiss the other." After "pecking" for a few hands, Townes wanted to go somewhere else with her. "He was so drunk," Jeanene recalls, "that I said, 'man, I can't take you to any bar. We'll get arrested!'" They ended up at the Continental Club, where she knew someone she thought would get them in, and the familiar greetings that Townes got from people in the club were Jeanene's first indication that Townes was a well-known figure in Austin. At the end of the night, she took him home with her.

"I already had it in my head that he's mine," Jeanene says. As she tells the story, Townes climbed into her bed, while she remained up, doing things around the house. Finally, Townes asked her, "Are we gonna get laid or not?" Jeanene responded, "You are way too skinny and dirty to lay me," beginning what she called "the eight-day war." She insisted that Townes eat something and take a bath; he said, "Well, I ain't takin' no bath," and Jeanene replied, "Well then … you ain't gonna get laid." She cooked him steak, eggs, and hash browns, which he "wolfed down," then they went to sleep. They spent a second night together, at Cheatham's house. As Jeanene put it, "no washy, no fucky." Eight days went by—"and he's a-stinkin'," Jeanene recalls—before Townes relented and bathed. As Jeanene bluntly summarizes, "I cleaned him up … then I fucked him."

Townes moved in with Jeanene, with Mickey White occasionally crashing on the living room couch, and they began what Jeanene refers to as "a three-month bar-hopping tour" of Austin. "You gotta meet Blaze," Townes told her; "You gotta meet my buddies!" She says she was "just trying to keep up, and keep him out of jail, and keep food in him. He was my assignment. God had given him to me. I had to take care of him."

Jeanene reminded Mickey of Leslie Jo Richards. "They had the same kind of spunky attitude," White says. "They were kind of the same size and [had] the same kind of hair. They were both real feisty girls. My gut feeling when he met Jeanene was that she'd be somebody who'd take what he could dish out with relative impunity. I think that's kind of what Townes required."

Some of Townes' other friends seemed less able to understand Townes' attraction to Jeanene. One old friend believes that Jeanene simply "didn't have anything going" and "saw a dollar sign on Townes' forehead." Her speculation was that Townes "wanted it so nobody would want to be around him or mess with him. And believe me, none of us wanted to hang out with Jeanene."[9]

There wasn't much money for Townes and Jeanene to worry about in the bleak months following John Lennon's murder, at the gray dawn of the Reagan era. Townes and Mickey were playing in Austin and Houston, making a few hundred dollars on a good night, but little of that money lasted long. Mickey, however, was making plans for something more expansive. He had recently seen an uncle of his dying of cirrhosis in a hospital, causing him to begin to examine his own intake of alcohol. "I'll never forget walking into that room and realizing, hey man, alcohol's serious business. I'd seen guys fall by the wayside behind heroin and cocaine and speed and all that kind of stuff, but it was the first time I'd seen somebody really fall by the wayside on alcohol, seeing that it took that long to do it but that it was just as bad." He was determined to get back on the road, and he discussed the idea of a west coast tour with Townes.

"It came together really quickly," White recalls. "I was able to coordinate dates at McCabe's and at the Great American Music Hall within a few days of one another. Once you book those core dates, you start filling things in, and that's your profit. Pay your expenses with your main gigs. We were back to double guitars, which is where we started in the first place, and we had the Colonel, and not a lot of expenses to get us out there and back. And right about that time, we ended up booking the Vancouver Folk Festival as well."

Before the tour began, Townes returned briefly to the farm in Franklin to retrieve some of his belongings. Mickey accompanied Townes on the trip; as he recalls, "His mom had this white Ford Toronado, so we rode up to Tennessee in that and got Geraldine. The dog was still up there, holding down the farm, faithfully and loyally. He kind of put the last shit down on the farm, and we got the truck, the Colonel. And we had two CBs—that was really a hoot.... and we kind of convoyed back down to Texas."

As the time came for Townes and Mickey to leave for Vancouver, which would be the first stop on the tour, Jeanene was increasingly upset at being left behind. Jeanene says Townes told her, "No slits on the road!" As she tells the story, to get back at Townes for this slight, she approached a "bag boy" at the local market. "I took him aside and I said, 'Hey, how 'bout you and me get together?' And he went, 'okay!'" She returned home to tell Townes that she had a date that night, and found him packing up the truck to leave. When she told him about her "date," Townes went out to the truck and brought in a copy of *Our Mother the Mountain* and flung it at her. "I said, 'You have records?'" She put the record on to play as Townes left, "and I was sitting there bawling ... I was crying ... I couldn't believe what I was hearing. I still kept my date, but ... all I did was talk about Townes the whole time I was there. Then I wanted him back, because I decided, okay, I'm keeping him."

Townes and Mickey covered hundreds of miles together in the Colonel, going up to Vancouver then back down the west coast before returning to Texas. "I remember Townes had this little bitty tape recorder with one little auxiliary speaker on it," White says. "We had two tapes, Robert Johnson and Utah Phillips. We listened to Robert Johnson and Utah Phillips for days upon end." The gigs were overwhelmingly successful, including a performance opening for Ramblin' Jack Elliott at his fiftieth-birthday celebration at McCabe's in Los Angeles. "Townes' reputation for blowing gigs came from playing Houston and Austin. If he played Gerde's Folk City or the Great American, he would never even consider blowing a gig like that," White points out.

Van Zandt and White headed into the desert from California. "We had to go through up near Tahoe into Carson City and then across the desert to Salt Lake," White says. "We stopped at Carson City, and Townes and I of course immediately hit the tables." White lost all his money fairly quickly, but he assumed that Townes was "holding on to the payroll and had enough money to get us to the next gig." White's main concern was whiskey. "We were playing two nights later, so I figured there'd be whiskey money. So I tracked Townes down about two or three in the morning and said 'Townes, man, loan me another hundred.' And he says, 'Man, I don't have any money at all.' He'd lost every single penny—the entire payroll—shooting craps. Fortunately, we'd paid for the hotel room before we started gambling, so at least we had a place to sleep that night."

The next morning, the two broke musicians made a play. Townes approached a man in the hotel elevator and asked him if he had the time. According to Mickey, "He said, 'I don't have a watch.' I said, 'Well, maybe you'd like to buy mine.' I had a Timex on, and I sold it to him for ten bucks. So that bought us a pint of booze and five dollars' worth of gas in the car, which is enough to go up the mountain to Tahoe. So we drive the Colonel forty miles or so up into the hills. At least it would be cool up there, and we could sleep in the car and be comfortable. When we pulled into Tahoe the next day, we didn't have any money at all."

Again, Townes had a plan. Seeing from the marquee that Christopher Cross was playing at Caesar's, with the comedian Gary Muledeer opening, they walked into Caesar's, and, according to White, "Townes picks up the house phone. 'Uh, give me Christopher Cross's room please.' 'One moment, sir.' You see Townes kind of waiting. 'Well, thank you very much. Could you try Gary Muledeer's room?' … there's a little pause. 'Hello? Is this Gary Muledeer? You might not know who I am. My name's Townes Van Zandt. Yeah, that guy.' Apparently, he made a connection. So they start talking back and forth, and Townes hangs up the phone, and he says, 'Look, man, Gary Muledeer says if we can get backstage after his second show, he'll loan us a couple of hundred bucks.'" Unfortunately, the attempt to get backstage at Caesar's Tahoe was unsuccessful.

They had one option left. "I had this lucky buffalo nickel taped to the inside of my wallet.… I stuck our last nickel in the slot machine and pulled the handle. Lemon, bar, cherry, click. The ominous sound. I said, that's it. So we headed out to the Colonel. It was our last nickel." Townes was reduced to phoning Peggy Underwood and asking her to wire them some money. He and Mickey headed back down the mountain and stopped at Western Union, where they picked up the money and hit the road again.

That summer, as a new single, Emmylou Harris released a recording of her duet with Don Williams on "If I Needed You," the second of Townes' songs she'd covered. The record quickly registered at number three on the country charts, and Townes' name was again before the public as a songwriter of note. One of the first things Townes did when he got the news about the hit record was to phone Fran. The song had been special to her since Townes started writing it on the occasion of J.T.'s birth, and she felt that Townes recalled that feeling in his late-night call to her years later.

Townes saw Fran and J.T. only infrequently after his move to Nashville. Fran recalls, "J.T. always had this great sense of loss. Granny, as we called her—Townes' mother—took J.T. a couple of times to go see him [in Franklin]. Once it was really good and once it wasn't so good." When Townes moved back to Texas, he was able to visit with J.T. more often, and he was more in touch with Fran, so a call from Townes was not a shock, but the timing was a surprise. As Fran recalls, "Townes called me in the middle of the night, like three o'clock in the morning. It was a Saturday night. I'll never forget because I had just gotten home from my honeymoon with Ronnie." Fran's new husband answered the phone. "He gave me the phone and Townes said, 'Babe, we've made it. We finally hit the big time. Now we can buy your dad that Cadillac!' He was so sweet. We talked for a long time. He finally said, 'Who was that guy? I hope he's a nice guy.' And I told him I'd just gotten married."[10]

Interestingly, like Doc Watson's earlier recording of the song, Harris' version altered the lines in the third verse about Loop and Lil, Townes' parakeets. Instead of the original "Loop and Lil agree/She's a sight to see/And a treasure for the poor to find," Watson sang "Surely you will agree/She's a pretty sight to see/And a treasure indeed for a man to find." The Emmylou Harris/Don Williams version was "Who could ill agree/She's a sight to see/And a treasure for the poor to find." According to Harris, Don Williams was perplexed by the Loop and Lil reference and insisted it be changed.[11]

Townes appeared on Ralph Emory's Nashville Network TV show shortly after Emmylou's record hit the charts, and, before playing the song, while sitting next to Bill Monroe, he once again told the story of how "If I Needed You" was the only song he had ever written in his sleep. Bill Monroe seemed unimpressed.[12] Townes also told the story and performed the song—as well as "Pancho and Lefty"—on his second appearance on *Austin City Limits* in 1982.

Townes was invited back to play the Vancouver Folk Festival in the summer of 1982, and he and Mickey decided to take Jeanene and Mickey's new wife, Pat, along with them. According to White, "Pat was a drinker, too, as was Jeanene, so it got pretty wild, to say the least. But we had a pretty good time, and we played well." After Vancouver, they went to Seattle, then played the Casper Inn, near Mendocino, then the Great American Music Hall in San Francisco and McCabe's in L.A. Next, they headed back to Texas for a couple of gigs in El Paso. White says, "In between those two gigs, we went over to Juarez one day ... and Townes spent—I mean literally—every penny that he had from the entire tour. It was one of those things where he was kind of getting at Jeanene."

At a bar, Townes began tipping the waiters, bar staff, and wandering children extravagantly. "Soon, you could just tell that the word had gone out, because, here it is like one or two o'clock in the afternoon, and out of nowhere, the mariachi band shows up. Jeanene's screaming at Townes at the top of her lungs, 'We gotta get out of here, we gotta get out of here,'" White says. "So we end up getting a cab, and this horde of kids is following us. And Townes has this big blue sombrero that's about three feet wide, little stuffed dolls and pinatas and all this kind of stuff just hanging all over him. The kids are following behind, and whatever money he had left, he rolls down the window right as the cab is pulling out and says, 'Here, take this home to your mama,' and throws all the money out the window."

This episode took place after lucrative paydays at major venues like the Great American Music Hall and McCabe's, so "hundreds and hundreds of dollars" were involved, according to Mickey. "Fortunately, we had a gig that night, so we made enough money to get home," he says. "But, of course, Jeanene was counting on paying her rent with that money when she got home…. She ended up hauling Townes out of there, but by that time, Townes knew that he had her going. And once she made herself vulnerable, in that sense, once she showed that the money was important, that was Townes' leverage."

By this time, there was a new development that Townes and Jeanene couldn't ignore: Jeanene was pregnant, and she was determined to have the baby. At some point, Townes revealed to Jeanene that he was still a married man and that he didn't know where his wife was. Townes acknowledged that he would have to get a divorce from Cindy sooner or later, and that, with a baby on the way, it would likely have to be sooner.

Townes was also deeply troubled by another family issue: his mother had been diagnosed with cancer, and the prognosis was grim. Townes visited her at her apartment in Houston that summer, where he also discussed with Bill and Donna plans for caring for their mother. He went back and forth between Austin and Houston to visit Dorothy numerous times over the course of the next few months, both before and after she was hospitalized, as she soon was, at the nearby University Medical Center.

According to Jeanene, Dorothy encouraged Townes to marry her. "He always talked about how she never took her [wedding] ring off, and on her fucking death bed she took that ring off and handed it to him and said, 'you know, I have never taken this ring off. I want you to go home and marry that girl.'[13] He came home and I was taking a nap, and super pregnant, and he told me what had happened and handed me the ring. And I'm bawling because he was always so impressed that she never took her ring off; that was a big thing."

According to Fran, when Townes came down to visit her and J.T., he mentioned Jeanene; "he said nothing was ever going to happen [with Jeanene] because his mom really didn't like her. You could tell even after the wedding." Fran had remained very close to Townes' mother, J.T.'s "granny"; "I got called in for all the family circle things," Fran says. "I was there for J.T., plus I loved Granny. She was something in my life. I felt separate from

the family but I knew everybody much better than Jeanene because we did stuff with them. So it was kind of awkward. I think
where Jeanene may get her story is that, being in a very Southern family, Granny was horrified that they weren't married and
she was pregnant. She said to Townes, 'You're going to do the
right thing and honor that baby.'"

As they settled back in Austin, however, Townes and Jeanene
returned to their familiar pattern of drinking and partying while
Townes played the local bars and clubs. Finally, in August, Townes
checked himself into the Starlite Recovery Center Drug and Alcohol Rehabilitation Program—at Kerrville, of all places—where he
underwent rehab until early October. Townes recalled later that
this was his longest period of sobriety, the three months from
August to October, 1982.[14] But soon he was drinking again.

Mickey and Pat also fell easily into an unhealthy pattern: "Pat
and I had gone back to shooting drugs, like speed," Mickey recalls. "And by that time, I was really peaking on my alcoholism and all that stuff. Man, I was nuts, cross-eyed nuts. It was a
little much even for Townes. So he decided he was gonna use a
different guitar player." For roughly the remainder of the year,
Townes worked with Elliot Rogers, who was half of a local two-
person band called the Ramblers. White played lead guitar on a
dozen or so gigs around Texas with Jimmie Dale Gilmore over
the next months, while Rogers played local gigs with Townes.
"Elliot was a good player," according to White, "but he couldn't
play with Townes like I could."

In January of 1983, Willie Nelson released a recording of his
duet with Merle Haggard of "Pancho and Lefty." This event was
to prove a major turning point in Townes' career, although not
in the way many people expected at the time. The song had
come to Nelson through a fortuitous sequence of connections.
Peggy Underwood was a good friend of Lana Nelson's, Willie's
daughter, and Peggy suggested that it would be a great song for
Willie to cover. Lana agreed, and played the song for her father
during an evening recording session. Willie liked it so much he

immediately learned it, then, late that night, woke Haggard up and had him come to the studio to record the song. The recording was done on the first take, and Haggard claimed it was the only song he'd ever recorded before he really knew it.[15]

Once Peggy Underwood had come through with this success for Townes, and once some real money started to come in, she naturally became more interested again in seeing that Townes' business affairs were being run properly. "After 'Pancho and Lefty' happened," she recalls, "we tried to get Kevin [Eggers] off the publishing. They had a corporation, and Kevin hadn't paid his corporate taxes … he wasn't helping Townes at all, and then all of a sudden, he's gonna make all this money from Willie and Merle's record. If he wanted to still be part of the publishing, he could have been paying the franchise or the corporate taxes in New York City."

Peggy tried to do the same kind of investigating that John Lomax had done to get to the bottom of Townes' publishing and recording contracts, and she ended up hitting the same brick walls that Lomax had. "Basically, we got this other lawyer and we were trying to get Kevin out, but it didn't ever happen," she says. "I was trying to legally get him off the boat so that Townes would own it again. [The publishing] should have reverted to Townes when Kevin didn't keep the corporation going."

The income that Nelson and Haggard's recording of "Pancho and Lefty" generated for Townes was a windfall. "When [Jeanene] first hooked up with Townes, he was just mainly getting gig money," Underwood recalls. "But he was getting some pretty good mechanical royalties" from "Pancho and Lefty." Underwood also profited from the record, through a "handshake deal" that recognized her part in making the record happen. "When that money started coming in, we were still hooked up, and he was still paying me my part," Peggy says. "We bought a big old sailboat, and we would all go out on the lake and ride around. Jeanene had never had anything like that."

During this time Jeanene attempted to retrieve some cash from their account through the Nashville accountant who was taking care of Townes' financial affairs. "And there wasn't any money in that account," Peggy recalls. "That guy hadn't filed any tax returns for a few years, and he'd been sticking all the money in his pocket. If that happens here, there's nothing you can do about it."

"I heard that Townes looked for me for a couple years, didn't know where I was," Cindy says. "At one point, I went from Montreal to Nashville to get my things." Cindy returned to Texas at the end of 1982 and stayed at her mother's house, north of Houston, while her mother was going through a divorce. "He finally tracked me down and showed up," Cindy recalls. "I didn't really want a divorce, at that point. But Peggy had drawn up our divorce papers, and I remember him coming up finally, with his hands shaking, wanting me to sign them. He said that maybe he'd gotten somebody pregnant. He wasn't sure. I thought, well, who am I to stand in the way? There's a child. So I signed the papers."

Peggy Underwood had taken care of Townes as a friend for some years, and it was Peggy whom Townes turned to when he needed to find Cindy. "She knew I was taking care of his business and that he wanted to be divorced and was looking for her," Peggy remembers. "She called me from Canada and I told her about everything. He didn't care, but Jeanene wanted him to get divorced." The divorce was finalized in Travis County, Texas, on February 10, 1983. Townes celebrated his thirty-ninth birthday a month later.

That same week, the doctors caring for Townes' mother determined that her cancer was inoperable, and gave her roughly six months to live. Her eldest son married the nearly-nine-months-pregnant Jeanene Lanae Munsell a week later, on March 14, 1983, in a small outdoor ceremony, with his friend Bo Whitt, an Austin artist, as best man. "It was almost like a present to my mom," Townes' sister Donna says, "so she knew they were married when her next grandchild was born."[16]

The very next day, Townes flew to Nashville for an appearance on Bobby Bare's TV show. Before he left, Jeanene gave him one piece of advice: "Whatever you do, Townes, don't say 'I just got married and we're having a baby.' Pick one or the other."[17]

Townes had known Bare for some years, originally through Mickey Newbury, and Bare—another prolific and creative Nashville rebel—had recently released an album that included a version of "Pancho and Lefty" as well as songs by Guy Clark and J. J. Cale. On the show, Bare asks Townes about the story behind "Pancho and Lefty," and Townes tells of writing the song in a motel room outside of Dallas while both Billy Graham and the Guru Maharaji were appearing in town. He says there were no hotel rooms within forty miles of the city, so he was forced to stay way out of town, and, with nothing to do for three days, he wrote the song. "I used to say it was about them," Townes tells Bare, referring to Graham and the Guru, "but I don't say that anymore."

They talk about Willie and Merle's cover of "Pancho and Lefty," and about the video that Townes appeared in briefly. ("I was the captain of the federales," Townes says very seriously. "All I had to do was look at people in contempt and disgust.") They also discuss Emmylou Harris' "If I Needed You" and what it's like to have a song in the charts. Bare says, "You can't gear your life to those charts, it'll drive you nuts," to which Townes quietly protests, "I'm *already* nuts."

As they wrap up their on-air chat, Townes says, "I'm supposed to mention that my wife Jeanene and I are having a baby any minute." He goes on: "There's a law in Texas where once you get divorced you can't get married for thirty days, and it was getting close. We got married a couple days ago, but it was getting close, and I thought, well, we could always go up to Oklahoma. And I phoned my mom and I said, 'Look, with this thirty-day law we might have to rush up to Oklahoma to get married.' And she said, 'Now don't you do that, Townes; you don't want that baby born in Oklahoma.'"

William Vincent Van Zandt—a healthy, handsome baby—was born to Jeanene and Townes on March 24, ten days after they were married. Townes left town almost immediately after the birth, accompanying Blaze Foley on an ill-fated trip to Muscle Shoals, Alabama, ostensibly to record an album, but in fact to spend an inebriated week in a motel room. The escapade culminated in a paranoid Blaze tearing his motel room telephone cord out of the wall and both Townes and Blaze being arrested for disorderly conduct.[18] Townes managed to talk himself out of the situation and caught a bus back home.

That July, when Will was four months old, Townes took Jeanene and the baby to the old family "fishing camp" in Galveston to spend a week with his sister and his mother, who were there for the month. Dorothy was weak, but alert and determined. "We all knew at that point she was dying," Donna says. "Over the years, she had taken a lot of things to my uncle's place. So, we spent part of that month cleaning out, room by room, drawer by drawer, just making sure we got her things out of there so my Uncle Donny wouldn't have to worry about it."

To Donna, who believed that she knew the extent of her brother's alcoholism, Townes seemed fairly "in control" as she puts it. "To look at him, he didn't seem drunk. He didn't seem different. But his mind ... depending on the time of day, his mind was not as sharp as it had been." After Townes, Jeanene, and the baby left, Donna was cleaning their room and made a discovery. "Over in back of the bed, kind of out of sight, there was a little bottle of whiskey. I didn't tell my mom because I figured she didn't need to worry about that. But he didn't look like a drunk. He just kind of sipped a lot, I think." Donna had seen her brother perform in Boulder and in Denver and had tried to gauge his condition by the quality of the performances. "There were some of the songs he wrote early on that were real intricate and difficult for him to sing when he was having problems with the drinking."

Townes' "drinking problems" came to a head at the end of that month. Very likely at the urging of his dying mother, or in some attempt to please her, Townes called Peggy Underwood, who took him to the Alcoholism and Drug Abuse Treatment Center at Brackenridge Hospital in Austin, where Townes voluntarily checked himself in on July 27. According to hospital records, Townes claimed that he had been in treatment eleven times previously.[19] The attending physician's notes state that Townes "has been drinking for 15 years but he states that it has not really been a problem until 10 years ago," and that he "stated further that it is not really a big problem." Townes reported that he was drinking a pint of vodka every day. He said that his wife and his friends had encouraged him to admit himself. The doctor quotes Townes: "I've just got to straighten up—I've been crazy all my life."

Of Townes' mental status, the Brackenridge doctor's notes state that "He admits to hearing voices, mostly musical voices. He denies any suicidal ideations. Affect is blunted and mood is sad. Judgment and insight is impaired." Townes initially expressed some confusion about where he was; his speech was "rambling," and he walked with a "stumbling gait." On his second morning in the hospital, he was "more alert," and he told the doctor that "he will probably be staying for detox and does not want to stay for the program." Townes requested and signed his own release that same day. He was discharged "AMA [against medical advice]/Unimproved" on July 30, after only three days in the hospital.

Willie and Merle's record of "Pancho and Lefty" hit number one on the charts that same week. Townes had a scheduled "end-of-the-month rent gig" at EmmaJoe's the same night he checked out of Brackenridge, a Saturday. According to Townes' friend Larry Monroe, the well-known DJ at KUT in Austin, Townes had a rough time getting through his set that night. In the midst of "If I Needed You," he forgot the lyrics and was stuck, foundering. Blaze Foley was in the audience, and he "glided gracefully to his side and sang the words for him, then harmonized with him as Townes got back on track."[20] Monroe believed that he had witnessed an "energy transfer" from Blaze to Townes. Townes continued the performance, and made it through.

Dorothy Townes Van Zandt passed away two months later, in September 1983.

# 13

## No Deeper Blue

THE CALL OF THE ROAD did not cease for Townes after the birth of his second son; indeed, it grew stronger, just as it had around the time of the birth of his first son. Once again, Townes' self-destructive behavior was alarming his friends and family, as he was made explicitly aware of through the intervention they attempted before his mother died. The hospital had proven too strict a regimen and he again convinced himself that the road would make him "free and clean," as it had before. "Townes would go into rehab for other people, not for himself," according to Mickey White. "Anybody who's recovering can tell you, you can do that until the cows come home, but until you do it for yourself, you're not going to be saved."

Townes did not want to go back out on the road by himself, so early in 1984, he decided to form a band. He got back together with Mickey White and called in two friends, the Waddell brothers, Leland and David, to play drums and bass guitar, respectively. To change things up, Townes and Mickey decided to add Boston native Donny Silverman on flute and saxophone. "Townes always had a plan, some kind of direction," White says, "and the plan was, this time, to put together a band. We'd go out on the road and get tight, and then go into the studio and cut an album."[1]

The band began rehearsing around Townes' fortieth birthday. Mickey was "musical director" of the group, and there were often disagreements about arrangements, tempos, and other issues. White recalls, "I'd had experience with bands and producing records and all that kind of stuff ... so I was kind of being bullheaded about that. Leland had his own ideas about how things were going to be; David had his; so a lot of the rehearsals would become these arguing matches. But in between, we did come up with some pretty good arrangements on those songs." The group played in Austin, Dallas, and a few other spots in Texas. After a series of gigs at Anderson Fair and Hermann Park in Houston, it became clear that the full "blues band" approach was not working, and the Waddells were dropped.

"A lot of it was because we drank too much, a lot of it was because we couldn't agree on an approach to playing. It wasn't Townes' strong suit, playing with a band. It could have worked, in the long run, but only with a lot of compromising," says Mickey White. White, Silverman, and Van Zandt continued to play as a trio, gradually expanding their territory outside of Texas. "We kind of really got good about July of 1984," White says. "My last drink was July 31, 1984. I was really rededicated. I was really stable, and I wanted to really take care of some business and book some good tours, and get us back up into Gerde's Folk City and places like that." White—with some intervention by Harold Eggers[2]—booked a tour of east coast clubs for the following spring.

The first stop on this outing was an important one. The gig was in Nashville, at a club called Twelfth and Porter, on April 17, 1985. "This was kind of a 'welcome back to Nashville' gig," White says. "Rodney [Crowell] and [his wife] Roseanne [Cash] were there, Guy and Susanna were there, and Neil Young was there." Young was in Nashville recording and his attendance added a lustrous buzz to the already auspicious evening. According to the writer Robert K. Oermann, the Twelfth and Porter show was billed as "the return of the lost sheep to the songwriting fold," adding that Townes was "surely one of the lambs who has wandered astray. Indeed, he practically defines the personality of the ne'er do well tunesmith."[3] The sense of this being a momentous night was intensified because Harold Eggers had arranged for the show to be recorded for a possible live album.

Apparently, among his ventures at the time, Eggers was trying to promote Willie Nelson's daughter Susie as a singer, and he had the notion that he could somehow involve her in the current recording project with Townes and his band. Hence, he set up the evening's recording in a peculiar way. "They put me and Townes' guitars on the same track," White recalls. "It should have been Townes' voice on a track, his guitar on a track, my guitar on a track, and Donny on a track," White says. "How else would you do it? But because Little H wanted to have a separate track for Ms. Nelson to sing on, me and Townes' guitars got put on one track, and it eliminated our ability to mix them. The counterpoint and stuff that we were doing was buried."

White overdubbed some additional guitar tracks later, but he had mixed feelings about the final recording. Because the new Tomato label was already having financial difficulty, however, with Kevin Eggers falling somewhat into the shadows, the recording ended up being shelved until 1987, when it was released on the small Sugar Hill label as *Live and Obscure*.[4] Of some note is the fact that, for the first time, the "executive producer" credit on the release went to Harold F. Eggers Jr., with the added credit that the record was manufactured under license from something called the Eggers Group Inc. Eggers later stated that *Live and Obscure* was "the first album put out with myself as co-owner with TVZ."[5]

Another big name in the audience at Twelfth and Porter that night was Cowboy Jack Clement. "Jack really liked the act and proposed bringing us into the studio as a trio, as an ensemble, and just sitting us down in a circle playing these tunes, and he'd turn the tape on. Basically doing in the studio what we had done that night, just adding a bass and drums," White recalls. This sounded like an excellent plan to Townes, who had no other viable recording irons in the fire and was happy to work again with Clement.

A few months later, Townes, Mickey, and Donny were back in Nashville, where they stayed for about two weeks working on the first basic tracks for the record at Clement's Cowboy Arms Hotel and Recording Spa. Nashville pro Jim Rooney was the recording engineer, and the record's de facto producer. "This is Jack's approach to producing," White says. "He had this little xeroxed sheet that he gave us all. There were about eight bulleted items; the two that I remember were 'No headphones' and 'Remember, it only takes three minutes to cut a hit song.'" Clement spent minimal time in the studio after that, leaving the nuts and bolts of the recording to Rooney. Clement's approach, however—to have the musicians "sit around in a circle and play the songs"— was undertaken and accomplished. Among Townes' records, Clement remembers *At My Window* as "the best one I was ever involved in."[6]

As he had in the past, Clement again surrounded Townes with Nashville studio pros. Roy Huskey Jr. was recruited to play upright bass, and Kenny Malone played drums. Townes had recorded tracks with Huskey's father for his third album, *Townes Van Zandt,* and he was again pleased to be working with consummate professionals who were also warm, friendly people. The simple recording process went reasonably well. "We put Roy and Kenny behind [sound] baffles," White recollects; "We were never more than about five or six feet apart." White overdubbed some lead guitar parts—on "Buckskin Stallion Blues," for example—but most of the recording was live, with the regular exception of Silverman's flute and sax parts. "Once we started playing, Donny immediately bailed out on the concept, because there was just no room for error," according to White. "Mickey Raphael was hanging around, and I said 'hey Mickey, we got one for you,' which was 'Snowin' on Raton.' Everything was done hot, and Mickey did an overdub." Nashville veteran Chuck Cochran was also "hanging around" and added some tasteful piano lines to several tracks.

As White remembers, "Townes was trying to get the opportunity to record these songs the way he wanted. Unfortunately, from my perspective, I think that Townes by this time had started to lose his edge, certainly on his guitar playing. And his singing wasn't quite as committed as it had been. His voice sounded better, a little older, but he didn't have quite the commitment in his voice that he had had, say, for *Our Mother the Mountain*."

The production of *At My Window* was well conceived and well executed, the sound clean, the arrangements straightforward and appropriate—leaning gently toward the best contemporary country sound—and the musicianship superb. The songs themselves are a mixed bag, with some disarmingly strong new material (especially "Snowin' on Raton" and "The Catfish Song"; to a slightly lesser extent "Blue Wind Blew" and "Still Lookin' for You"), some more mundane new songs ("Ain't Leavin' Your Love," "Gone, Gone Blues," and "Little Sundance #2"), and some old songs, including a third revisiting of "For the Sake of the Song" and new versions of two major songs from the *Seven Come Eleven* sessions that were being released for the first time: the laconic, Robert Frost-inspired "At My Window" and the beautiful, strangely perfect "Buckskin Stallion Blues."

Danny Rowland remembers the seed of "Snowin' on Raton" being planted during a long drive from Colorado to Texas, through the Raton Pass overnight, to make it to the next gig.[7] "Snowin' on Raton" is one of Townes' best songs—if not *the* best—from what by this point can be called his "late" period. The song seems to explore a poetic question; something like, when the beauty of life and love are gone, will the memory sustain you in eternity?

The chorus—a simple melody cast on a framework of finger-picked blues chord changes—and the elegant movement of the words, stands as one of Townes' most moving, haunting statements: "It's snowin' on Raton/Come morning I'll be through them hills and gone." Townes, transient, will move on; eternity will not notice. As in other significant songs throughout Townes' canon to this point—notably, "Highway Kind"—the road is a dominant image here, Townes' old friend, for better or worse. Again the feeling is of the resignation and acceptance that comes at the end of life's journey, when you're almost "through them hills and gone," and silence is all that is left.

"When I first heard it, it just bowled me over," David Olney says of the song. "It's a beautiful song. It's like a real folk song. There's a line in it, 'Tomorrow the mountains will be sleeping/ silent 'neath a blanket green and blue.' Well, to me, when you think of snow-capped mountains, it would be a blanket of white. And I think that's visually probably what he saw, but *emotionally*, the blanket was green and blue." Olney also notes how the personal touch in the song is similar to that in some of Townes' other songs. "The verse about mother and little brother, that reminds me of 'Rex's Blues.' I didn't notice until I was singing both songs that they both mention brother and sister and mother and baby, or little darlin'. They're like recurring characters."

"The Catfish Song," like "Flyin' Shoes," originated by the side of the Harpeth River in Franklin, Tennessee, and has as its central image the murky depths of a riverbed. Also like "Flyin' Shoes," the changing seasons figure prominently, and the course of a relationship is likened to the course of nature. The mood of the song is tender regret, of dreams and even memories lost, but tempered with the comfort of being a part of nature. But it is implicit that the singer isn't planning on being around much longer, and he's leaving his hopes at the bottom of the "dirty old river."

Like Van Zandt's live recording project that year, the fruits of these studio sessions wouldn't see the light of day until 1987. In fact, for months after the initial sessions, Clement continued to add tracks to the tapes, remix tracks, and otherwise work on "finishing" the record. He shopped the project to a number of small labels, including Rounder Records, before the North Carolina label Sugar Hill Records picked it up and released it. As White recalls, *At My Window* "regenerated a little bit of enthusiasm on Townes' part. He'd added to his body of work, which he'd wanted to do for a long time; he felt good about the new songs; he got good reviews." He adds: "Butch Hancock told me that's his favorite Townes album. It's really Townes."

Not long after, Townes left on a brief tour of England and Scotland. It was on this tour that Townes began to develop a love of the British Isles and the British people that brought him back to England, Scotland, and Ireland numerous times in the next few years. He also became aware that he had a large audience outside of the United States, and that the road through Europe—an unexpected extension of the road he had been traveling all these years—might be the road that would carry him where he needed to go.

Back in Austin, on the afternoon of June 26, 1986, Townes Van Zandt and Bob Dylan chanced to meet. As Larry Monroe tells the story, Dylan was shopping in Electric Ladyland, a costume shop on South Congress. Monroe and his daughter were there, and they saw Blaze Foley come into the store and go into the room where Dylan was shopping. Some moments later, Foley appeared at Monroe's side and said, "Bob Dylan is outside talking to Townes. Come on, I'll introduce you to him." By the time they got outside, as Monroe wrote, "the drifter had escaped." Foley told him that "he had walked up to Dylan, introduced himself and said Townes was out front. Dylan had wanted to meet Townes, and they had immediately gone outside. Blaze had seen me on the way out and had come back in to get me after he introduced Dylan to Townes."[8]

Peggy Underwood remembers that both Blaze and Townes—who were near the end of a days-long drinking campaign at the time—were very excited by the meeting with Dylan. "Dylan definitely knew who Townes was," she says. "There was some talk of recording something, but it never happened."[9] Mickey White recalls a vague connection with Dylan mentioned by Kevin Eggers some time before. "Kevin told me years ago, back in the seventies, that Dylan was real interested in Townes and was proposing something," White says. "But, you know, I think Townes would have been real uncomfortable doing that with anybody, much less Bob Dylan."

Susanna Clark agrees. "Townes was funny," she says. "Bob Dylan was a big fan of Townes. Every time Bob Dylan came to town, his people would call the house and say, 'There's a backstage pass ready for you at the Dylan concert.'" She also recalls hearing that Dylan's "people" extended overtures to Townes. "They would call, and Dylan would want to write with Townes. Townes never did accept that invitation. He didn't write with people very well." Susanna also notes that Townes was inherently "not impressed" with Dylan's stature, although he admired his writing. As she recalls, "Townes kind of made a joke. He said that when he ran into Bob Dylan on the street, Bob Dylan said, 'Oh, I have all your records.' And Townes said, 'Apparently.'"

Toward the end of the year, Jeanene began looking for a place to live in Nashville. Once again, the Austin environment was proving too toxic for Townes; it was too hard for Jeanene to keep him reasonably sober there, especially while raising a small child. In addition, she was interested in seeing Townes pursue the career opportunities that she figured would be knocking in Music City. She knew Townes' history in Nashville, but she believed that it was the place to be. "It was a big choice in his life right then," Townes' friend Lyse Moore remembers. Moore, a Texan, had moved to Nashville from Houston, where she had been an owner of the folk club Anderson Fair. "But he told me he was going to go to Nashville with Jeanene. That's what Van Gogh would do, he said. He was really in his Van Gogh period."[10]

That Halloween, the Van Zandts—Townes, Jeanene, and three-and-a-half-year-old Will—moved from Austin to 313 Town Park Drive, Nashville, near the airport outside of town. Lyse Moore recalls that Jeaneane "made the trip up with Will and a girlfriend of hers, and Townes followed in a few days. She had had a vision of a yellow house, and she found one by the airport." Townes renewed his acquaintance with his old friend Bob Moore (no relation to Lyse Moore), with whom he had been close since he lived in Franklin. Bob observed that Townes joked about his new Nashville home, "saying that he had the perfect place to live; he was right by the airport and there were two liquor stores—he called them 'LSs'—and a mental hospital all within walking distance."[11]

Lyse Moore credits Jeanene with making the right move in leaving Austin and coming to Nashville. "I did not like Jeanene at first. I didn't like where she was from, I didn't like what she did, but she earned my respect through time.... She got him out of Austin. He was about to go down there; he would have just drunk himself to death. He was sitting around the house with his entourage of drunks and folks that he'd have fetch and do things; it was sort of embarrassing to watch."

Townes continued to tour heavily throughout 1986 and into 1987, including a number of shows sharing the bill with Guy Clark, and some with David Olney. He played the prestigious West Virginia *Mountain Stage* live radio program, hit both the Winnipeg and Edmonton folk festivals in Canada, and went to Europe for gigs in England, Scotland, Ireland, and the Netherlands in the fall.

In a typically literate and perceptive article in the June 7, 1987, *New York Times*, Robert Palmer paid prominent tribute to Townes, comparing him outright with Hank Williams: "both men live in their music, as if singing and writing and being human were the same thing and all as natural as breathing. Their songwriting craft and vocal musicianship are exceptional, but what you hear is beyond all that; it seems to be the direct, untrammeled expression of a man's soul. You can hear the South and Southwest in the accents, the casually mentioned names of towns and rivers, the music's unforced swing. But the highway runs from one end of America to the other, and for men like these the highway is heritage and home."[12]

*At My Window* was finally released—complete with a display quote from the Palmer article and a cover sticker displaying the famous and soon famously overused Steve Earle quote about standing on Bob Dylan's coffee table in his cowboy boots proclaiming Townes "the best damn songwriter in the whole world," much to Townes' dismay. A nervous-looking Townes made an appearance on the Nashville Network TV program *New Country* with most of the session band from the album, including Jack Clement on keyboards and dobro.

Keith Case, a well-established Nashville agent who also worked with Guy Clark, had started booking shows for Townes, which caused Mickey White some consternation. "He started squeezing me out, because it was more practical and easier for him to get Townes around without shipping a duo or a trio," White says. "I was a little bit pissed at Townes because he didn't really step up and say anything about it."

Townes turned forty-four on the road, and he continued to bounce from east coast to west coast all year—still working with Guy on many shows, including a series of joint radio appearances in California. This touring regimen, while meant to keep him moving and in a stable condition—which it did for some time—was beginning to wear on Townes. Once destinations outside of the United States began to enter into the arithmetic of the road, the "getting there" became harder and harder, requiring more of an effort at compensation from Townes, and that compensation was again taking the standard form of heavier and heavier drinking. It was showing in his performances—which could, as always, be brilliant one night and disastrous the next—and it was showing in his personal life, as he struggled with the knowledge of his family responsibilities even as he traveled the world far away from them.

In October 1988, Townes set off for a brief series of gigs in New Zealand, accompanied by Mickey White. "Jeanene is the one," White says. "She called me up and said look, Townes is trying to pull up and keep from drinking, and he's got this little tour in New Zealand, and I think it would be a good idea if you went along. And Townes just kind of let it happen. I don't think he was really enthusiastic about it. But we had a good time, the reception was good.... This is when I was playing my very best, at the top of my game," White says. "We were in New Zealand for about ten days, and they took really good care of us." Upon his return, after a show with Guy Clark at the Great American Music Hall in San Francisco and an early December show in Louisville, Kentucky, Townes was home for only three months before going back to Europe.

The months at home were a mix of attempted domesticity and minor tumbles back into the wild life. "In those first few years when they were out by the airport, he'd get Will off to school, and Jeanene was learning the music business from Jack Clement," Lyse Moore remembers. Nashville agent Pam Lewis had taken on a management contract with Townes, and Jeanene was serious about getting Townes' business affairs in order, much as John Lomax had been, although she had a much larger stake in the outcome. But Townes also spent a lot of his time at home drinking with his friends, including his good friend Jimmy Gingles—a Kentucky native living in Nashville and working as a club DJ and as a magician on the side. Gingles recalls the house on Town Park Road more as a scene of good-natured but sometimes edgy partying than of domestic bliss. One night, after hours of drinking tequila with Jimmy and a houseguest from Texas, Townes had gone to bed. Out of the blue, the houseguest, drunk, lost his composure and head-butted Jimmy.

"I just left," Gingles remembers. "I walked up the street and called a taxicab.... Townes called me the next morning and wanted to know what happened to me and everything, so I told him what happened. Well, he got a little irritated that his houseguest had pulled a stunt like that." Townes spoke to his houseguest, who had been so drunk that he'd forgotten everything that happened the night before. "This guy carried a .25 automatic revolver with him all the time, which I didn't know," Gingles continues, "and this guy couldn't remember nothing from the night before, and there was a creek that ran beside his

———•◆•———

house, and [Townes] said, 'Y'all got in an argument … you took a shot at him, and he's somewhere down in the creek….' And he had this guy walking up and down the creek looking for my corpse…. Townes wanted to teach this guy a little lesson on trying to be a human being."

Bob Moore recalls one night at the Town Park Drive house: "We were in the house and drinking, and Townes picks up the BB gun, which was a gift from Susanna and Guy from a long time before," Moore says. "And he shoots out one of the lamps that were mounted on the wall. Then he hands it to me and says, 'I bet you can't do that.' So I did. Then we started shooting other things in the house." Jeanene, struggling to hold things together, was not amused. "She tried to keep him motivated, but he was way past that," according to Jimmy Gingles. "In all fairness," Bob Moore says, "Jeanene put up with a lot." But Jeanene could only put up with so much; she also knew that she had to try to help Townes stay alive. Around this time, with help from friends, she began to look into treatment options for Townes' alcoholism.

Townes invited Bob Moore to go on the road with him toward the end of 1988, and they travelled extensively in Moore's new Honda Civic, with Townes doing most of the driving. "We hit the Birchmere, near Washington, D.C.; we went to New York City, to a place called the Wetlands Preservation; and to Café Lena in Saratoga Springs, and to Buffalo," Moore remembers. "Once we drove over to Columbia, South Carolina, about 500 miles I guess. And we went to Austin, Dallas, and Houston two or three times." One long drive was extended in an odd way. With a gig in Burlington, Massachusetts, set for the next night, Townes opted for an adventure. "I think both of us knew that 'MA' was the abbreviation for Massachusetts, rather than Maine," Moore says. "But we pretended it wasn't, and instead, we went to Maine." They made it all the way to Bangor, Maine, "and as we got farther and farther up the road, we realized, there's nothing here. But I knew, I'm pretty sure I knew, I mean, neither of us are stupid. He had some friends near Portland who had a restaurant named Pancho's Choice, and I think that he wanted to see them, so we went and visited a little bit then drove on up to Portland and spent the night. And about midday the next day, we realized we'd better get back. And he made the show."

The first week of February 1989, Townes was booked at Poor David's Pub in Dallas, then at the Cactus Café in Austin. As he and Moore were getting ready to set out from Nashville, Peggy Underwood called from Austin to tell Townes that Blaze Foley had been shot and killed.[13] He was thirty-nine years old. "We decided that Jeanene and Will and all of us would go down in their van," Moore remembers. "When we stopped in Texarkana to sleep, it was like, sixty degrees and raining, but when we woke up the next morning, it was solid ice all over everything. And I think it's about a hundred and sixty miles from Texarkana to Dallas, and it took us thirteen hours to get there. The heater didn't work in the van, and Will was in my sleeping bag, and most of our clothes were covering up the rest of him. But Townes drove all the way. And, I mean, it was stress city. But he was so determined that he wasn't gonna miss the gig. He was really serious."

Austin writer Michael Corcoran beautifully describes the day of Blaze Foley's funeral, an icy February 4 in the Texas capital: "At the jam-packed service, guitarist Mickey White passed out the lyrics to 'If I Could Only Fly,' Foley's trademark song, and as the ragtag congregation sang those words about wanting to soar above human limitations, the song grew spiritual wings.... Someone at the gravesite busted out a roll of duct tape, Foley's favorite fashion accessory, and folks started adorning the casket. Some of his friends made duct tape armbands or placed pieces over their hearts. Kimmie Rhodes started singing an old gospel song as the casket was lowered, and the tears nearly froze before they hit the ground."[14] Photographer Niles Fuller recalls shooting some pictures that day of a very somber Townes Van Zandt "looking into the tent where Blaze's duct-taped and white-flowered casket lay."[15] Lyse Moore recalls that "[Blaze] was a wonderful soul and spirit; that's why Townes loved him. You know, if you're true of heart, Townes would love you; if not, he'd just play with you a lot."

Soon after their return to Nashville, Townes and Jeanene—with concerned input from Guy and Susanna Clark—decided to make another attempt at drying Townes out. This time, they were all determined that this was going to be a serious effort. In fact, it would be the most serious, sustained effort of Townes' life, and it would be the last serious, sustained effort. As Susanna recalls, "He was picked up in a limo and taken down to Huntsville, Alabama. And when he got back, they had done a good job."[16]

Townes entered a full forty-five-day detoxification and rehabilitation program, which involved treatment at a number of different facilities. Jeanene visited on most weekends, as well as for a "family week" near the end of the program. One weekend, though, Susanna Clark visited Townes at the request of Jeanene. "There was a reason for my going," she says.

> They had put him on these very powerful barbiturates that were making him crazy, because they said he was having hallucinations. And I said, "I don't think you are." I said, "What are they?" And he said, very quietly, "Well, one of them, I looked out my window and there was an Indian woman and her husband, an Indian man, and a little baby Indian. And the little baby Indian was sitting in the tree. And a plane flew over, and the little baby Indian pointed up at the plane and said, mommy, what's that, what's that? And the mommy said, oh, that's just some humans who think they can fly." And so I said, "Townes, those aren't hallucinations. You're seeing spirits. That's real." And he said, "Really? Oh, that gives me hope." I said, "You're connected to another part of the world." And he said, "Oh, that makes me feel so much better.... That gives me a reason to stay sober ... knowing that I'm connected to a spiritual world, now I have something to look forward to when I get out of here." ... He was convinced that he wasn't crazy after all.

Mickey White thought a great deal about the issues facing Townes as he fought his alcoholism, and he and Townes discussed many times the concerns surrounding both of their struggles. "He'd spin out his lines and his bullshit and all that kind of stuff," White reflects, "but after you'd traveled hundreds and hundreds of miles ... you'd get some pretty animated, honest introspection coming from him. I think that people who recover from alcoholism with things like AA, the twelve-step approach, tend to be the most successful. But Townes, he was so completely about his spirituality, that that was going to be the vehicle that was going to lead him to recovery."

White believes that Townes' bipolar disorder was a real factor, but that it wasn't always clearly evident because Townes was "always drunk." "Townes' main problem was that he was an alcoholic," White insists.

> I think that it makes it a little harder for people to recover if they suffer from clinical depression, because when they quit drinking, it just becomes so much more evident. And true, people have recovered who had much more serious, deep-seated psychological problems than I think Townes ever had. People tend to make that a reason that Townes couldn't recover, but I think that the main reason was that he was never motivated to in the first place. And I don't think that that had to do with his depression as much as it had to do with his world view, and just the way his life developed, and his outlook on certain things. I think a lot of that had to do with death taking people away from him and things like that.... I think that he believed in Armageddon. I think that he believed in redemption. I think that he was raised on that stuff and it created a conflict he never could really reconcile.

Bob Moore recalls that when Townes came home from Huntsville, he was changed. "Somehow, they got through to him," Moore says. "And I realized that if I want to be around him, I can't drink. And he was very supportive of that, and until he died, he was very protective of me."

Townes played a scheduled show at the Bottom Line in New York shortly after being released, staying with his friend, the folk singer Eric Andersen. The gig was well attended and successful, but Townes was somewhat tentative and uncomfortable with his sobriety. He returned to Nashville before his next series of gigs, and he asked Bob Moore to accompany him. "I said yeah, and we went up to the Birchmere and then to a folk festival in Staunton, Virginia." Moore says. "And then after that, pretty much, any place he went that wasn't too far to drive, we went together. And, you know, we just talked and talked."

Moore was impressed to the core by Townes' gentleness and kindness, which he began to take particular note of during this period of sobriety. "He taught me so much," Moore says. "Once, I remember, Will was really little, and he bumped into the downspout on a gutter, and all these red wasps came flying out of it, and he was terrified of it. Then, later, these yellow jackets showed up down the bottom of the hill, and I said, 'well I'll get rid of them, I'll just pour some gasoline down in their hole, and that'll kill them,' and Townes said 'No, if we don't go down there, no harm will come, and there's no need to kill them.' He was incredibly spiritual. He made you constantly appreciate the balance of nature.... It was like he'd already been where I was and he knew the way better than I did."

At the folk festival in Staunton, Virginia, Townes was on the bill with the country-folk singer George Hamilton IV, "an extremely nice gentleman," as Bob Moore recalls. "He had recorded 'I'll Be Here in the Morning' years and years ago. And this is just Townes' second trip after being in the treatment center in Huntsville. It was almost like George Hamilton could sense it, that Townes was so nervous. We had to go by a liquor store to get there, which was hard. He was just trying to get it over with; he hadn't gone on yet, and George Hamilton IV came over and said, 'You know, Townes, there's a chord or two I can't remember on "Close Your Eyes I'll Be Here in the Morning."' I know that he knew it, but he was just being incredibly perceptive."

On the drive back from Staunton, Moore recalls that Townes talked a great deal about his parents, seemingly examining their lives as a source of strength. "He said that when [his mother] died, he realized that his first instinct was to call her to tell her that his mama died," Moore says. "And he told me about his father, that before he died … his father, he looked at him, and said, 'It's a rough old world out there, and I'm not sure you're ready for it.' And he said that when he started doing music in clubs, he was doing Bob Dylan stuff … and his father told him, 'I believe you have a good start, and if you're going to do this, you ought to write your own songs.'"

Townes got his sea-legs back on a European tour that spring, turning in a series of excellent performances in the U.K. and Germany. He continued to tour through the end of 1989 and into 1990, but he stayed closer to his old home axis, Tennessee and Texas. He was not drinking, already now for the longest period of his adult life.

Around this time, Kevin Eggers approached Townes and Jeanene with the idea of re-recording all of Townes' material in pristine new studio versions, including duets with some major artists. Jeanene had already learned enough about Townes' previous arrangements with Eggers that she was wary. As one writer later reported of the projected sixty-song, multi-CD box set project, "Jeanene says her husband only began work on the much-delayed set after Eggers agreed to 'make good' contracts for Poppy and Tomato back royalties."[17] At any rate, the sessions were arranged at the Fire Station studio in San Marcos, Texas, in the early spring of 1990. Eggers would produce, with Eric Paul as engineer, and he brought in a crew of top-notch musicians, including Augie Meyers on accordion and Ernie Durawa on drums, both associates of San Antonio stalwart Doug Sahm; the great New Orleans bassist Irving Charles; guitarist John Inmon from Jerry Jeff Walker's Lost Gonzo Band; plus the parade of guest artists that began to line up: Doug Sahm, Freddy Fender, Jerry Jeff Walker, James McMurtry, Kimmie Rhodes, Emmylou Harris, and Willie Nelson, among others.

Among the first of the duet tracks recorded were Freddy Fender's beautiful bilingual Tejano take on "Pancho and Lefty" and

"Quicksilver Daydreams of Maria," joined by Ruben Ramos and the Texas Revolution and Fender's Texas Tornado bandmates Sahm and Meyers; and Sahm's own sparkling Texas-perfect, laconic reading of "Two Girls." Some of the recording shifted to Nelson's Pedernales Studios, including the session for Willie's mellow duet with Townes on "No Lonesome Tune." After a few weeks of steady work the sessions became more sporadic, apparently due to financial issues troubling Eggers.

A few days after his forty-sixth birthday, Townes appeared on Larry Monroe's radio program on KUT in Austin. As they talk, Monroe notes Townes' sobriety, saying "A lot of people know you had a drinking problem. You've been clean and sober for a couple years, now, right?" Although Monroe overstates the timeframe, Townes responds, "Oh yeah, I'm doing real well.... It's a whole different ball game." Townes then plays a new song, and it's instantly clear that he has not lost any of his abilities as a songwriter.

"Marie" is as harrowingly good as anything Van Zandt ever wrote, using a first-person narrative—using it in a straightforward, prose-like manner new to Townes' songwriting—to tell the story of a homeless couple and, more broadly, to address the issue of homelessness. Townes had exhibited concern for the poor and homeless since his childhood, and he still made it a habit to give money—often his entire earnings from gigs—to street people. Over a familiarly melancholy finger-picked minor-key chord pattern, Townes tenderly sings the story of a nearly broken homeless man and his pregnant girlfriend, Marie ("In my heart I know it's a little boy/Hope he don't end up like me."). Marie dies in her sleep one night ("just rolled over and went to heaven/My little boy safe inside"); the man lays her body "in the sun" and hops a freight train, concluding, "Marie will know I'm headed south/ So's to meet me by and by." Townes' simple, concrete writing and deadpan delivery perfectly evoke world-weariness without ever crossing the line into sentimentality, and "Marie" stands with "Snowin' on Raton"—a very different kind of song—as among the best of his work from the 1980s and '90s.

Townes tells Larry Monroe that he was in San Francisco with Guy Clark when he wrote "Marie."[18] "One morning this song just kind of … there it was," Townes says before going on to confirm that he wrote the song for Blaze Foley. "I had a gig here, it would have been a year ago, the first of February, when I played that frozen weekend at the Cactus. I couldn't wait to get down here and play it for old Blaze. Then the news came." Monroe asks about Townes' current "extensive" recording project, and Townes describes the proceedings: "It's gonna be sixty or sixty-five songs, it's gonna be on Tomato, it'll be a three-CD set of all my songs, all re-recorded," he says. "We have about forty-one songs so far, and we go back in to start and finish up in about two weeks." In fact, while more work was completed on the project, Kevin Eggers' financial problems once again intervened, and it would be years before any of the recordings saw the light of day.[19] Townes later told an interviewer, "It's either going to be a giant tax write-off, or some company with a lot of money is going to release it."[20]

Two months later, Townes embarked on an adventure that had the potential to expose him to a whole new audience and a new phase of his career. The band Cowboy Junkies—who made a national impact with their debut album, *The Trinity Sessions,* in 1988—were booked for a twenty-five-city tour to support their newly released third album, *The Caution Horses,* and they needed an opening act. "We felt a little weird, because we felt that we should be opening for Townes, you know, if art was the criteria," according to Junkies' songwriter and guitarist Michael Timmins. "But we realized at that point that obviously we had the draw, and he was more than happy to do it. We were [traveling] in a bus, and he asked us if he could get on the bus as well, because it would make it a lot easier for him. So that was great, because we really got to know him. It's a pretty intimate setting, a bus, buzzing around North America."[21]

The tour kicked off on the first of May at Toad's Place in New Haven, Connecticut, one of the more intimate venues of the tour, which included a mixture of bars and theaters. After a theater show in Pennsylvania, they played the Beacon Theatre in New York City, then Boston and Springfield, Massachusetts, then Lisner Auditorium in Washington, D.C. The tour progressed across the south—Atlanta, Tampa, Birmingham, and other stops—then jumped back north to Ann Arbor, then headed west to St. Louis, Chicago, and Minneapolis, among other cities, then up into Canada for multiple dates before hitting Portland, Oregon, then Saratoga, California, then a final show at the Paramount in Austin at the end of June.

"There's always something on the bus during a tour that catches on, and everybody gets addicted to it," Michael Timmins says. "On that tour, it was craps. Townes was a big craps player, and he taught us all to play, and we played nonstop." Timmins wrote a song about the trip, which he called "Townes' Blues." The song documents a stretch of their tour bus trip from Boulder, Colorado, to Houston, Texas, a trip that Townes had taken many times. "It was an overnight drive, and we played craps the whole time. The longer you play, the more you lose or the more you win, and you just have to be lucky enough to stop when you happen to be winning."

Timmins notes that the "in" joke in his song is the reference to the Raton Pass. "Throughout the whole tour, during Townes' show, he'd play his song, 'Snowin' on Raton,'" Timmins says. "Before that song, he'd always introduce it as, 'You know, the Raton Pass is the quickest way to get from Colorado to Texas, and I've travelled it many times.' Just coincidentally, we happened to be doing that trip from Colorado to Texas, but our driver decided that he didn't want to go through the Raton Pass, he wanted to stay on the superhighway. So he went all the way around and all through Kansas. And about eighteen hours into the trip, Townes is saying, 'If we took the Raton Pass, we'd be there by now!'"

Timmins remembers Townes being mostly—but not entirely—sober for the tour and turning in excellent performances. The band was aware of Townes' history of drinking problems, and they had concerns, but, Timmins says, "There was absolutely no problem. He might have gotten drunk a couple of times on off days. But he certainly never missed a show and he never screwed up a show and he was never too drunk to play, that's for sure." Townes did better at the theater shows than at the bar shows, where the crowds were often not paying close attention to the opening act, but on the whole his sets were well received. "I think it was, for Townes, a pretty sober period…. He would certainly go through periods where he was pretty dark … not mean or anything like that, just very inward. You can hear that in the songs, and you could see it in his personality at times…. He'd often give fairly cryptic but—as a songwriter, for me—pretty incisive descriptions of how he came to write certain songs…. I think what he taught me was that no matter how lyrical or poetic a song is, it should always be grounded in a place or an event."

Townes was writing during this period, and he expressed considerable satisfaction that he was doing so again after a "dry spell"—a "dry spell" that included "Buckskin Stallion Blues," "The Catfish Song," "Snowin' on Raton," and "Marie," among others, but that was in fact much less prolific than his great creative burst in the late sixties and early seventies. One of the songs Townes began working on during the tour was "Cowboy Junkies Lament," a light, surrealistic ballad with dark undertones, in the style of "Two Girls" and "You Are Not Needed Now." Townes later said it was the only song he ever wrote specifically *for* anybody.[22] As Timmins recalls, "He said, 'I'm writing one about you guys.' He said, 'I'm almost done, but I want to finish it up.'" A month after the tour ended, Townes sent Timmins a tape of the finished song. Timmins says the band, "flattered and blown away," tried to decipher the lyrics together, but couldn't figure it out. "So one day I called him, and I said, 'Townes, you got to tell me, give me a hint … what's it about?' And he said, 'Well, the first verse is about you, the second verse is about Margo, and the third verse is about Pete.' That was it. And when I went back and started to look at it, it began to make sense."

Timmins pegs "Cowboy Junkies Lament" as "a very Townes song. There's a lot of insides, and a lot of cryptic comments and turns of phrases that begin to make sense. Townes was an observer. That's what he did. He was a very quiet man. He would sit there and he would take in what was going on around him."

Bob Moore remembers Townes stopping in to see him in the midst of the tour. "He just looked worn out," Moore says. By the time Townes returned to Nashville in July, he was exhausted. And he was drinking again, after nearly a year of sobriety.[23]

He was only home for a matter of weeks before hitting the road for some gigs in the south and the west, most with Guy Clark and Robert Earl Keen, including a show at one of Townes' old stomping grounds, the Chautauqua Park in Boulder, Colorado. The recording of that performance displays Townes as close to the top of his game as he had been in some time. If he was drinking again, it was not evident that night. Townes is clearly in good spirits; he notes how glad he is to be back in Boulder, at Chautauqua, where he spent so much time in his youth ("We used to stay in cabin one-eleven," he notes; "Forty years and I've come about fifty feet."). He also gives spot-on readings of some old songs—"Fraternity Blues," "Lungs," ("a blues song," Townes says), an amazing, precise "Mr. Mudd and Mr. Gold"—and several newer songs, including a beautiful "Snowin' on Raton," a lovely, lilting "Buckskin Stallion Blues," and a brand new composition called "The Hole," a surrealistic yet honest account of Townes' struggle with his demons.

In September, Townes headed for a destination as far from home as he could get: Australia and New Zealand. He played a series of shows across New Zealand, including Auckland and Wellington, then flew to Australia for gigs at the Rose, Shamrock & Thistle (known as The Three Weeds) in Sydney; Moruya Hall, a small town five hours down the south coast from Sydney (where he played for his largest crowd of the tour, a group of about 300, most traveling a considerable distance to see him); and Madigans in Melbourne.

Keith Glass, an Australian singer–songwriter and recording artist, booked the tour, and remembers meeting Townes at the airport when he arrived in Australia. Glass drove Townes to the Koala Hotel and left him there to rest. First, though, Glass says, Townes "insisted on scouting the street to purchase a walking stick, as his leg was troubling him." Townes began having attacks of gout around this time, not unusual in heavy drinkers; he was photographed carrying a walking stick in subsequent years. Glass arranged to meet Townes later in the day. "When I came back, he had already drunk the entire contents of the room's mini bar—every small bottle of whatever. I had neglected to remove it; I was told he was no longer drinking. He blamed the need to do this on the fact that I had turned up in dark sunglasses at the airport and it had freaked him out."[24]

Once Glass established himself as a fan of Lightnin' Hopkins, Townes became more comfortable with his host. Townes asked to go to a Chinese restaurant, where he ordered a steak, then to a strip club. "Townes had purchased a stemmed rose under plastic from one of those people that come around tables, and we wandered out of Chinatown up to Kings Cross, the seedy redlight, strip-club area, to go to this place," Glass says. "It was in a side street and really sleazy looking.... The price of admission was a five-dollar can of Victoria Bitter beer, which everybody clutched through the show of about six girls, grinding away on the table tops." They retired early, however, and went to the zoo the next day. "Townes had an almost childlike fascination with the Australian animals, especially the Tasmanian Devils; he went ape-shit," according to Glass. "I realized later it was because of the cartoon character."

Glass found Townes "a bit antsy" and in need of distraction from drinking on his days off. "One day, I resolved to get him out of any reach of alcohol, at least until the show." Glass decided they should go fishing, and Townes insisted on renting the smallest rowboat they had; "I went along with it, but I doubt we ever made it more that a couple of hundred yards away from the jetty. But for the next four hours we dropped a line over the side, took bets on imaginary scenarios, and sang David Olney's song, 'Jerusalem Tomorrow.'"

Townes was drunk for the show that night, but "still, the crowd hung on every word." The other gigs went better, particularly the Melbourne show. "I had a support group to take the babysitting pressure off," Glass says. "The two [Melbourne] shows were the best. Townes pulled out some new songs and was telling great stories."

Townes was turning in some stunning performances during the earliest years of the 1990s. In contrast to the many shows he struggled through in the late eighties, he seemed to briefly achieve a higher level of consistency, along with a new—and still growing—depth of world-weariness that showed in his voice as well as his playing. As always, humor played a prominent part in Townes' performances, as it did in his personality, and as he progressed into the "late" period of his craft, the humor became more clearly a yin to the yang of the dark side of his nature. Finally, the humor became a struggle to sustain, and for the most part it fell away. But for a while in the very early nineties, Townes seemed to be once again running on all cylinders in many of his performances.

Townes' show at the Quasimodo in Berlin in October 1990—later released as *Rain on a Conga Drum*—is one example of a nearly flawless performance from this period. The writer Michael Hall recalls that Townes was "sober, which was a surprise" as well as "soulful and funny, which wasn't." A show in Roscrea, Ireland, on the last day of August 1991, is another example of Townes near the top of his form. The shows on the brief British tour that included the Roscrea gig featured John Stewart, Peter Rowan, and Guy Clark playing before Townes, then a solo performance by Townes, then Townes and Guy playing together, telling stories, joking, and trading songs, projecting honest good humor. Townes was clearly in good spirits throughout, and in good voice, and his playing and delivery were focused and incisive. A show in Munich in late October 1992 was similarly solid, and included a surprise performance of one of Townes' earliest compositions, "Waitin' for the Day," a song Townes played only rarely.[25]

But as good as these and other isolated performances were, this period was as uneven as any in Townes' career. Michael Hall contrasts the 1990 Berlin performance with what unfortunately became more of a typical performance, a night at La Zona Rosa in Austin two and a half years later, remembering that Townes was "so drunk he couldn't finish a single song during the entire abbreviated set. Embarrassed fans started filing out after fifteen minutes as he fumbled with chords and slurred his words into gibberish. Some stuck it out to the end, feeling guilty for watching." After the show, Hall writes, "he collapsed." According to Hall's account, immediately after the La Zona Rosa show, Townes consented to let his friend Steve Weiner "take him to a Nashville treatment center—but not before having a drink in the Dallas airport. 'Amigo, I've been drinking for thirty years,' Townes told him. 'You can't feel guilty that you can't stop me.'"[26]

# 14

## Flyin' Shoes

A T A HOTEL IN DUBLIN, while on tour at the end of October 1990, Townes printed on a sheet of wrapping paper, in his usual all-capital-letter style, the lyrics to a song he titled "Ruester's Blues," then he signed it, wrapped a package with the paper, and sent it to his friend Danny "Ruester" Rowland in Kentucky. Ruester was always glad to hear from Townes, who was fairly good about keeping in touch as he traveled, but these lyrics were somewhat disturbing. "Don't want to be here when the reaper comes," the song begins; "Don't want to hear his machine no more/Don't care where he's goin'/where he's from/I just gotta be away from here." The second verse—illustrated with Townes' drawing of a moon with a face—is equally dark: "Tired of the rising/tired of the felling [sic]/Forgotten the moon/the sunshine too." He goes on with a personal message offering at least some grim hope: "Seems all my friends be ripe for plantin'/Listen my friend, good luck to you."[1]

Townes Van Zandt—road-weary yet needful of the freedom of the road and almost always *on* the road—careened down that same road toward his fiftieth birthday and didn't pause to look back. The years of touring—and the years of heavy drinking—had for some time been manifested in Townes' singing voice and performing style, but now the damage was becoming more starkly reflected in his deeply lined face and his increasingly frail, seemingly shrinking body as well—his "skin like iron" and "breath as hard as kerosene."[2] The toll Townes was paying was evident in his whole demeanor. Photographs from the nineties show a man who looks considerably older than his late forties or early fifties.

The Townes Van Zandt who was performing Hank Williams' "Lost Highway" regularly in the nineties sounded like he had lived the song in the deepest, most intimate way. At least once—at a show in Manchester, England, in 1994—Townes introduced "Lost Highway" by quietly saying "This has nothing to do with me," but the audience sensed something different as they listened to his dry but passionate reading of the song. The spirit of Hank Williams was close by.[3]

Townes had grown into some of his older songs by this time; he was able to invest them with a new sense of truth. For example, his performances of "To Live's to Fly" in the early to mid-nineties had a *gravitas* that earlier readings lacked. Similarly, later performances of "Waitin' Around to Die" cut closer to the bone. Later performances of "Nothing" could be chilling, even terrifying. As the chances for good performances seemed to deteriorate with Townes' condition, songs like these touched audiences all the more deeply, often to the point of inducing tears. Townes also became more and more prone to weeping on stage. Sometimes he would attempt to turn an emotional collapse into a joke. He would often play "Old Shep"—the chestnut about a boy who has to euthanize his faithful dog—as a dark comedy, mocking the song's melodrama; then, part way through the song, he would actually break down crying; then he would turn around and laugh at his own emotionalism, which came finally as a relief to uncomfortable audiences as well as to Townes, who many people correctly sensed was struggling to get through his set.

It got worse. Many performances from this period feature Townes talking considerably more than he plays—sometimes offering long, rambling stories, sometimes stumbling through songs, fumbling chords and forgetting lyrics. He often acknowledged to the audience that he was talking too much, and he would invoke the advice his mother had given him about performing: "Play, Townes; don't talk. Play." At least once an audience member shouted back, "She was right!" During this period, an audience might collectively guess that they were at a train-wreck of a show if they found themselves listening to Townes doing a twenty-minute, part-talking, part-singing version of "The Shrimp Song," barely able to get through a line without some absurd distraction.[4]

As a credit to Townes' perseverance and ingrained professionalism, however, for a while, the good performances could still be very good. On a brief tour through the Netherlands in the fall of 1991—with Jeanene (who was pregnant with their second child) and young Will along and time for sightseeing, including a trip to the Van Gogh Museum in Amsterdam—Townes left behind him a trail of good shows.[5] A gig at the Milky Way in Amsterdam was captured by a Dutch film crew, and the film shows a solid, confident performance. Mickey White—who had not played with Townes for three years—was in Europe at the time and came to see his old friend at the Milky Way. Townes invited Mickey up to play some songs ("I really think he did that for me," White says), which ended up being the last time the two played together. White was concerned about Townes' physical condition, but heartened by his performing energy and focus. "As the years went on, singing became more and more difficult for him physically," White reflected. "On the other hand, his ability to entertain became more and more seasoned."[6]

White believes that Townes was more in control of some of those "train-wreck" performances than a casual observer might have thought. "He was building his legend," Mickey says. "I've seen Townes sober as a judge before a gig, and he'd go up there and right in the middle of the second song he'd stop and start talking, and I'd know exactly what he was doing. He hadn't taken a drink all day long, but he had to do what he felt was the best thing to maintain interest. He would never do that at big gigs, only at the gigs he played on a regular basis—Anderson Fair, Cactus Café, places like that." White recalled one particular example, a gig in Arkansas booked by Townes' friend Linda Lowe. "He blew that big gig, but the reason he did that was because she was just hanging on to him so much, and she was so nervous about this gig she was promoting."

While in Holland, Townes was interviewed on Dutch MTV. The interviewer asked him, "Are there any goals left for you?" Townes reflected for a moment. "Well, I'm gonna do this new album, with all new songs," he responded slowly. "And then, uh, you know, I mean I have a lot of goals...." He paused, very thoughtful, and gazed downward. "You know, I'm a father, and, uh, that's a goal in itself. That kind of stuff." He seemed to be taken aback somewhat, and within just a few moments, the depth of thought with which he was addressing the question became compelling. Then, he seemed to realize that he was getting too "heavy," and—just as he would do in a performance—he quickly lightened the mood, concluding, "But I'd like to write some songs that are so good that nobody understands them. Including me."

Townes finished 1991 and started 1992 on the road, back and forth between the United States and Europe. Jeanene later told an interviewer that she had essentially been Townes' road manager since Will was born and "Townes decided he didn't want to leave me and Will to go on the road, so he fired his band and the three of us hit the road together for five years."[7] Jeanene and Will accompanied Townes on numerous trips, both in Europe and in the United States. Townes was at home in Tennessee, though, on February 14—Valentine's Day—when Jeanene gave birth to a lovely, dark-haired daughter whom they named Katie Belle (with a nod to Townes' paternal grandmother, Bell Williams Van Zandt). Neither Townes nor Jeanene took a long break from business after the birth, however. From their new home in Smyrna, Tennessee—which they jokingly called the Ponderosa after Jimmy Gingles remarked that it looked like the ranch house on *Bonanza*—Jeanene had been working for some time on consolidating her and her family's interests in Townes' catalog of songs.

"By 1987, I was the business manager and song plugger," Jeanene said. "In 1992, Townes gave me half interest in the publishing...."[8] On February 16, 1992, records show that Jeanene obtained a *Certification of Transfer of Copyright from Townes Van Zandt to Jeanene Van Zandt for "Blaze's Blues" and 13 Other Titles.*[9] This was one of the first steps in what was to be an ongoing effort by Jeanene to secure her financial position, and thereby to ensure that her family—Will and Katie Belle—were taken care of should anything happen to Townes, the family's only breadwinner.

The breadwinner was back on the road the week after his daughter's birth, on the west coast, then in Canada, then playing some Texas gigs with Guy Clark—at Gruene Hall, then the La Zona Rosa gig at which Michael Hall described Townes as "so drunk he couldn't finish a single song"[10]—then—after the aforementioned detour in the Nashville alcohol treatment facility—back to Europe.

In 1993, the sessions originally recorded in 1974 to become *Seven Come Eleven* were finally released on Kevin Eggers' Tomato label as *The Nashville Sessions*, to little notice. Also, an assortment of live recordings made in 1978 of Townes, Ruester, Jimmie Gray, and Owen Cody was released on the Sundown label as *Rear View Mirror* (which was to become one of Townes' consistently best selling albums, containing as it does most of his best songs up to that point, beautifully performed with sympathetic musicians and straightforward arrangements). In 1994, a companion album of cover songs recorded around the same time with the same group was released as *Road Songs* on Sugar Hill. In 1993, Townes told DJ Larry Monroe that he was beginning to believe that "If you do enough live albums, people will think you're dead."[11]

The pattern seemed well set, and the story of the next few years of Townes' life is told in large part by his touring itinerary. After a break between December 1992 and March 1993,

April started Townes off in the Midwest; July took him through England, Scotland, and Ireland; August and September found him back in Austin, and at Kerrville again; by October, he was back in Europe—Germany and Holland—then in November and early December he went to New York, Pennsylvania, and back to Texas—the Cactus Café on December 2 and 3—then, by December 6, England, Scotland, and Ireland again. (Of his just-completed European tour, Townes told Larry Monroe in a radio interview: "I had a good time. I don't think I got paid, but I had a good time."[12])

The following year—1994—took up the same pattern. With Harold Eggers at his side, Townes was on the road playing gigs all spring, again concentrating on the British Isles, then the western United States; in the fall and throughout the winter it was back to Europe: Norway, Holland, Germany, Austria, Switzerland, Slovenia, Italy, then back to Britain. A December 12 gig in Perth, Scotland, was followed by a December 17 gig in Chicago, Illinois. A month later—January 15, 1995—Townes was in Hanau, Germany; the next week, he was playing the *Mountain Stage* radio program in Charlestown, West Virginia, then was back at the Cactus in Austin.

Behind the still fast-moving story of Townes' life on the road was the deteriorating reality of Townes' family life. There was no chance of Townes settling into any kind of domesticity in the limited time between tours—usually from a few weeks to no more than a couple of months—and the time he did spend at home became increasingly contentious. Friends recall a number of incidents during which Townes—in a drunken state, hallucinating—frightened young Will. "You could have a conversation with Will when he was five years old just like you could with the most intelligent and educated adult you ever ran across," Jimmy Gingles says. "But I remember one night, Townes scared Will to death. He jumped up and yelled 'There's spiders! They're on the floor!' And Will, he jumped up and grabbed onto my neck and just held on."

Will later recalled this period: "My early memories have to be bad, bad memories, definitely," he says. "I don't think he really understood that you need to treat a child differently than you do an adult. And to him it wasn't anything, but to a six-year-old boy it's scary, you know."[13] Another friend confirms this scenario. "He and Will were not getting along," according to this account. "Will would call his daddy terrible names, and they would get in fights, and Townes would be just too drunk. So Jeanene made a very hard decision. She still loved him dearly when she did it, but she made the decision, and he signed all of his publishing over to her."[14]

Townes had been out gambling at Merv Griffin's new Riverboat Casino in Metropolis, Illinois, near the Kentucky border, with Jimmy Gingles one night in the early spring of 1993. Gingles traces the couple's breakup to that night. "It was when he called her from my apartment," Gingles recalls, "and told her he'd lost $1400. He was freaked out, boy, he was just sick. 'What am I gonna tell Jeanene?' And I told him, 'Call her and tell her the truth,' and Jeanene said, 'Well, that's just great! I just bought you a new truck'—which was a secondhand truck—'and when you get back to Nashville, you can load your stuff up in it, and you can get outta here!' And she said, 'I want you to keep gambling, and I want you to keep drinking, because I bought some stock in Merv Griffin's casino, and every time you lose, I win.' That's what she told him, point blank."

Jimmy and other friends attest that the relationship between Townes and Jeanene on the whole was extremely volatile by this point. "The truth is the truth," Gingles says, "and on more than one occasion, in front of me, over at their house, I heard Jeanene tell him, 'I can't wait 'til the day you're dead, because then you're gonna be worth more to me than you ever was alive.'"[15]

Other close friends experienced the same kind of volatility and explosiveness around Townes and Jeanene. Bob Moore recalls, "Jeanene actually told him she could hardly wait until he was dead, because he'd be worth a lot more dead than alive. I heard her say that right to his face." Moore balances his account by giving Jeanene credit: "She prepared the meals," he notes. "Will was in school, Katie was a baby, and she acted like a housewife."[16]

Moore does remember, however, what he thought of as a turning point in Townes and Jeanene's relationship. During a visit at the house in Smyrna, Moore says Townes took him aside and told him something in confidence. "He said, 'I got up the other morning and Jeanene put these papers in front of me and said, here, you need to sign these papers, and it turned out I was signing away my song catalog and everything else.'"

Townes told Moore that he had said to Jeanene, "You're edging me out, aren't you?'"

The story of Jeanene "tricking" him into signing his song publishing rights and all of his worldly possessions over to her became a part of Townes' stage routine almost immediately. As he told it to a live audience at a 1993 taping of *The Texas Connection* TV show in San Antonio:

> Those Stouffers breakfasts, those are dangerous little units, man.... I've gotten to where I love 'em, and they're so easy, and I don't have to wash the dishes. [My wife]'s gotten to where anything she wants me to sign, in the morning she just hands me one of them Stouffers and then pushes the paper over and, "Sign this right here, Townes." So far I've signed away all my entire publishing enterprise.
>
> If I ever upset her, all I have left is this little johnboat—kind of a big rowboat—and a little, small motorcycle, and my guitar. And I've been thinking about, how am I going to tie this big guitar on that little motorcycle and park them both in that stupid boat? And sit out there on the lake and freeze to death. So watch out for them Stouffers.[17]

Townes elaborated in a later interview, when the interviewer noted that his song, "Katie Belle Blue" is "something your daughter's going to have after you're gone." Townes replied, "She also has all the publishing and the Buick and this house and an acre of land. I signed all that over." He went on: "I have a pickup truck, an eighty-nine GMC with a new motor and a good undercarriage, and a J200 Gibson. Everything else has been signed over. I keep the gig money and the family keeps the ASCAP, the publishing, and the recording money. It's all set up."

Townes continued that interview in a more philosophical vein. "Between taxes and liability insurance and this and that, we ain't in it for the money, man ... we're out there for one guitar chord, one note, one beam of light in somebody's mind. We travel 600 miles a day to do it. It's not the money."

By all accounts, Jeanene demanded that Townes leave the family home in Smyrna and find a place of his own.[18] He ended up in a rented room at a place in downtown Nashville known affectionately as the Rock'n'Roll Hotel. "The Rock'n'Roll Hotel was some rented rooms over a restaurant that had been known earlier as Spence Manor, where music groups touring would be catered to, so everything they needed would be right there," according to Bob Moore, who helped Townes move into a small, dark room there. "It turned out to be kind of a flop house," Moore says, "and when Townes was there, construction was going on and whoever had bought the place was turning it back into a restaurant. I thought at the time that there were some pretty sleazy people that came by."

Townes' life at the Rock'n'Roll Hotel tended to be as seedy and unpleasant as his surroundings—a "grubby place full of grubby people," according to Susanna Clark. As one extreme illustration, a friend recalls Townes telling about an incident there that he said forever put an end to his use of heroin, which he still dabbled with occasionally. "These two chicks—he wasn't really with either one of them, they were just chicks he knew, and he always had people around, some were using him, some he was using, and I'm suspecting these were a couple of users—but these two chicks came in there with some heroin ... and the one chick hit up the other chick, and she OD'ed. And as soon as she did, the one chick pulled the needle out of her arm, stuck it in her own arm, and took the rest of the dose. But Townes luckily had the knowledge of how to revive the chick that was OD'ing, so she didn't die.... Then he told them to get their shit out of there, he didn't want any of it, and he said he didn't do any more heroin after that."[19]

Bob Moore went through similarly traumatic times with his friend during the Rock'n'Roll Hotel period. "Townes fell over there one time and had to have his head stitched up," Moore says. He agreed to go to nearby Vanderbilt Hospital, but he refused to go back to get the stitches out when the time came. Bob took Townes to a girlfriend's house. "I knew she could do it, although she's not a nurse," Moore recalls. "But he wasn't going to get the stitches taken out, and she took the stitches right out of his head." Another time, Townes phoned Bob from the Rock'n'Roll Hotel; "It was late in the night and he was frightened," Moore says, "saying there were all these black demons surrounding him. But a white angel, he said, was standing between him and the black demons. I know once I heard Jeanene say that he'd be alright if he stayed on Zoloft."

Townes spent much of the early spring of 1994 playing shows in Texas. He celebrated his fiftieth birthday with a party in Austin, he played the Cactus Café, and he played a "Writers in the Round" concert in Houston, among other gigs. Back in Boulder, Colorado, later in March, he recorded his second show for the *E-Town* radio program, which aired the following month. By that time, Townes was back in Europe. He kept up a grueling schedule for the rest of the year: From Britain to California in the spring; from Texas to Scandinavia in the fall; then a stretch of shows in Germany, Austria, and Switzerland, finishing the winter with gigs in Slovenia and Italy, then back to Britain, then back to the United States.

In the works for some months, a Final Decree of Divorce was granted to Jeanene Lanae Van Zandt from John Townes Van Zandt on May 2, 1994, in the Chancery Court for Rutherford County, Tennessee ("upon the Wife's Complaint for Absolute Divorce ... on the grounds of irreconcilable differences").[20] The

Certificate of Divorce recorded that the last date the couple had resided in the same household was the first of April, 1993. That household—the "Ponderosa" in Smyrna—was now by decree "divested out of the Husband and vested solely in the Wife."

The centerpiece of the divorce decree, however, was the award to Jeanene of "undivided One Hundred Percent (100%) interest in all of the Husband's right, title, and interest in and to the musical compositions, including but not limited to the copyright and all renewals and extensions thereof for the United States of America and all countries of the world": and what follows is a listing of 126 Townes Van Zandt songs—divided by the three established publishing catalogs: Townes Van Zandt Songs (sixteen titles), Silver Dollar Music (fifty-nine titles), and Columbine Music (fifty titles).

Nor does the next paragraph of the decree fail to command attention: "Husband also assigns to the Wife, thus relinquishing, all royalties due the Husband as the so called 'writer's share' of the above referenced compositions including all revenue paid from any publisher, administrator or licenses and all revenue, including but not limited to bonuses, payable by any performing rights organization, including but not limited to ASCAP."

Susanna Clark voiced a common reaction among songwriters to this relinquishment of "writer's share": "That was an unfair thing. You don't get writer's share from somebody, leaving somebody with the only source of income they had [being] what they made on the road." Clark continued this thought with a personal memory: "But even then, he would come over and, after he got off the road, he'd come over and give [Jeanene] all the money he had in his pockets. I mean, he didn't care anything about money. He was very drunk all the time there, and he signed every piece of paper she stuck in front of him. He didn't read it.... I would say that she did do a lot of things to try to give him a home. But it was very difficult."[21]

Townes' on-stage cataloging of his remaining worldly possessions was always fairly accurate, as reflected in the official account of his "sole and separate property, free and clear of any claim of the Wife." The decree lists "the 1989 GMC Truck and Camper, 1984 Honda Shadow Motorcycle, and the 1983 Starwind 22 foot boat and trailer." But there was one other thing in which Townes remained vested; he retained "sole ownership in all oil lease and mineral rights presently in his name acquired through inheritance." Through someone's insistence—either that of a knowledgeable, sympathetic lawyer, a close friend, or, one might still reasonably imagine, Townes himself—the Van Zandt family inheritance—the "old money," such as it was—was kept out of litigious hands and remained with Townes Van Zandt.

Jeanene was granted sole custody of Will and Katie Belle, and Townes was ordered to pay "One Thousand Forty Five Dollars … per month … in compliance with the Tennessee Child Support Guidelines based on the Husband's monthly net income." Townes was awarded "liberal visitation" rights. Both Townes and Jeanene were required to place their respective stocks and bonds in trust for the children's education.

Bob Moore remained close to Townes during these months, and he has further recollections illustrative of this period of dissolution and decline. "Once I was gonna take Townes to the airport. He was going back to Austin, going to a treatment center, and when I came in he was lying on the bed and I didn't know if he was alive or not. He sort of sat up and asked me to go get him some vodka, which was in walking distance. I started just bringing miniatures back, and I soon found out that wasn't enough." Moore asked Townes about his flight arrangements, and Townes managed to phone the airport. "He was calling the airline about his flight, and even as sick as he was, he was very courteous with the customer service person at the airport. She was having trouble understanding him because he was slurring his words. But the flight he was supposed to be on started with 'DT', and she could never understand him, so finally he said, 'detox,' which was where he was headed."

Before he could take that flight, in early June of 1994, Townes was admitted to Vanderbilt Hospital. Bob recalls that the ongoing construction at the Rock'n'Roll Hotel had been having deleterious effects on Townes for some weeks. "They were tearing out all sorts of stuff to remodel the place, and he had to move from one room to another," Moore remembers. Susanna Clark recalls that Townes had a brown blanket, "and he would wake up in the morning and all this white stuff, which it turned out was asbestos, would be all over his blanket. He was breathing that in every day." In addition, "What finally got Townes into the hospital was he had left some Chinese food with shrimp in it out overnight, and he had gotten up and eaten that, and he had bad food poisoning."

Bob Moore happened to know one of the nurses attending Townes before he was admitted to the Hospital. "She said that she had been working there at Vanderbilt for years, and she said she had never seen anyone come in in as bad a shape with DTs as he was." Apparently, Townes did not reveal to the doctors that he was an alcoholic. Susanna says, "They found him on the floor having seizures, and they didn't know what was happening." Susanna was at home recovering from dental surgery and was unable to do anything. "And so I called Jeanene. Jeanene was—and I don't blame her, you know, she was pretty tired of dealing with his things, but he was in the hospital—and I said, 'Jeanene, get down there and tell them he's an alcoholic. Lie to them; you know, tell them you're his wife." Jeanene agreed to go. Once the doctors realized "that they had a late-stage alcoholic on their hands," according to Susanna, "they had him in a room that had a glass wall so that the nurses could keep an eye on him at all times. And apparently they were giving him such strong drugs to make the withdrawal seizures not come that he had to be on a respirator." Bob Moore recalls visiting his friend in the intensive care unit, "in some room where it was almost perfectly sterile, and you had to put on all this stuff over your shoes and wear a gown and wear a mask."

Detoxifying an alcoholic in Townes' "late-stage" condition can be a difficult endeavor, but it is one that is routinely undertaken for alcoholics every day in hospitals and other medical settings, and the detox regimen that Townes was put on at Vanderbilt was not unusual. Within a two-week period, the patient would face up to a week of medical detoxification, with close observation of side-effects and other medical problems and a protocol of healthful eating followed by a full physical and emotional rehabilitation regimen. In the full program, psychiatric problems would be brought to the surface and dealt with once the alcoholism was addressed.

In the eleven years of their marriage, Jeanene had been through numerous attempts to dry Townes out, but none had been as harrowing as this one. Part of her reaction to the stress of this extreme situation was to blame the hospital staff. "[T]hey almost killed him," she reported later, "and he was in intensive care for six days. The doctor told me that if we ever tried to dry Townes out it would more than likely kill him."[22] If Jeanene was distinguishing between the possible circumstances of Townes trying to detoxify on his own—at home—versus doing it under medical supervision—at the hospital—her point could be salient. If she simply believed that Townes could never dry out, that he was doomed, it is possible that she was either misinformed or misunderstood what the doctor was telling her. A physician familiar with dealing with families of alcoholics suggests that it would be reasonable to imagine a situation in which a conversation between an alcoholic patient and his doctor might go like this: "'If you continue drinking you are going to die.... However, if you quit on your own you will die too. You need to come in and be detoxed in a hospital.' A lot of alcoholics will relate this story by saying, '[The doctor] said if I quit drinking I would die.'"[23]

Rex Foster—a Texas folk musician with roots in the pioneering 1960s psychedelic band Rachel's Children—became friends with Townes when they were both in the alcohol rehabilitation program at Starlite in the eighties (where they also formed a short-lived musical group called the Starlite Drifters). Foster summarized his view of Townes' struggles with recovery by noting that "He was doing the best that he could.... You know, I think that Townes' destiny ran itself out, and part of the map of that destiny was that he had some trouble in recovery that he couldn't quite get past. But he's not unusual. See, that's the thing. Townes is not unusual. He is a unique artist, and a unique human being, as we all are. But in his final demise, and in this burden that he carried all his adult life, he is not unique at all. He's very textbook, actually."

"When he got out, he had pneumonia from the hospital," Susanna Clark says. "Jeanene took him home with her and helped him, kind of nursed him back. But he was drinking, sneaking little sips in.... We weren't going to let him go back to that place [the Rock'n'Roll Hotel], so Guy and I sold him our house on the lake." Guy and Susanna had lived in the modest, cabin-like house on Old Hickory Lake—in Mt. Juliet, Tennessee, about fifteen miles northeast of Nashville—for some years before moving back into town, and the house had been the scene of many an hour of partying and music-making.[24] "Oh, it was so nice at the lake house," a friend remembers. "Wood floors, a fireplace—and Townes always liked a fire going, no matter how hot or cold it was, and he'd always keep a pile of wood out there."

"We called it the 'Bayou Self,'" Jimmy Gingles recollects. "We had a nice sign somebody made that said 'Bayou Self,' but somebody stole it.... It was a place he could relax, although he always had people out there. He had a great library there, you know. He really enjoyed everybody coming by, and it was super good for him."

As he had when he lived near Lake Travis in Austin, Townes indulged his fondness for sailboats, keeping a small, two-man Snark at the house on Old Hickory Lake. Gingles recalls, "We would go out on the Snark and he would teach me sailing stuff—you know, 'Comin' about!' And he gave me a book on sailing. He was a good sailor." Townes kept his twenty-two-foot motorized Starwind—the *Dorothy*—on J. Percy Priest Lake, just south of Mt. Juliet (the "Town Between the Lakes"). "Most of the time, what he would do is, he would just motor it out and anchor it. Just to get away," according to Gingles.

This was, of course, a troubling period for Townes' children, especially Will. "Will got on a kick when he came out to the Bayou Self," Jimmy Gingles remembers. "He got a can of spray paint and was spray-painting obscenities in the street. One of the neighbors called and the cops came out, and they made Will go scrub down the street." Katie Belle, still a baby, felt less direct impact, but Townes mourned what he considered his doomed relationship with both of his children. "Townes used to cry over her, because he said he knew he was gonna die at an early age," according to Gingles.

According to Townes, while he was still living at the Rock'n'Roll Hotel, he had a dream that woke him up late one night. In the dream, he told himself, "You're too old, too tired, too road-weary. You know what to do; you don't need to take any orders about anything from anybody." He concluded: "You need to go to Ireland and make a record with Phillip Donnelly."[25] Donnelly—an Irish guitarist who had been a staple Nashville session man for some years before returning to Ireland and becoming a producer—had played guitar on *Seven Come Eleven (The Nashville Sessions)* and *Flyin' Shoes*, and Townes and he had kept in touch over the years. Townes got up in the middle of the night and phoned Donnelly, who answered the phone and immediately and enthusiastically agreed to produce Townes' next record—in Ireland.

As Townes had played more and more shows in Ireland in the 1990s, he had come to enjoy and appreciate the Irish people, the pubs, the music, the countryside, and the idea of Ireland. "People from Ireland and people from Texas ... can both get real sad," Townes said, explaining his affinity. Both peoples "rebound," he went on, "when they realize they've got the blues forever." Townes told an Irish writer of his affinity for Shane MacGowan—leader of the Irish punk band the Pogues and Ireland's greatest living songwriter—and said that one of the songs on the new album was written about him.[26] MacGowan's own affinity for what he called "piss artists"—great artists who are

———◆—◆———

also alcoholics (he cites James Joyce, in particular)—makes it easy to imagine his reciprocal affinity for Townes.[27]

"Most of the songs were pretty much written by the time I got over," Townes said. Townes and Harold flew to Ireland in May. Phillip Donnelly met them and drove them from Dublin to Limerick, where they had booked ten days at Xeric Studios. The musicians were "top of the line players," according to Townes. "Donovan played harmonica. That was the first time I got to meet Donovan. He's really good guy and a very fine harmonica player."[28] Donnelly led the effort in the studio and played guitar. The musicians were Irish, except the bass player, Sven Buick: Robbie Brennan and Fran Breen on drums, Brendan Hayes on keyboards, beautiful pedal steel guitar work by Percy Robinson, Paul Kelly on fiddle, Mairtin O'Connor on accordion, Brendan Reagan on bazouki and mandolin, and Declan Masterson on penny whistle and Uileann pipes. Townes overdubbed his vocals and did not play guitar at all—an absence that is felt on the final recording more acutely than Donnelly must have imagined during the sessions, even though it was his only option, given Townes' unsteady condition and declining instrumental skills. "The whole ten days was a real treat," Townes said; "And it was just me and Harold and the boys. After that Harold and I went on a twenty-day tour of Ireland and England and then back home. And Phillip got down to the mixes and all that."

Townes had been playing many of the songs on the album for some time before recording them. He had played "A Song For" live on the air on Larry Monroe's Austin radio program late in 1993, saying "Wait 'til them Irish guys get ahold of it!" The song leads off the album, setting a somber tone. Jeanene later wrote to Townes that she remembered "waking one morning to find your writing pad on the coffee table. You were still asleep so I felt safe sneaking a peek. As I read the words to what later became 'A Song For,' I was brought to tears.... It was so tragically beautiful. You came running from the bedroom and asked, 'What's wrong babe?' I said Townes, this new song is so beautiful. It's bound to be my favorite. You replied, 'Song my ass, that's a suicide note.'"[29]

In an interview on German radio, Townes was asked to play a song "even more desperate than 'Nothin'." He plays "A Song For," saying "It's beautiful in a way, in its own way. It's a song for somebody, I'm not sure who. I don't think it's for me, because of my daughter, Katie Belle, and my son Will, and my son J.T., and my friends." The song is as grim as anything Townes ever wrote, a final declaration of resignation, of having reached the end of the road, "weak and weary of sorrow." Townes writes of trembling and stumbling, saying directly, "I'd soon as be dead." The conclusion indeed sounds like last words, from the schizophrenic "myself going crazy the way that it does" to the final "too late to wish I'd been stronger."

Another song that Townes had been playing for some time before recording was "BW Railroad Blues," which he explained to Larry Monroe was about his friend—the best man at his wedding to Jeanene—the artist, Bo Whitt, who had recently committed suicide.[30] "Blaze's Blues" had also been around for a while. Townes always said he wrote it on Blaze Foley's guitar, and it springs from the saga that Townes often recounted of his adventure with Blaze in Muscle Shoals, Alabama, just days after Townes' son Will was born. "Hey Willie Boy" was written—quickly—on commission for an album on Sugar Hill Records of fathers' lullabies to their children;[31] "Katie Belle Blue" is a more finely crafted song—one of Townes' best late compositions—and a beautiful tribute to his daughter: "There's no deeper blue in the oceans that lie/As deep as the blue of your laughing eyes."

"Marie" appears in a crisp, well-recorded take; "Lover's Lullaby," "Cowboy Junkies Lament," "The Hole," and "Niles River Blues" (a studio composition) are similarly well done. "Billy, Boney and Ma" is a bizarre turn for Townes, a darkly humorous fantasy with an Irish spirit and an Irish studio treatment. "Goin' Down to Memphis," "If I Was Washington" (which Townes told a writer he wrote "a couple of wives ago"[32]), and "Gone Too Long" round out the collection on a lighter note. The album, which took its title from "Katie Belle Blue," was called *No Deeper Blue*, and was released in November 1994. The cover art was a painting by Bo Whitt's widow, Jeanette (Jet) Whitt, called *Snake Eyes*, of a colorful Townes Van Zandt, an ace of broken hearts up his sleeve, throwing a pair of dice, coming up with snake eyes.

Neil Strauss wrote in *The New York Times*: "When it comes to putting out new albums, Townes Van Zandt is often too busy living his songs of pain and desolation to record them in the studio. Though this Texas songwriter has never stopped performing since the 1960's, as many as 10 years have elapsed between his albums. Last week, *No Deeper Blue* (Sugar Hill), his first studio recording in seven years, was released." Strauss cites the record's "half-spoken stories" and "sparse ballads," and quotes Townes on his dream that was the origin of the project: "From the time I had that dream until somebody handed me the finished cassette was about a year. I can't believe I pulled that together."[33]

In mid-1994, Townes told an interviewer about his immediate plans: "We're going to Texas to this studio that we know real good and just make up songs and call it *Sky Songs*.... I'm pretty good at that sometimes with, you know, a little shot of hooey (picks up mini-bottle of vodka). I can really do it. There's three on the new record (*No Deeper Blue*)." He goes on to say that he wished Ernest Tubb had recorded "Don't You Take It Too Bad," "but he died." Then he concludes the interview with an expression of surprise: "You know, I don't have any idea where I got this shirt or that jacket. I just woke up with them on. Plus I got a big lump on my head and a broken toe."[34]

Not only did Townes continue to tour incessantly in 1995, but he stepped up his schedule. In January, he covered Germany, West Virginia, and Texas. In February, he was in California, Nevada, and the Pacific Northwest, then Alaska. In March, he was touring the Northeast; in the summer, it was back down South, then back to Germany, then back out West, then back to Germany, Switzerland, and Belgium. In September, Townes played a benefit at the Bluebird Café in Nashville for a local dental clinic—one of Susanna Clark's favorite charities—along with Guy, Steve Earle, and Emmylou Harris.[35] That fall, he returned to western Europe, then closed the year playing Renfrew Ferry in Glasgow and the Borderline in London.

Townes' son J.T. accompanied his father and Harold Eggers on their trip through California and the Pacific Northwest to Alaska in February 1995. As he had in the past, J.T. got a close look at Townes at his best and at his worst. "You couldn't control him," J.T. said of his father during this period. "A lot of my role on the road with him would be to ration out his vodka with water. There were times we were left in awe trying to figure out what Townes' magic was under this totally unmanageable shell of a forty-five to fifty-year-old stubborn-ass traveling songwriter."[36] According to J.T., Townes was "a total spoiled brat" on the road. During the time J.T. was with Townes, he recalled that, many mornings, "when I'd wake up, he would be on my bed, sitting on the foot of my bed with his head in his hands nodding back and forth going, ' ... bitch,' and crying. And a lot of that was the alcoholism—the ride that that takes you on is pretty unpleasant, but he had that even before the alcoholism."

J.T. believes that Townes' great writing was done before his addictions got the better of him, that "alcoholism didn't take effect until the last ten years of his life," adding: "I've never seen someone more able to in the worst circumstances, in the worst stage of personal abuse, be able to ... convince someone that they were not only not able to help him, but that they had lied to themselves as well, and that their life was a sham and that they should also start drinking heavily."

A more sublime moment came for J.T. when Townes played the Northern Lights Church in Juneau, Alaska, in February 1995. J.T. recalls his father believing that he sometimes saw "white angels or goblins." "I would always dismiss it as dementia," J.T. said. Harold Eggers had made the Juneau show's promoter, an Alaskan songwriter, aware that "she was going to have a big role in making sure the show went down, because Townes at this point was like having five kids under five years old on your hands." J.T. told the woman that he would disappear a half-hour before the show with Townes' bottle of booze, and that Townes was not allowed to have a drink before going on. At show time, Townes started to scream, "If I don't see 'T, I ain't going on"; but, according to J.T., "he was too skinny to fight this big Alaskan songwriter chick and she just pushed him out there." Townes received a thundering ovation from the crowd, "and he became very humble and played the most amazing show on the whole tour."

Townes got through the gig, then, before he had a chance to have a drink, "the promoters brought this old Alaskan shaman up to meet him, because she had something to tell him. She told him through an interpreter that the only reason that he was able to balance on his stool all night was because there was this angel supporting him from behind with her wings spread." Townes looked at the shaman and told her, "I dig; I'm hip."

On German radio in November 1995, Townes answered questions from the program's host, a woman named Sabina. "We get home on December the fourteenth," he told her. "It's funny, Sabina, you get home, and boy—you wake up: 'Where's my guitar? Where's the suitcase? Where we going?' And I realize, I'm in my own room. The only thing to do is feed the dog and feed the birds. That's it. And nothing to do for three weeks." Townes goes on: "It's been a long tour, and it's still going. It'll be through Christmas. I try to get them to book me through Christmas. I'd like to spend Christmas in Morocco, or somewhere else. Anywhere but home."

Then, this exchange:

Sabina: What do you think was the most challenging, the hardest time in your life?

Townes: I can't think of an easy one.

Sabina: You think life is hard and not sweet?

Townes: Well, it's hard and sweet. Like rock candy.[37]

In November 1995, in Hanau, Germany, a small town near Frankfurt, Townes first met an attractive young woman from Darmstadt named Claudia Winterer. Townes invited Claudia, an executive in a bank in Bonn, to some of his upcoming shows in Cologne then Krefeld. The two spent hours talking after the Krefeld show. "That night, Townes asked me to join him on the rest of tour," Claudia recalls. They met up again in Bonn. "We fell in love with each other. We travelled together to Berlin, Dresden, and other German cities. One week later, Townes called me at home from England, in December, and we met again in London, where he played two shows in a club called the Borderline."[38]

Townes returned home and started 1996 on familiar ground, playing January gigs at the Cactus Café in Austin, the Mucky Duck in Houston, and Poor David's Pub in Dallas. He spoke to Claudia on the phone frequently, joking to friends that his monthly phone bill was higher than his rent.[39] That March, Claudia accepted Townes' invitation to visit him in Tennessee. She arrived in Nashville the day after Townes' fifty-second birthday. "Townes and Richard Dobson picked me up at the airport," she recalls. "It was wonderful to stay with Townes at the place where he lived and to see what he had been telling me so many times on the phone before, his dog Feather and the beautiful red cardinals he used to feed every morning."

Among the many local friends to whom Townes introduced Claudia were Jim and Royann Calvin. The Calvins were Townes' neighbors in Mt. Juliet, and both were accomplished bluegrass musicians. Jim had been a member of the New Christy Minstrels in the late 1980s; he married Louisiana native Royann and they formed a duo—Royann on guitar and Jim on mandolin and fiddle—playing gigs at the Bluegrass Inn and other Nashville establishments. Bill Monroe came to one of the Calvins' shows and even played with them; they became friends, started visiting at Monroe's farm, and ended up "still playing shows, but also three or four days a week out with Bill Monroe," Jim Calvin recalled, "driving him to the Opry on weekends, Royann cooking and cleaning, me mending fences and feeding the cows, and writing songs and picking with Bill in the evenings." The Calvins played several shows with Monroe before his final illness, and as a duo toured Louisiana, Florida, and Texas. Townes met them through mutual friends at a Mickey Newbury show in Nashville. They realized they were neighbors and became friends quickly after jamming at Townes' house on the lake.

Jim recalls, "He was really impressed with our music, but he started to go through a couple of his songs, and we had no idea. We knew 'If I Needed You' and 'Pancho and Lefty,' and that was about as much as we knew about Townes Van Zandt at the time. But that didn't bother him, that we were innocent to his legend."

Jim and Royann threw a big party for Townes and Claudia at their house in Mt. Juliet. Jim remembers, "I said, 'Now let's put on a good show for this girl, she's from Germany, man, she's never probably heard this heavy-duty picking like we do here at Polecat Hollow.' We just pinned their ears back, and boy, Townes was just so thankful for this great show for Claudia. We had barbecue and he ate all this food and everything—more than anybody had seen him eat before—and they just had a hell of a time." Townes and Claudia stayed in the Calvins' guest room that night. According to Jim, "Good grief, he was a new man when he was around her. He stayed sober enough to drive."

Townes also introduced Claudia to Susanna Clark and to Bob Moore. He took her to his show at the Bluebird Café, then she and Townes drove to Texas and met Harold Eggers in Austin. "We stayed at Harold's place, where we also met Townes' son J.T.," Claudia says. "I enjoyed it very much to see father and son together." Before leaving Austin, they stopped at Butch Hancock's place for a visit. Then they drove to Santa Fe, New Mexico, for Townes' gig at the Old Santa Fe Music Hall with Guy Clark on March 21. "It was a great show," Claudia recalls, adding that Townes "got standing ovations." They visited late into the night with Guy, then Claudia had to return home.

Townes played shows primarily in Texas that spring, including a May gig at the Old Quarter in Galveston, a cozy new version of the old Houston watering hole run by that establishment's original owner, Townes' old friend Rex Bell. A June performance at the Birchmere in Alexandria, Virginia, was startling to long-time fans and frightening to the club's owner, who questioned Harold about Townes' health and safety and got the standard response: Townes was just "on medication." In a radio interview, Townes gave away this common ploy: "'He's on medication' is usually just an excuse my road manager uses to get me out of trouble."[40]

# 15

# The Blue March

T HAT SPRING OF 1996, TOWNES was surprised to hear from
Steve Shelley, the drummer for the New York band Sonic
Youth, that members of the group were interested in making a record with him. A major label, Geffen, was backing the
project through its Ecstatic Peace imprint, which was an outlet
through which members of Sonic Youth could sign and record
artists that they thought deserving. After recording some bands
that didn't make much of an impression, they sought out Townes.
Shelley's side project, a duo/sometime trio called Two Dollar Guitar, was to back Townes on the sessions, which Shelley would produce. The idea had potential, although there were downsides.

Geffen A&R man Ray Farrell, who was in charge of the project, had looked into Townes' last few recording efforts, had spoken to people involved, and had some idea of what he was up
against. Townes Van Zandt clearly was not a well man. There
was already some sense that the planned sessions might turn
out to be not only a physical and emotional drain on Townes,
but also a financial drain on the label. They weren't sure that
Townes would like the idea of playing with the young musicians

in Two Dollar Guitar, or how their styles would mesh. Farrell brought Townes down from Nashville to Memphis in early fall to discuss the project and meet the band, and he had doubts that any of it would work out.

Townes was frail and shaky when he met Farrell and the band in Memphis, but he seemed to enjoy himself, staying up late talking and playing poker. Even with the research he had done, it was eye-opening for Farrell. He hadn't realized that Townes always traveled with a "caretaker"—Harold Eggers—and with Eggers absent on this trip, Farrell had to learn quickly to fill that role. Farrell remembers Townes being emotionally up and down, but warm and friendly. One night at dinner with the group, Townes suggested that they all write a song together, on the spot. Townes threw out the first line, then they went around the table until everyone had contributed lines and they eventually played the idea out. Farrell was impressed by Townes' ability to create this atmosphere, to make everybody part of the party.

A few days after he returned home to Nashville, Townes let them know that he was ready to go ahead with the project. He was flattered that these young musicians wanted to play with him. He had heard Mudhoney's recording of "Buckskin Stallion Blues," and been very happy with it, and proud. "I'm the mold that grunge was grown in," he had said.[1] The recording sessions were scheduled for the end of the year.

Later that month, Townes and Harold returned to Europe. Although the first shows were in Scotland, they flew straight to Germany, where Claudia met them at the Frankfurt Airport. "I cooked gulasch, Townes' favorite German food. Townes visited my ill brother in the hospital. Then my other brother took us to the airport and we took the plane to London and then to Glasgow." Claudia and Townes were inseparable for the rest of their time together. Her recollection of their itinerary is detailed: "I remember the show in Glasgow best, where Townes played on a laid-up ship [Renfrew Ferry], which brought a special atmosphere and mood to the show. Then we came back to London, where Mike Weston King picked us up at the airport. We went to the Cambridge Folk Festival, where Townes played on two nights for forty-five minutes each. And we also met Peter Rowan, Chris Smither, Alison Krauss, and other artists there. After Cambridge, Townes played shows at some more English places before we left England and travelled to Ireland. There he played in Dublin first, at a very beautiful old place where most of the people seemed to know him from a long time ago [Whelan's].... After the gig[s], we had some days left like holidays. We spent these days in a very nice hotel at the coast together."[2]

A few days after his last show in Ireland, Townes was in California, then Reno, Nevada, then back to California for a gig at the Ash Grove in Santa Monica that same month. In early September, he went into Flashpoint Studios in Austin with Jim and Royann Calvin and recorded five tracks, including one of Royann's songs, "Love Is Where You Find It." Two of the songs were released on a vinyl single in a limited-edition British pressing of 2,000 copies on the German label Exile: extremely creaky versions of Michael Weston King's "Riding the Range" and Ewan MacColl's "Dirty Old Town," which had been a big record for Shane MacGowan and the Pogues.

Along with the Calvins, Townes played Eureka Springs, Arkansas, the last week of September, then, the first week of October, the Mucky Duck in Houston. There, Townes had a chance to catch up with someone he had not seen for some years: his second wife, Cindy. "Harold was there with him, being real protective. Townes had a half-pint, and Harold said, 'Don't let him have more than part of that, because he can't handle it any more.' And he was so skinny; he had shrunk. He wasn't the tall guy that I remembered falling in love with."

Cindy and Townes talked long into the night. "He said he had to go back on tour overseas, and he wanted me to go with him," Cindy recalls. "For a minute I thought, yeah; I haven't been overseas, and this was a chance to go. Then, at that point, the whole history came flashing back, and I'm looking at a man who's basically withered away to nothing."

On June 23, 1996, Townes played his first and only show at Nashville's venerable Ryman Auditorium—the "Cathedral of Country Music"—at a tribute concert for songwriter Walter Hyatt, who had recently been killed in a plane crash. This was Townes' first major gig with the Calvins supporting him. They continued to rehearse together in preparation for some shows in Texas that fall. As Jim Calvin remembers, "This was the time when he was getting into 'Sanitarium Blues.' He was laying that on us, just starting to include that in his shows. He just did it like a poem. He never played the guitar with it." The Calvins were not used to material as dark as "Sanitarium Blues," but they were committed to Townes.

"Harold just showed up when it was time to go on the road," Jim Calvin says. "He would fly into Nashville and stay at Townes' house for a day or two, make sure the truck was running good, and they'd take off. Or they'd meet up at some airport if they were going to Europe. Harold would be constantly trying to take care of business and keep Townes away from his bottle and stuff, or keep him from getting in too deep before a show, and that kind of business. It was definitely a love–hate thing by the time I met them. They'd test each other, but you could tell they were friends. They would have quit each other in disgust long ago if there wasn't a whole lot more to it, I think."

They kicked off their mini-tour of Texas at Rex Bell's Old Quarter in Galveston, with Richard Dobson opening the show. Dobson remembers that Townes "looked very tired." Rex hosted them all at his beach house on the Bolivar Peninsula, across from the end of Galveston Island. "He's just six months older than me," Rex recalls marveling of Townes. "I've got thick grass at my house, and he stumbled and grabbed me, so I helped him across the yard. It was like I was helping an older person, he was so frail. And we were so worried about him, because he was just skin and bones, and he wouldn't eat. Harold would hide his vodka, and then make him drink Ensure before he could have his vodka, so he'd just guzzle the Ensure so he could get his vodka."

Bell says the show was memorable: "Other than the fact that he was very weak, he really did a good show that night. He did as good as he could do in his physical condition. When he wanted to, he could still sing beautifully. His picking had slipped; as you remember, early in his career he was a fantastic guitar player. He wasn't flashy, but he was just so pristine, so clean. But he made up for it in later years, in my opinion, with his sincerity about how he approached music."

Jim Calvin recalls Townes and Rex enjoying their time together as if they knew it might be the last. "They were just the dearest of old friends," he says. "It was real pleasant. With Townes, there was times we were sitting around his house and he'd start swinging his arms, trying to keep these ghosts and demons away. I mean he was seeing them, saying 'Get away! Get away!' But when we were over at Rex's, I just never saw him so calm and relaxed and normal, you know. The demons were gone."

At the next show, at Poor David's Pub in Dallas, the demons returned. Townes' friend Roxy Gordon lived near Poor David's, and he and Townes began drinking early in the day. "I got the impression that he was enjoying to see how drunk they could get," Jim Calvin says. "I mean, they were barely able to walk." Showtime came, and Townes was not at the club. According to Jim, that evening's show was "by far the worst performance that I was ever associated with." Royann Calvin remembers the scene as "the most hellacious time we ever had with Townes," and she tells the story vividly:

> We found Townes at Roxy's house, and they had been drinking for about five hours, and smoking a little dope.... I think they had britches and stuff on underneath, but they were both wearing reindeer pelts when we got there. Normally Jim and I would do thirty to forty-five minutes. Well, we get through with our set, and Townes, sitting right at the edge of the stage, is screaming, "Play another one! Play another one!" Well, this kept up for an hour and a half. Finally I said, "Alright folks, in just a few minutes, Townes Van Zandt will be putting on a bril-

liant performance," and we got off the stage and I ...
set up his guitar, and he tries to get on his stool and
almost falls face forward with his guitar in his hand.
So I catch him before he falls over, and he's starting
to get bitchy: "I told you I didn't want to do this!"

He started doing some of his songs, except for
half of it was in tongues, and half of it was just
howling. He howled one song for fifteen minutes.
And I'm not talking about like, bad singing, I'm
talking about literal dog howling.

Harold's freaking out. He's ready to pull him off
the stage and turn on the lights and give everybody
their money back. And I got up on the stage, turned
off the mic, and said, "Townes, look at that little
boy, sitting there in front of the stage." There was a
kid about nine years old there. I said, "This is someone who's never seen you before, whose parents are
fans of yours or they wouldn't have brought him
here at this hour of the night. Please, if nothing else,
show this child something." And he came to for a
minute and played a few songs in a row without
saying another word.... But then he went into the
howling thing again.

The crowd is watching this with their mouths
open, and they're just astounded, and some are disgusted, some are humiliated, and the little boy was
figuring it was pretty cool, watching someone go insane right before his eyes. So that's where we quit. I
said, "Okay Harold, I give up, you win, turn on the
lights." And nobody wanted their money back. As
soon as he finished, they all came up and talked to
him, asked for autographs; the little boy bought an
album, got an autograph. Nobody acted like anything weird ever went down. Several of them I even
saw a couple days later. They showed up at the Cactus Café to try it again.

The Cactus gigs were better, but again, longtime friends and
fans were concerned at Townes' condition. Larry Monroe had
Townes, Jim, and Royann in the KUT studio after the second
night at the Cactus; Griff Luneberg, the Cactus' manager, was
there for the late-night session as well. Townes sounded tired
and a little drunk—not completely out of it, but out of it enough

to elicit some concern. "I've had so many concussions in the last month that I can't even count 'em no more," he tells Monroe at one point. "I've lost about half my thinking process. I'm gettin' to where I can barely catch airplanes." He stops and asks Monroe, "Do you have any idea where we are now?" When Monroe assures him that they are "in the heart of Austin, Texas," Townes says, "Oh good, I feel better."

Townes plays a few songs with the Calvins, including a ragged "White Freightliner Blues" and a wobbly "Lost Highway." Townes observes that "Hank Williams was such that it's hard to comprehend. It's a hard act to follow. You know, the one thing I've thought about Hank Williams—he was able to write the funniest songs and the saddest songs ever. I try to write funny songs and they come out dismal." Monroe notes that many of Hank's songs were based on his ex-wife, Audrey. Townes, not missing a beat, responds, "Well, where was she when I needed her?"

Townes cites his favorite music—Muddy Waters, Mozart, Lightnin' Hopkins, the Rolling Stones, Hank Williams, and Bob Dylan—then tells the story of how he heard Dylan singing "Pancho and Lefty" with Willie Nelson on TV for Willie's sixtieth birthday celebration. (Townes was asleep and Will ran in to wake him up when Dylan and Willie launched into the song, then, "I went back to sleep ... back when I used to sleep in my own bed.") Townes notes that Dylan, instead of singing "Livin' on the road, my friend," sings "Livin' on the edge, my friend."

About halfway through the visit, Luneberg—a friend of Townes' for more than fifteen years—takes the microphone and, in contrast to Monroe's easygoing style, asks Townes some direct questions. He starts by saying that it was great to have Townes at the Cactus the past two nights. "Thanks," Townes says; "it's kind of my home club—that and the Paradiso in Amsterdam."

Then, Luneberg goes on: "People are always asking me ... Townes, how come you're waitin' around to die?" Townes dodges the question, slowly telling a story about the old man who inspired him to write "Waitin' Around to Die," but Griff tries again: "People are always asking me, though ... I know you're happy most of the time, but people are always asking, 'What's wrong with Townes?' And I'm going, ah, he's gonna outlive us all." Townes replies quietly, "No, I don't think so." Griff presses: "I mean, do you feel tortured, or upset, or ... ?" Townes says, "Pretty much."

Griff: I mean, if I was as revered as you are ...

Townes: I'm not revered.

Griff: Well, you're certainly revered. You're nice to paupers and you're nice to kings and you have no pretensions and that's what's beautiful about you.

Townes: I thought it was my eyes.

Griff: ... We're all concerned, but I think you're gonna outlive us all. I just want to reconfirm that.

Townes: Well, I hope so....

Griff: Okay, good.

Townes: ... My goal is to write one song good enough to rock the Lord off of his throne and have him look down and say, "That was a good job. You just saved a little girl's life." If I could do that— I don't care about the money or anything along those lines....

I wrote one perfect one and I recorded it and never sang it again.[3] If I could write another one like that, everything would be okay. I could go back to the ranch. I could do anything.... I'm gonna have to take better care of myself and all that if I'm gonna be able to do it....

If I could just do something like that, then I could lay down and go to sleep [his voice cracks on the last word].

Before leaving for Europe, Townes and the Calvins recorded some tracks at Michael Catalano's home studio in Nashville to round out a collection of live recordings that Harold Eggers was preparing for release on Sugar Hill, to be titled *The Highway Kind*. With Royann playing tight rhythm guitar and singing occasional harmony and Jim taking soulful turns on mandolin and fiddle, they recorded sparse, grim versions of Hank Williams' "(I Heard That) Lonesome Whistle," Roy Acuff's "Wreck on the Highway," and Guy Clark's "Dublin Blues." During the session, according to Jim, "Townes was getting loaded, and he was doing an okay job, but he wasn't being as good as he was capable of, I'm sure. I thought him and Harold was gonna be about done with each other that day. Townes was determined to have a good time."

Around this same time, Townes ran into his Texas friends Joe Gracey and Gracey's wife, singer Kimmie Rhodes, in Nashville. Gracey had been a well-known disc jockey at Austin's KOKE-FM in the seventies, pioneering the "progressive country" format, and had turned to record production under the tutelage of Cowboy Jack Clement. Kimmie had been recording with Willie Nelson, and for her upcoming album, which Gracey was producing, she was featuring duets with Willie and with Waylon Jennings. They were recording at Clement's studio the next day, and they asked Townes if he would like to sing something with Kimmie on the record. Townes readily agreed, and Kimmie picked her song "I'm Gonna Fly" to sing with him.

"We sent my brother out to pick him up" for the session the next day, Gracey recalls. "He made them go by his favorite weird little place to get whiskey, and by the time he got to the session he was well on the way." Kimmie showed Townes the song, and they tried to run through it a few times, but Townes was unable to play the guitar. "We abandoned the concept of a live duet between the two of them," Gracey said. "She sat next to him and squeezed his hand when it was his turn to sing a line, and he was able to get a take done. But he was both deeply moved by the song and drunk, so he kept crying when he came to the line '[the songbird] can only make one sound.'"[4]

The schedule for the November tour was as grueling as the previous European tours. Again, Townes and Harold flew to Germany a few weeks before the first shows so Townes could be with Claudia in Bonn. "At the weekend, we drove to my hometown, Darmstadt, where I had a nicer place. In Bonn we were sometimes sitting on the 'banks of the old river Rhine' watching the ships go by. In these days, he often used to play his song 'Fraulein' for me."

Claudia accompanied Townes on his trip through Germany: Berlin, Dresden, Solingen, Bonn, Hannover, Bielefeld, Utrecht (Netherlands), Munich, Wurzburg, Schorndorf, Nurnberg, Burghausen, Cologne, Bochum, and Offenbach. The performances were for the most part typical of this final period of Townes' decline: often rambling, stumbling, drunken disasters. Claudia was certainly around Townes enough to understand what she could expect from a relationship with him. "She's an intelligent woman," Jim Calvin says. "She knew what she was getting into, and she was willing to go there. I'm pretty sure she wasn't gonna try and change him. She was gonna try and make sure he ate right, and things like that, which he needed.... She definitely loved the guy like crazy. And he talked about her all the time."

"It was the second of December at Frankfurt airport when I saw Townes for the last time," Claudia recalls. Townes and Harold flew to London, where Townes was booked at the Borderline on the next evening.

By this time, Townes was exhausted. His performance at the Borderline was a train-wreck, although somehow his utter sincerity managed to come through. There was a palpable sense in the audience that they were witnessing the real thing—a human being *in extremis*.

At one point, to lighten the mood, Townes related the story of "Katie Belle Blue," saying he'd written three lullabies in his life: "One for a full-grown woman, who divorced me ... I guess that one didn't take ['Lover's Lullaby']; one for money," for his son, Will ("Hey, Willie Boy"), "who thought it was the stupidest song he'd ever heard ... and one genuine lullaby," which he then played, haltingly. "Marie" followed, blending seamlessly into "Waitin' Around to Die," then "A Song For," each song more stark and grim than the last.

After telling an old joke, Townes launched abruptly into "Sanitarium Blues." The audience had probably gone farther into Townes' dark state of mind than they wanted to, and this harrowing spoken-word piece proved too much. There was nervous laughter at some of the most grim lines and a clear sense

of relief when Townes finished the recitation and began the familiar "Tecumseh Valley." At least the audience could sing along
with this story of misery, disappointment, and untimely death.

As Harold helped Townes from the stage at the show's end,
audience members turned quietly away, cumulatively stunned
and embarrassed by this display of frailty—and of mortality. If
this wasn't the blues, they'd never see the blues.

Incredibly, immediately upon returning from London and the
exhausting month-long tour, Harold Eggers took Townes to Austin for a late-night recording session at Flashpoint, where the
harrowing evidence of Townes' final deterioration was committed to tape. Nothing from the session was commercially releas-
able; in fact, it was almost impossible to listen to the recordings
without cringing or weeping.[5]

After the quick, grim detour to Austin, Townes returned to
Tennessee, to his home on Old Hickory Lake. Five or six days
before Christmas, weak and unsteady, he fell down the concrete stairs outside the house and hurt his hip so badly that he
couldn't stand up or walk. He had fallen recently in Germany,
in the bathroom, and sustained a large bruise on his thigh as
evidence, but this was much worse.[6] After lying outside for an
hour or more, he dragged himself inside and phoned Jeanene.
He told her he had pulled a muscle in his leg while tossing and
turning in his sleep from a bad dream. Jeanene called Jim and
Royann Calvin—to whom she had not spoken for some time—
and asked them to look in on him.[7]

Townes was clearly in great pain when Jim and Royann arrived at the lake house, but he refused to see a doctor. Jim, a big
man, gently loaded him into the cab of their pickup truck and
took him back to their house. Townes insisted to the Calvins
that he had just pulled a muscle falling out of bed, and that it
was getting better, but after a few days with Townes on their
couch—unable to get up to go to the bathroom—Jim and Royann realized they were in over their heads. They had a wheelchair delivered so they could at least move him around more

easily. They continued, first gently, then more insistently, to try to convince him to go to a doctor, but he stubbornly refused. He was drinking steadily, as usual, and his mood fluctuated between very dark and very light. He had some new songs, some of which he had recorded demo versions of in Nashville with Jack Clement a few months earlier, and he was quietly determined to make the upcoming Memphis recording sessions, come hell or high water.

On December 23, from the Calvins' couch, where he had been drinking and watching religious fundraising programs on television, morose and obviously in significant pain, Townes suddenly announced that he wanted to have a party. Jim Calvin saw this as a positive sign and phoned some friends, who came over with guitars. Townes perked up. "Man, he sat up, grabbed the guitar, and did his whole new album without stopping. I mean without taking a damn break." He "couldn't quit grinning after everybody left."

But the high spirits didn't last. Townes spent Christmas Eve and then Christmas Day still on the Calvins' couch, by now absolutely despondent. "I was getting beside myself, you know, I'm sitting here arguing with him. I was mean with him even," Jim Calvin says. "After a while though, he decided he really wanted to see his kids. And he calls Jeanene up. He had a bicycle for Katie Belle and a hundred-dollar bill for Will, and he wanted to give them their Christmas presents. And she just said, 'No, I don't want you here. I'm busy. I'm having this big party here, and I don't want you here, you'll ruin it.' And that left me and Royann just aghast. Like, oh boy, we don't like Jeanene no more, what the hell is this? And he said, 'No, no, no, no, that's the mother of my children. Don't you ever paint her in a bad light.'" Jeanene was firm in her determination to keep Townes away from the family when he was drinking.

When Harold Eggers arrived at the Calvins' house at the appointed time a few days later to accompany Townes to Memphis for the upcoming sessions, Jim and Royann politely but firmly expressed their concerns to him about Townes' condition. Eggers seemed to treat their concerns with some disdain. "He said, 'Hey, don't worry. I appreciate you looking after Townes, but I got him, I've been doing this for years. He just wants attention, and you guys were suckers enough to give it to him.' And he didn't realize; he just didn't understand. But we had to load Townes into the truck, and it was painful; he was hollering in pain. And I was frankly relieved to not be responsible, because I felt like, damn, he would not go to the hospital, and we couldn't make him." Townes told Harold that he was going through with the sessions no matter what, and that he would see a doctor as soon as he got back, and they set out on the three-and-a-half-hour drive to Memphis.

Nobody knew for sure what would come of the recording sessions booked with Steve Shelley and Two Dollar Guitar at Easley Studio in Memphis for the last days of 1996. For *No Deeper Blue*, the last Townes Van Zandt studio album, the arrangements were done and most of the instrument tracks were laid down before Townes even arrived at the studio. All he had to do was sing the songs, with fewer chances for disaster, and a better chance to come in on budget. Understandably, that record had turned out to be somewhat sterile, despite some strong material. Now, in Memphis, every opportunity was being provided to make these sessions different. Whether or not Townes somehow knew that the upcoming recording would not be his big major-label break, but would more likely be his last record, is open to speculation.

Some of those involved in the Easley sessions had heard that Townes was in a wheelchair, but seeing his condition when Eggers wheeled him into the studio was a shock for everyone. He was pale and unshaven, gaunt, trembling. The writer Robert Gordon dropped by the studio and was stopped in his tracks. "He was a very heavy drinker," Gordon says, "and I remember when he took a shot during the sessions, you could hear it going through him. You could hear it moving through his blood going into his body and then out again. It didn't change his behavior radically, but you could hear the change—in his slur. It was almost like this wave that went across him."[8]

An engineer on the sessions remembers Townes and the group working for three days, starting each day around noon, working for two or three hours, then taking a break while Townes had a nap, and returning to continue around six or seven o'clock. Townes and Eggers were at odds the entire time. "I was the mother superior with the stick," said Eggers.

A look at the songs Townes planned to record gives an indication of his state of mind.[9] One was the bleak, haunting "Sanitarium Blues," which he had been performing on his last tours and had recorded as a demo in Nashville, as a spoken-word piece. Townes sets a basic rhythm with his taut, metered speech, reciting in a sorry, broken tone the story of a man who would "as soon be dead" taken to an asylum against his will by people he knows are less sane than he himself is; he's strapped to a table, hosed down and shot full of drugs, then given up on as incurable. The desperation in his voice is made all the more terrifying by the resignation his words reveal, the feeling that it's too late to do anything but succumb. Clearly, this was not destined to be a hit record. Nor was "Screams from the Kitchen," with the chorus "Goodbye to the highway, goodbye to the sky, I'm headed out, goodbye, goodbye."

Another selection was one of Townes' old favorites, Blind Willie McTell's "Dying Crapshooter's Blues," the mere title of which seems to speak volumes, and which Townes, an avid gambler, was clearly interpreting autobiographically. Also on the list was a song that Townes wrote with Eric Andersen a decade before, "The Blue March": "Old Black Bush gonna carry me down/ Throw me into the burying ground/The ground be wet, my eyes be dry/Just don't let me hear my baby cry." The last song of the last evening session was a blues piece, with Townes, uncharacteristically, playing heavy solo electric guitar. There were technical problems with the recording equipment, which forced them to call a halt for the night, but everyone saw it as a way out. They felt that they were pushing Townes too hard, "getting into territory that none of us could handle," Geffen A&R man Ray Farrell said. Townes was not unaware of the situation. He told engineer Stuart Sikes that he would like to go back to Nashville and try to clean up in a detox program.

Early the next day—New Year's Eve—Steve Shelley phoned Jeanene, who still controlled Townes' business affairs, and told her they were cancelling the sessions. Townes hadn't been told of the decision when Jeanene called him at his hotel to tell him, and while they were talking Harold Eggers came in and confirmed what Jeanene had said. She then spoke to Eggers and told him to get Townes back to Nashville and to a doctor, even if he had to drag him kicking and screaming. Before leaving Memphis, Townes phoned Claudia in Germany. "He told me that he had to stop recording because of his aching leg and that he wanted it to be checked by a doctor at home in Nashville," she recalls. Eggers says he pleaded with Townes on the trip back to Nashville and finally got him to agree to go to a "convenient care" emergency center, Townes knowing that they couldn't keep him there.

The doctor who finally examined Townes was alarmed. He told Townes that he was seriously injured, that he might have a blood clot from his injury, which could kill him, and that he had to get to a hospital immediately. Instead, Harold Eggers took Townes home to Mt. Juliet, then called Jeanene and told her that Townes had finally agreed to go to the hospital, but only with her. Jim Calvin drove Harold to the airport. According to Calvin, "Harold said, 'Oh, Townes will be fine. Let's all hope we make a bunch of money this next year, and we'll get you guys out on tours, we'll get you over to Europe this year with him,' all this. Just pep talking, business talk more than worried about Townes. But I was worried about Townes."

Meanwhile, Jeanene rounded up Will and Katie Belle and made the forty-five-minute trip out to Townes' house on the lake. When she arrived there was a fire burning in the fireplace, as Townes always liked. She found him talking on the phone to Jimmy Gingles. Jimmy later said that Townes had called him and told him that he was "surrounded by spirits." He asked Townes whether they were friendly spirits, and Townes told him that he thought so, but that he was afraid that they would push him into the fireplace if he bent down to stoke the fire.

Townes tried to put off the hospital trip until morning, but Jeanene was insistent, asking him, "Do you want to be wheeled out on stage the rest of your life?" He finally relented, and Jeanene once again called the Calvins and asked them to stay with Will and Katie Belle and to help get Townes into the car. It was just before nine o'clock when they reached the Summit Medical Center in Hermitage, just north of Mt. Juliet. Townes had been drinking all the way over and was in fairly good spirits when they arrived, but he was anxious. He was taken in for x-rays. When the doctor emerged he told Jeanene that Townes had an impacted left femoral neck fracture—a common variety of hip fracture—and that he would need surgery right away. Jeanene was stunned. How could he have a broken hip for nearly two weeks and not know it?

Townes had always hated hospitals—and according to Jeanene he had come close to dying while undergoing detox at Vanderbilt just a couple of years earlier—and now he was afraid. He made Jeanene promise that she would take him home right after the surgery. He looked helpless as they wheeled him into the operating room, turning to Jeanene and saying "Well, babe … looks like this is it." Jeanene went home to wait. She got a call at around two-thirty in the morning from the doctor saying that the operation had gone well and that Townes was resting.

But when she arrived with Will and Katie Belle later in the morning, Townes was suffering delirium tremens, sweating, convulsing, and hallucinating. Jeanene spoke to a doctor, who insisted that Townes be put into alcohol detoxification and rehabilitation, saying it was the only way to save him, but she believed that Townes was too weak for that now. Even though, just the day before, Townes had himself expressed the desire to enter detox, Jeanene had come to believe that detox would kill him. Plus, she said, she had promised Townes that she would take him home. She was insistent. The doctor was equally insistent in his response, advising her against removing a late-stage alcoholic from medical care so soon after a major operation, especially in his extremely fragile, unstable condition.

The doctor directed a nurse to sedate Townes, which the nurse did. Jeanene told the nurse to get the paperwork ready, she was taking Townes home, even though it was strictly against medical advice. The nurse, dismayed, tried to comfort Jeanene. Her own father, she told her, was an alcoholic who had recently fallen and was hospitalized with a broken hip. There are many critical issues involved with medical care for an alcoholic, and the doctors know what they're doing; he'll be okay in the hospital, she said. Jeanene remained insistent.

She went home to get organized, again calling on the Calvins to help with the kids and with moving Townes. She filled a flask with vodka and went back to the hospital. Townes was awake, trembling badly, hallucinating. Jeanene whispered in his ear that she had a jug in the car, and that he'd be going home soon. Townes reached out for the jug, then began frantically searching his bed for it. Telling the hospital staff that she was his wife, Jeanene signed Townes out of the hospital "AMA (Against Medical Advice)."[10] They got Townes to the car, where Jeanene lifted the flask and helped Townes take a drink, "which went against everything I had been through with him all those years trying to keep him away from the bottle," Jeanene later wrote. "It was too late for that and I had to put that dream behind me and just accept what was and love him as he was."

By the time they got to the lake house, about a twenty-minute drive from the hospital, Townes was feeling better, though still shaky. Jim Calvin again helped get Townes into the house, where he insisted on sitting up in his wheelchair, and within an hour or so, sipping vodka the whole time, he was laughing and telling jokes. They shared a joint, and Townes seemed at ease. When Jeanene soon realized that the only medication they had prescribed for Townes at the hospital was antibiotics—no pain medication—she called the doctor. Knowing that Townes had left the hospital against medical advice and that he would drink, the doctor would not prescribe pain medication, which would be dangerous mixed with alcohol; he suggested instead that they give Townes an over-the-counter analgesic. Jeanene got Townes into bed, then, with Jim and the kids staying to watch him, went with Royann to get the medication and do some grocery shopping. They were gone for two hours, picking up a good supply of food along with a bottle of Tylenol P.M., and Townes seemed to be feeling pretty good when they got back.

Jim and Royann went home for their New Year's Day cabbage and black-eyed peas. Jim told Royann on the way home that one unusual thing had happened while she and Jeanene were out—that while he lightly dozed in front of a football game on TV, he heard Will calling out from Townes' room, fearfully. "You okay?" Jim had quickly called. As Will later remembered, "I went and got Jim and I was like, 'We need to check on dad.'" Will recalls that he was watching his father lying in bed and "his arm flew up like that [gesturing], like real sporadically, and I was like, 'Hold on, something's not right.... We went in there and I asked him if he was alright, and he said, 'Yeah, yeah, I'm fine....'"[11] Jim later wondered whether Townes might have suffered some kind of convulsion or seizure, then recovered.[12]

Jeanene brought Townes his Tylenol, and he asked for three, saying quietly, "it's starting to hurt pretty bad." The kids stayed with him while she went to fix him a plate of cheese and crackers, grapes, sliced apples, and roast beef, food that he could eat without having to use a knife and fork, as his hands were still trembling badly. Bob Moore phoned, "to try to find someone home that could tell me how he was. Jeanene answered the phone, and she said, 'Townes, it's Bob, do you want to talk to Bob?' And he was evidently in the process of moving out of his wheelchair and on to the bed, and he just said, 'I am so tired....' Then he caught himself, he didn't like the way it sounded, and he said, '... moving out of this chair and into the bed.' But I think he meant, 'I'm just so tired.'"

Jeanene asked Townes if he needed anything else. "Thanks babe, this is great," he said. Jeanene went to call Guy and Susanna Clark, as Townes had asked her to, to let them know he was doing okay. According to Susanna, "She wanted to believe he was okay, but she knew. I mean, she shouldn't have taken him out of the hospital. The doctors told her not to; everybody told her not to. But she did. I was shocked when she called to say he was at home."

Katie Belle was with Townes, talking to him playfully, when Will asked his father if he needed anything, then went into the bathroom. "No thanks, son, I'm fine," Townes said. Jeanene was talking on the phone to Susanna. Susanna could hear clearly when, a few minutes later, Will rushed into the room with Jeanene and said, "Mom, you better look at dad, he looks dead!"

Jeanene hurried in. She knew as soon as she saw Townes that "his spirit was no longer in the room."

"Jeanene said, 'Oh, my God, oh, my God, Townes, Townes, Townes,' and then she said, 'Hang up, Susanna, I've got to call 911,'" Susanna says. "I slammed the phone down."

Meanwhile, the Calvins arrived back home. "When we got home, the phone was ringing," Jim says. "It was Jeanene saying that he'd had a heart attack, and the medics were there, and please come right back. So we drove back like crazy. It's hard to talk about it. We drove back there, and we seen an ambulance heading towards the hospital, but they didn't have their lights flashing and they weren't driving real fast, and I said, 'Oh, man.' And Royann, boy she just started crying." Jeanene had called Susanna back, too. "She was crying," according to Susanna, "and I stayed on the phone with her the whole time, until they got him in the truck. And she kept telling me, 'Oh, the truck is out there, it's moving slowly, it's moving slowly.' And I said, 'We'll meet you at the hospital.' So I went and woke up Guy."

Jeanene had tried to revive Townes, shaking him, screaming his name. She performed CPR for the fifteen minutes it took a fire–rescue team to arrive. The fireman was hesitant to perform mouth-to-mouth resuscitation, and Jeanene told him to do chest compressions while she continued mouth-to-mouth. Paramedics arrived a few minutes later and took over the efforts, directing Jeanene to look after the children. A defibrillator brought a brief heartbeat.

"Royann stayed there with the kids, and me and Jeanene went to the hospital," Jim Calvin recalls. "We got to the emergency room, and we was maybe fifteen minutes behind them or something. And this one doctor comes in this room, and boy he was just real upset. He was mad. He said to Jeanene, 'What the hell were you doing? What were you thinking when you took him out of this hospital?' And this other doctor just grabbed him and jerked him out of the room. And he says, 'Unfortunately, Mr. Van Zandt did not survive.'"

When Guy and Susanna arrived, a nurse took them to the room, where they found Jeanene, who said simply, "He didn't make it."

Back at home, Katie Belle explained to Royann that "Daddy had a fight with his heart."

In the emergency room at Summit, Susanna Clark immediately asked to see the doctor who had attended to Townes. As she recalls, "The doctor came in, and I said, 'What happened?' And he said, 'He never should have left the hospital. It's as simple as that.' Think about it. He had all those drugs from the hospital still in him, then she'd given him vodka, then the nurse says to get him Tylenol P.M., and Jeanene told me that he took four of them. And damn, you know, he just laid back. Jeanene said that he had his hand on his chest and was just very peaceful. There wasn't a peep out of him. He just laid back."

The autopsy report states that "The patient died of a cardiac arrhythmia. The manner of death is natural." In fact, "cardiac arrhythmia," which is a disturbance or irregularity in the heartbeat, cannot reliably be diagnosed post-mortem—it is an effect, not a cause. The term is often used by medical examiners as a catch-all phrase when no cause of death is immediately evident.

There was no "heart attack," as such; the autopsy cites a "normal" heart, with no indication of significant coronary disease.[13]

On the summary page of the autopsy report, "myocardial ischemia"—constriction of the coronary arteries and deprivation of oxygen to the heart—is listed as the second cause of death, though this condition does not show up in the body of the report. Myocardial ischemia is another commonly cited cause of death on death certificates, and ischemia and arrhythmia are very frequently cited together when no other clear cause of death can be determined. These kinds of deaths occur most often outside hospital settings, since patients being monitored in hospitals are normally defibrillated at the first sign of a cardiac arrhythmia, and saved. There was no diagnosis of either condition either before or after Townes' surgery, and there is nothing in the autopsy report to indicate the mechanism of ischemia.[14]

The toxicology report revealed the presence of diphenhydramine (likely from the Tylenol P.M.), promethazine and diazepam (likely from the shot administered by the nurse before he left the hospital AMA—promethazine to quell post-op nausea and diazepam to treat alcohol withdrawal), and traces of "marihuana metabolite." His blood alcohol level was 0.02, consistent with the reports that he had only been "sipping" in the hour before his death.[15]

John Townes Van Zandt signed and executed his Last Will and Testament in October of 1988. No new will was prepared between then and the time of Townes and Jeanene's divorce in 1994, but a codicil with three alterations was added. The first alteration was to a paragraph wherein J.T. and Will would share the inheritance of any of Townes' assets in succession of Jeanene—the new version removed J.T. and left only Will in line for inheritance. The second alteration gave more details about the intended distribution of Townes' song copyrights, specifying an intent that the Songwriters Guild of America administer the copyrights. The final amendment reads, in full: "It is my intention that Lara Fisher receive nothing under this my Last Will and Testament."[16]

Jeanene was originally named executor of Townes' will but was precluded by law from serving in that capacity once she became Townes' ex-wife. In September of 1997, the probate court appointed Guy Clark as executor, but he declined to serve and offered a statement to the effect that Jeanene, as the guardian of two of Townes' "residual beneficiaries" and "primary manager of most of the deceased's property," should serve instead. The court then appointed J.T. (also a residual beneficiary) as co-executor, along with Jeanene.

There was a funeral in Nashville, at Belmont Church, downtown near Music Row, "emceed" by Steve Earle and featuring eulogizing and performances by Guy Clark (who joked, "I booked this gig thirty-something years ago"), Lyle Lovett, Emmylou Harris, Nanci Griffith, Mickey White, and others. Jeanene distributed a printed collection of obituaries and quotes, led off by her own statement: "Townes' message to us was to Love and have Compassion for one another and to drink up Life both the Good and the Bad. My life is a thousand times richer and deeper for his precious words and the Love we shared." She rounded off her collection of tributes with a discography of Townes' work, then a handwritten pitch at the end: "More to come: 60 newly recorded songs w/guest Star Duets, Last Recordings of TVZ—2 day [*sic*] before he died w/spoken poetry and video, video, video...."

Claudia Winterer flew in from Germany shocked with grief, attended the funeral, and stayed for some days with the Calvins afterwards. "They were planning on getting married," Jim Calvin says of Townes and Claudia. "I think he was trying to save up some money or get another hit record where they could lay off the road for a while ... get some more of the 'Pancho and Lefty' kind of checks coming in, and have them directed at him instead of Jeanene. He talked about it seriously. There was this donkey farm out in West Texas, a little piece of land out there by Roxy Gordon's, and he was gonna get two females and a male, and they were gonna live out there and raise donkeys." Richard Dobson also recalls the donkey farm idea.[17]

According to Calvin, Townes planned to "just do some gigs, hang out, and drink, cook, make love.... He was gonna get out of Tennessee and go back to Texas, and he was gonna be on his little rancho for the most part, and if he was gonna come out and do a show, they were gonna pay good for it. He was gonna marry her and move out to the desert in West Texas and live happily ever after, and to hell with the world."

Whether or not the plans would have come to pass is impossible to guess, but his friends agree that Claudia brought a special joy to Townes' last months. "I'm sure that they would have gotten married," Bob Moore says. "She quit her job and was coming here. She called to tell Townes when she was gonna be arriving, and Will answered the phone, and he said, 'My dad just died.' Then she came on. She was a very nice lady. I remember Townes said he would hit passing gear on the truck and start going real fast and he said it would always make Claudia laugh," Moore recalls. "She told me, 'We were like kids, we were so much in love.' So at least he got that."

Cindy Van Zandt arrived at Belmont Church right after the funeral ended. Jim Calvin recalls, "Everybody's gone, and me and Royann and Claudia are sitting there. And this woman drives up in a bright red Camaro, and she's got reddish blonde hair, and it was Cindy. And she says 'It's all over?' And I says, 'Yeah, I guess so. But you're in time for a flower.' And I gave her one of the flowers that was left. And she took it, got in her car, and drove back to Texas."

There was another funeral in Dido, Texas, outside Ft. Worth, where Townes Van Zandt's deepest roots lay. The family service was attended by many friends as well, who all gathered near the Van Zandt plot in Dido Cemetery, where, on that cold January day, Townes' mortal remains were laid to rest.[18] His tombstone reads

*To Live's To Fly*

# Afterword

THE FIRST POSTHUMOUS TOWNES VAN Zandt tribute show was held a few weeks after his death, at the Cactus Café in Austin on two nights when Townes had been booked to play his "home club." Friends and fans gathered to hear Jimmie Dale Gilmore, Joe Ely, Kimmie Rhodes, J.T. Van Zandt (who attended a number of tribute shows and has become an accomplished performer) and others play Townes' music and remember his life. More all-star tributes followed quickly, including a notable show at the Bottom Line in New York and gatherings in Nashville, Houston, Seattle, and Los Angeles. Guy and Susanna Clark hosted a "Celebration of Townes Van Zandt" on *Austin City Limits* with Willie Nelson, Emmylou Harris, Lyle Lovett, Steve Earle, Nanci Griffith, Jack Clement, and others (including J.T.), which became one of the series' most popular shows. The Clarks were also prominently involved in an album project that was released in 2001 on Willie Nelson's Pedernales Records called *Poet: A Tribute to Townes Van Zandt*, which featured Guy, Willie, Emmylou Harris, Lucinda Williams, Cowboy Junkies, John Prine, Ray Benson, Billy Joe Shaver, Steve Earle, Delbert McClinton, and J.T., among others.

And every New Year's Day since the first anniversary of Van Zandt's passing, at the Old Quarter Acoustic Café in Galveston, Townes' old running buddy Rex Bell—"Wrecks"—hosts his Annual Townes Van Zandt Wake. Each year, the cozy barroom fills with fans, friends, family, and onlookers, and the tiny corner stage holds a parade of musicians young and old playing Townes' music, interpreting his songs, and making them new.

268

On the other side of the coin, the bickering, ill will, and lawsuits surrounding Van Zandt after his death mark the final and most unfortunate similarity between Townes and his hero, Hank Williams. As one of the principals admitted five years after Townes was laid to rest, "It's ugly—way uglier than you can imagine."

But, fifty years after Hank Williams' death, few remember the details of or the participants in the petty, transitory squabbles that arose on his passing. Hank Williams' legacy is secure. His complete works are available all over the world and his songs have become part of the American vernacular. It seems reasonable to imagine that the same could come to pass for Townes Van Zandt.

[Townes] basically went down in flames, but he stayed so true to his vision you can't fault him for anything. He was never hypocritical about the devotion to his music. He died in the course of living on the road and playing his music. There aren't going to be any new songs or performances. Once everyone is done rushing out whatever they have, the real test will begin. The test of time—and time is still ahead of him. That he makes it through the hype is all that's important. This is music that deserves to be treasured as genuine folk music for centuries. —*J.T. Van Zandt*

I remember having a conversation with Jimmie Dale Gilmore about him, and we both came to the conclusion that the only reason Townes was still on the earth at that point was to write songs and to sing them. It was like he had some connection with some very strange energy, whatever you want to call it, you know, his muse, that wouldn't let him leave until she or it was finished with him. He was the cipher for this expression that people had to hear. And it was almost like he knew that. He almost wanted to go, but he realized there was unfinished work to be done. And that was quite a few years before he died. And I think, near the end there, he was almost waiting to go in a weird way. "I've done my bit, I've had my say, now I've got to leave."

... Again, in some of his darker moods, he would talk very cryptically about things like that.

I think Townes knew what he was doing was pretty special. I do think he knew that. And I don't think it really bothered him that much one way or the other, whether people knew that or not, as long as he was doing that. I think he had an understanding of his place and of what he was responsible for, really. Which is unusual. —*Michael Timmins*

In his songs, Townes is usually talking metaphorically about consciousness and the primal, universal battle of darkness and light. Townes was so articulate about it, he was so passionately feeling that he spent a whole lot of energy trying to escape the intensity of his feelings. That's really clear to me, especially looking back on it. He had a lot of command of the language. He was a poet, and there's kind of a tradition of that, the depressed outsider. But he also had this incredible sense of humor, and despite the heaviness, that was a real common bond among all of us who knew him. He sidestepped his pain with humor. There was a mixture of darkness, light and slapstick going on. Townes could make us feel his pain, laugh and feel hopeful all at the same time. — *Jimmie Dale Gilmore*

# Endnotes

## Introduction

1. "No Place to Fall," *Picking Up the Tempo,* no. 17, no date but estimated late 1977.
2. Lola Scobey, "Biography," *For the Sake of the Song* (Houston: Wings Press, 1977).
3. Author's interview with Frank "Chito" Greer, September 1, 2001.

## Chapter 1

1. This is the version of the migration accepted by the Van Zandt Society at the time of this writing. There is a version that Jeanene Van Zandt recalls hearing from Townes' Aunt Sudi (Martha Ann Van Zandt Perryman, who died in 1998) that has Jacob, born in the 1750s, immigrating from Holland with the Moravian Colony and settling in Pennsylvania, then moving to North Carolina. The Society's Historian, Sally Van Sant, writes:
Jacob was the son of Garret and Mary Van Zandt (possibly the grandson of Albertus and the great grandson of Garret and Lysbeth Van Sant). Garret the great grandfather is the one who immigrated [to America] not Jacob. We have no proof that Jacob went with the Moravian Colony and in searching all the Moravian records there is no mention of any Van Sant (any spelling).
2. Frances Cooke Lipscomb Van Zandt (born 3/4/1816 in Virginia, died 4/1909 in Texas) was also a fascinating character who, toward the end of her life, wrote a book, *Reminiscences of Frances Cooke Van Zandt, Wife of Isaac Van Zandt.* She was known as Fanny, and a priceless transcript exists of one of her slaves, J. M. Moore, talking about his life with the Van Zandts:
My mistress was named Fanny and was one sweet soul. She had five children and they lived here in town but have a purty big farm east of town. My mother sewed for Mistress Fanny, so we lived in town. There were lots of niggers on the farm and everybody round these parts called us 'Van Zandt's free niggers,' 'cause our white folks shared with their darkies and larned 'em all to read and write. The other owners wouldn't have none of Van Zandt's niggers....

George P. Rawick, ed., *The American Slave: A Composite Autobiography*, vol. 5 (Westport, CT: Greenwood, 1979).

3. The Texas State Historical Association, "Civil War," "Van Zandt, Khleber Miller," The Handbook of Texas Online, www.tsha.utexas.edu/handbook/online.

4. Isaac Lycurgus Van Zandt died in 1935; Sara Ellen Henderson Van Zandt died in 1915.

5. Donna Van Zandt Spence recalls that her grandmother, Bell Williams Van Zandt, also had twin boys who died at birth before her aunts were born, and a boy, Jack, born before her father. These children's graves are in the Van Zandt plot in Dido Cemetery: "Infant Twins, December 6 1904" and "Jack Van Zandt, February 8 1911 – November 20 1916."

6. Sources for personal details on this generation of Townes' family include author's interviews with Townes' sister Donna Spence (March 27, 2000), brother Bill Van Zandt (March 28, 2000), and first wife Fran (now Lohr) (March 29, 2000; January 5, 2001; and January 12, 2002).

7. The Texas State Historical Association, *Handbook of Texas Online*, www.tsha.utexas.edu/handbook/.

# Chapter 2

1. All quotes from Bill Van Zandt and Donna Van Zandt Spence are from the author's interviews: Donna Spence, March 27, 2000; and William Van Zandt, March 28, 2000.

2. Fran Lohr, interview by the author, January 12, 2002.

3. Ibid.

4. In 1961, Frances presented the Van Zandt family with a longhand reminiscence of her years with the Van Zandts, which she titled "My White Family." Her recollections here are taken from that manuscript, which Bill Van Zandt has lovingly preserved.

5. Fran Lohr, author's interview.

6. Ibid.

7. Todd Musburger, interview by the author, July 9, 2001.

8. Townes told this story many times, including to DJ Larry Monroe in an interview included on the CD *Documentary: Townes Van Zandt*, Normal Records, 1997.

9. "Fraulein," written by Lawton Williams, was a hit for Bobby Helms and remained on the country charts for fifty-two consecutive weeks. It was later recorded by many other country artists, from Ernest Tubb to Mickey Gilley to Willie Nelson. Townes made a studio recording of the song for his 1972 release *The Late, Great Townes Van Zandt*.

The source for the statement that Townes learned the song during the week after Christmas is Townes himself, introducing the song during a live performance in 1990 in Berlin, Germany, later released as *Rain on a Conga Drum*.

# Chapter 3

1. 1977 interviews by Richard Wootton and Scott Giles, and material from Bob Claypool (*The Houston Post*, June 1, 1977) and Joel McNally (*The Milwaukee Journal*, May 1, 1977), were reprinted in "Townes Van Zandt," *Omaha Rainbow*, no. 15, December 1977.
2. The source of the story about driving from oil field to oil field listening to the radio is Paul Zollo's introduction to his 1990 interview with Townes in *Songwriters on Songwriting* (New York: Da Capo Press, 1997). The source of the quote from Townes about his deepest musical influences is that same introduction.
3. The sentence about the starving person is quoted by Michael Hall in his article in *Texas Monthly*, "The Great, Late Townes Van Zandt," March 1998.
4. As Townes told the story to Susanna Clark (interview by the author, March 28, 2000), after he shot the deer: "he looked up at his father, which was very hard for him to do, and said, I'm never going to do this again, ever. And his father said, Okay." The following statement from Bill Van Zandt (interview by the author) should also be taken into consideration: "The shame of it was Townes was real good at— Townes had really good reflexes. Later we went duck hunting, and Townes would kill all kinds of ducks without any trouble."
5. This story was recounted by Susanna Clark in her interview with the author.
6. Bill Van Zandt interview.
7. This story was recounted by Fran Lohr, interview by the author.
8. Academic transcript for Townes Van Zandt, Boulder High School, 1958–1959 class record.
9. Jeanene Van Zandt relates this story, as Townes told it to her, in an article in the *Guardian UK*, August 1998, called "Legend of the Fall."
10. Bill Van Zandt interview.
11. Townes is quoted telling this story in Nashville in 1990, by Paul Zollo in his book of interviews, *Songwriters on Songwriting*.
12. This story is also told in Zollo, *Songwriters on Songwriting*.
13. Academic transcript for Townes (John) Van Zandt [*sic*], Barrington High School, 1958–1959 class record.
14. All quotes from Todd Musburger are from the author's interview, July 9, 2001.
15. All quotes from Luke Sharpe are from the author's interview, August 21, 2001.
16. All quotes from Marshall Froker are from the author's interview, June 22, 2001.
17. Bob Myrick, interview by the author, February 12, 2001.
18. Quoted in Hall, "The Great, Late Townes Van Zandt."
19. Luke Sharpe interview.
20. Academic transcripts and records for Townes Van Zandt, Shattuck School, 1960–61 and 1961–1962.

21. Bill Van Zandt, author's interview. According to Townes' Student Activity Record at Shattuck, the name of the play where he made his one and only dramatic appearance was "Down in the Valley," part of the Winter Carnival Folk Opera.
22. What Froker remembers as "Train I Ride" was probably "Mystery Train," which Townes would have known from Elvis's recording on Sun Records.
23. Townes told this story to a doctor at the University of Texas Medical Branch, where it was reported in the Discharge Summary for Mr. Townes Van Zandt, 1964.

## Chapter 4

1. Quoted in *Omaha Rainbow*, no. 15.
2. Townes recounted this story of his "false start" to his doctor in 1964, who recorded it in his records: Medical records for Mr. Townes Van Zandt, University of Texas Medical Branch Hospitals (UTMB).
3. William Hedgepeth, "Townes Van Zandt—Messages from the Outside," *Hittin' the Note*, May 1977.
4. All quotes from Bob Myrick are from the author's interview, February 12, 2001.
5. Academic transcripts for John Townes Van Zandt, University of Colorado, Spring Semester 1962–1963.
6. Luke Sharpe, author's interview.
7. All quotes from Fran (Petters) Lohr in this chapter are from the author's interviews, March 29, 2000; January 5, 2001; and January 12, 2002.
8. Some of Townes' other early talking blues songs were "Talking Karate Blues," "Talking Birth Control Blues," "Talking Thunderbird Blues," and the unrecorded "Talking Burial Blues" and "Talking Eight Day Beauty Plan." Similar, although not in the "talking" blues form, was his early "Mustang Blues."
9. Bill Van Zandt, author's interview.
10. Tom Barrow, a fascinating character, died in 2000 after a long battle with cancer. A native of Billings, Montana, he had a long career as a world-class balloonist. "I like the idea of going where the wind takes you," Barrow said in an interview in *Balloon Life*, 1997.
11. Donna Spence, author's interview.
12. Medical records for Mr. Townes Van Zandt, UTMB.

## Chapter 5

1. Grace K. Jameson, M.D., "A Brief History, Department of Psychiatry and Behavioral Sciences," UTMB, 2001.
2. Quotes from Dr. Grace Jameson are from the author's interview, January 3, 2002, and from a transcript of Dr. Jameson's speech, "A Brief History, Department of Psychiatry and Behavioral Sciences," UTMB, 2001.

3. Dr. Charles Gaston, Psychological Reports for Mr. Townes Van Zandt, March 23, 1964, UTMB medical records.

4. A diagnosis of "acute schizophrenia and manic-depression" has been widely reported as the reason for Townes' hospitalization; this is the diagnosis recalled by Fran Lohr in the author's interviews. The diagnosis has been reported elsewhere as "manic-depression with schizophrenic tendencies," which is most likely a later interpretation of Ms. Lohr's recollection of the diagnosis.

5. Frank "Chito" Greer, interview by the author, September 1, 2001.

6. Sources for the discussion of manic-depressive illness, alcoholism, and the relation of both to creativity include Kay Redfield Jamison, *Touched with Fire: Manic-Depressive Illness and the Artistic Temperament* (New York: Free Press Paperbacks, 1993); Charles L. Bowden, MD, "Update on Bipolar Disorder: Epidemiology, Etiology, Diagnosis, and Prognosis" (University of Texas Health Science Center, San Antonio); www.nimh. nih.gov/publicat/bipolar.cfm; www.mayoclinic.com/health/alcoholism/ DS00340; and *Diagnostic and Statistical Manual of Mental Disorders* (Washington: American Psychiatric Association, 1994) (DSM-IV).

7. University of Texas Medical Branch Hospitals Discharge Summary for Mr. Townes Van Zandt, 1964.

# Chapter 6

1. All quotes from Fran Lohr are from the author's interviews, March 29, 2000; January 5, 2001; and January 12, 2002.

2. All quotes from Dr. Grace Jameson are from the author's interview, January 3, 2002.

3. Academic transcript for John Townes Van Zandt, University of Houston, Houston, Texas, spring 1965 – fall 1966.

4. Bianca DeLeon, author's interview, April 20, 2000.

5. All quotes from Bob Myrick are from the author's interview, February 12, 2001.

6. The practice of assigning a different order of call based on marital status ended in 1973.

7. All quotes from John Carrick are from the author's interview, August 17, 2000.

8. "Townes Van Zandt," *Omaha Rainbow,* no. 15.

9. Ibid.

10. All quotes from John Lomax III are from the author's interview, April 21, 2001.

11. Larry Monroe, prod., *Documentary: Townes Van Zandt.*

12. All quotes from Rex Bell are from the author's interview, January 2, 2002.

13. All quotes from Guy Clark are from the author's interview, January 8, 2000.

14. Darryl Harris, interview by the author, January 7, 2002.

15. "Townes Van Zandt," *Omaha Rainbow,* no. 15.

16. Available for years as a bootleg, this recording was released in 2004 on the German label Normal Records as *Live at the Jester Lounge: Houston, Texas 1966.* For some reason, the order of the songs on this release was altered from the original performance; the original order is cited here. The 1966 date cited on the Normal release is almost certainly incorrect.

17. In Hall, *Texas Monthly,* March 1998, Fran recalls the doctors "calling him 'an acute manic-depressive who has made minimal adjustments to life.'"

# Chapter 7

1. All quotes from Mickey Newbury are from the author's interviews, May 4, 2000, and July 10, 2000.

2. Townes Van Zandt, interview with Larry Monroe, KUT radio, March 1990.

3. All quotes from Jack Clement are from the author's interview, June 19, 2002.

4. From Tomato Records press release, March 2002.

5. Mickey Newbury, liner notes, *For the Sake of the Song* (Poppy, 1968).

6. Townes Van Zandt, quoted in "Space Cowboy: Townes Van Zandt," by Robert Greenfield, *Fusion,* no. 30, April 3, 1970.

7. Bianca DeLeon, author's interviews, April 20, 2000, and January 10, 2001.

8. Townes Van Zandt, quoted in Greenfield, "Space Cowboy."

9. Emmylou Harris was in the audience at Gerde's one of these nights. "I had never really seen anything like that before," she said during the 1998 *Austin City Limits* tribute to Van Zandt; "I thought he was the ghost of Hank Williams, with a twist."

10. Quoted in Greenfield, "Space Cowboy."

11. Van Zandt's other co-writes include "Gone, Gone Blues" with Mickey White, "Heavenly Houseboat Blues" and a song called "Sapphire" with Susanna Clark, "German Mustard" and a song called "Bloodstream" with Rocky Hill, a song called "The Pining I Keep for You" with Royann Calvin, and four songs with Eric Andersen, written in the late eighties and beautifully recorded by Andersen on *You Can't Relive the Past* in 2000: "The Meadowlark," "The Road," "Night Train," and "The Blue March."

12. All quotes from Rex Bell are from the author's interview, January 2, 2002.

13. Vince Bell, "Remembering the Old Quarter," *Vince Bell's Journals: Out Here on the Edge of the Desert,* no. 4, March 17, 1997, www.mindspring.com/~vincebell/edge04.htm.

14. Vince Bell, interview by the author, February 14, 2001.

15. Dale Soffar, interview by the author, January 5, 2002.

16. A recording of Townes' performance at Carnegie Hall was released in 2002 on the Dualtone label as *A Gentle Evening with Townes Van Zandt.*

17. According to Bob Myrick, Townes appeared once on Steve Allen's TV show and felt that Allen had been cavalier and somewhat abusive, joking dismissively after Townes mentioned that his music received airplay mostly on "underground" radio stations.

# Chapter 8

1. All quotes from Susanna Clark are from the author's interview, March 28, 2002.
2. All quotes from Fran Lohr are from the author's interviews, March 29, 2000; January 5, 2001; and January 12, 2002.
3. Bianca DeLeon, author's interviews.
4. Lyse Moore, interview by the author, April 23, 2001.
5. Jack Clement, author's interview.
6. All quotes from Mickey White are from the author's interview, August 12, 2001.
7. All quotes from Rex Bell are from the author's interview, January 2, 2002.
8. Bob Fass radio show, WBAI-FM, New York City, October 20, 1970.
9. Bob Myrick, author's interview.

# Chapter 9

1. Zollo, *Songwriters on Songwriting*.
2. All quotes from Rex Bell are from the author's interview, January 2, 2002.
3. All quotes from Mickey White are from the author's interview, August 12, 2001.
4. All quotes from Dale Soffar are from the author's interview, January 5, 2002.
5. All quotes from Susanna Clark are from the author's interview, March 28, 2002.
6. Zollo, *Songwriters on Songwriting*.
7. Ibid.
8. All quotes from Bianca DeLeon are from the author's interviews.
9. Richard Dobson, interview by the author, May 10, 2000.
10. "Townes Van Zandt," *Omaha Rainbow*, no. 15.
11. Zollo, *Songwriters on Songwriting*.
12. From "Gibby Haynes vs Willie Nelson": http://ngro_obsrvr.tripod.com/articles/gibbyvswillie.html.
13. "Townes Van Zandt," *Omaha Rainbow*, no. 15.
14. Richard Dobson, *The Gulf Coast Boys* (Bryan, Texas: Greater Texas Publishing Company, 1998).
15. *Omaha Rainbow*, no. 15.
16. Ibid.
17. Ibid.
18. Townes Van Zandt, interview with Larry Monroe, KUT radio, December 1993.

19. The source for this discussion of "Pancho and Lefty" is Paul Zollo's interview with Townes in *Songwriters on Songwriting*.
20. Paul Zollo, *Songwriters on Songwriting*.
21. All quotes from Peggy Underwood are from the author's interview, January 9, 2002.
22. All quotes from Earl Willis are from the author's interview, January 5, 2002.
23. All quotes from Cindy Van Zandt Lindgram are from the author's interview, January 11, 2002.

# Chapter 10

1. Frank "Chito" Greer, author's interview. Chito also made the following cogent observations:

   Oh shit, the son of a bitch could walk into a bar, twelve sheets to the wind, be the biggest, most obnoxious asshole there, but still, that son of a bitch could pick up the best-looking chick in the bar. Every time. There was just something about him … women wanted to take care of him. He brought out the mother instinct in them. Big time.

   And how do you think he gets them girls out of them bars? Just like that…. Just like that! The son of a bitch is the *best* at conning. And that's okay, because it's an art. Now, *that*'s an art; because he's a liar and a cheat; and it's the art of *creating* the whole deal.

2. All quotes from Mickey White are from the author's interview, August 12, 2001.
3. Bob Myrick, author's interview.
4. Cindy Van Zandt Lindgram, author's interview.
5. Earl Willis, author's interview.
6. John Lomax wrote before the record was released that the record was "tentatively titled *Deader Now Than Ever* by yours truly." (John Lomax, "No Place to Fall," *Picking Up the Tempo* no. 17, no date, but estimated late 1977)
7. Jack Clement, author's interview.
8. All quotes from John Lomax III are from the author's interview, April 21, 2001.
9. Rex Bell, author's interview.
10. The source of the discussion of the Rocky Mountains tour is Richard Dobson, *Gulf Coast Boys*.
11. Ibid.
12. The Texas State Historical Association ,"Clarksville," *Handbook of Texas Online*, www.tsha.utexas.edu/handbook/online/articles/CC/hpc1.html.
13. All quotes from Peggy Underwood are from the author's interview, January 9, 2002.
14. Chito's girlfriend, Mary Ann, contributed insights and reminiscences during the author's interview with Frank "Chito" Greer, September 1, 2001. All quotes from Mary Ann are from the author's interview with Chito.

15. William Hedgepeth, "Townes Van Zandt—Messages From the Outside," *Hittin' the Note*, May 1977.
16. Ibid.
17. Brackenridge, the oldest public hospital in Texas, is also the only hospital in Austin that accepts uninsured patients in the emergency room.
18. *Heartworn Highways*, DVD, directed by James Szalapski (1977, 2005).
19. Townes Van Zandt, interview with Larry Monroe, KUT radio, March 1990.
20. Darryl Harris believes that this is Kathy Tennel, not Ivy, but others are certain that it is Ivy.
21. Townes' performance of "Pancho and Lefty" was cut from the film, but it appears as a special feature in the DVD version released in 2005. Interestingly, Townes gives one of his best "explanations" of how the song came to be written. Introducing it as "a medley of my hit," he says he wrote the song "about two Mexican bandits I saw on TV two weeks after I wrote the song."
22. Townes Van Zandt, quoted in "Townes Van Zandt," *Omaha Rainbow*, no. 15, December 1977.

# Chapter 11

1. Townes Van Zandt, quoted in "Townes Van Zandt," *Omaha Rainbow*, no. 15, December 1977.
2. Ibid.
3. All quotes from Cindy Van Zandt Lindgram are from the author's interview, January 11, 2002.
4. The Battle of Franklin is summed up on www.americancivilwar.com/statepic/tn/tn036.html.
5. John Lomax III, author's interview, April 21, 2001.
6. *Omaha Rainbow*, no. 15.
7. Hedgepeth, "Townes Van Zandt—Messages from the Outside."
8. Ibid.
9. David Olney, interview by the author, February 7, 2001.
10. According to Gray (in a conversation with the author), Jennings fired him for refusing to wear the band uniform.
11. Selections from these live soundboard recordings were eventually released as *Rear View Mirror, Road Songs*, and *Rear View Mirror, Volume Two*. These recordings constitute some of Townes' best work.
12. Quotes from Danny Rowland are from the author's interview, April 22, 2001, and from Rowland's own liner notes to *Rear View Mirror, Volume Two* (2004).
13. According to Cindy, while they lived at the cabin in Franklin, Townes taught her to play guitar. The first song he taught her was "Blue Eyes Crying in the Rain," the Fred Rose classic that was Willie Nelson's big hit from *Red Headed Stranger*.
14. Some of Townes' comments on his songs are light-hearted, some more serious. For "If I Needed You," Townes again claims that it's the

only song he's ever "written while sleeping." For "Lungs," he writes, "The darkness of disease and the fire of frustration. This song should be screamed, not sung."

15. John Lomax, *For the Sake of the Song*.
16. From *Omaha Rainbow,* no. 15, December 1977.
17. *Solo Sessions*, 1995.
18. The primary source for background on Chips Moman is Peter Guralnick, *Sweet Soul Music* (Boston: Little, Brown and Company, 1986).
19. Townes told this story many times as an introduction to playing the song.
20. Andy Langer, "Townes Without Pity: The Battle for Townes Van Zandt's Legacy," *Austin Chronicle*, June 14, 2002.
21. Quotes from J.T. from "The Tower Son," John Nova Lomax, *Houston Press*, October 17, 2002.
22. Hedgepeth, "Townes Van Zandt—Messages from the Outside."

# Chapter 12

1. All quotes from John Lomax III are from the author's interview, April 21, 2001.
2. All quotes from Mickey White are from the author's interview, August 12, 2001.
3. Mickey White, author's interview. According to Danny Rowland, the Colonel was named after the famous Confederate Colonel John Singleton Mosby, known as the "Gray Ghost."
4. All quotes from Cindy Van Zandt Lindgram are from the author's interview, January 11, 2002.
5. All quotes from Peggy Underwood are from the author's interview, January 9, 2002.
6. The Texas State Historical Association, "Foley, Blaze," *The Handbook of Texas Online,* www.tsha.utexas.edu/handbook/online/articles/FF/ffulm.html. Also, Lee Nichols, "A Walking Contradiction: *The Legend of Blaze Foley,*" *Austin Chronicle*, December 28, 1999.
7. It became a standing joke around Austin that the letters "BFI" (which stands for Browning-Ferris Industries), which adorned the front of every trash dumpster in town, actually stood for "Blaze Foley Inside."
8. Information on and quotes from Jeanene Munsell Van Zandt come from interviews by Ruth Sanders, who shared transcripts of her unpublished interviews from February 9, 2004, and May 9, 2004, and her notes.
9. The old friend quoted here is Peggy Underwood, from the author's interview. She added the following in relation to this period: "He actually tried to get me to go back with him, and I said, no way, because I didn't have the energy. I'd already done that. Plus I was already involved with another nut."
10. All quotes from Fran Lohr are from the author's interviews.
11. Emmylou Harris, as told in *Townes Van Zandt: Be Here to Love Me,* DVD, directed by Margaret Brown (Rake Films, 2005).

12. *Be Here to Love Me.*
13. Dorothy Van Zandt was not literally on her "death bed"; she didn't pass away until six months later.
14. Lustrica N. Amposta, M.D., Attending Physician's Discharge/Furlough Note for John T. Van Zandt, Alcoholism & Drug Abuse Treatment Center, Brackenridge Hospital, Austin, Texas, July 30, 1983.
15. *Be Here to Love Me.*
16. All quotes from Donna Spence are from the author's interview, March 27, 2000.
17. Quotes from Jeanene Munsell Van Zandt come from interviews by Ruth Sanders, February 9, 2004, and May 9, 2004.
18. Townes Van Zandt, interview with Larry Monroe, KUT radio, December 1993.
19. Hospital records, Alcoholism & Drug Abuse Treatment Center, Brackenridge Hospital, July 26, 1983.
20. Larry Monroe, "Blaze Foley," first printed in the *Austin Weekly* in February 1989. Also, www.larrymonroe.com/writings/writings01.html, 1999.

# Chapter 13

1. All quotes from Mickey White are from the author's interview.
2. Mickey White says of the first gig of that tour, at Twelfth and Porter in Nashville (which was recorded and became the album *Live and Obscure*), "I had booked that gig, then 'Little H' got a hold of it. This is when he kind of stepped back in," with "Little H" referring to Harold Eggers. White, however, credits Eggers with publicizing the show well.
3. The quote is from Robert K. Oermann's liner notes to *Live and Obscure* on Sugar Hill Records.
4. *Live and Obscure* was actually the first recorded but second released of Townes' albums on Sugar Hill, the second recorded, first released being *At My Window*.
5. Harold Eggers, "Twenty Years With Townes Van Zandt," www.townesvanzandt20yearshfe.com/timeline/.
6. Jack Clement, author's interview.
7. Danny Rowland, author's interview.
8. Larry Monroe, "Blaze Foley," first printed in the *Austin Weekly* in February, 1989, www.larrymonroe.com/writings/writings01.html.
9. Peggy Underwood, author's interview.
10. All quotes from Lyse Moore are from the author's interview, April 23, 2001.
11. Bob Moore, author's interview, February 13, 2001.
12. Robert Palmer, "A Hard Road, Seldom Taken," *New York Times*, June 7, 1987.
13. All these years later, his friends and fans still question the jury's verdict that acquitted Carey January of Foley's murder by reason of self-defense. "Derelict in Duct Tape Shoes: Fifteen Years After His Death, Blaze Foley's Legacy Is Secure" by Michael Corcoran, *Austin American-*

*Statesman* Staff, January 31, 2004, http://insurgentcountry.net/blaze-foley-15.htm.

14. Ibid.

15. Niles Fuller, from "Have Your Say—Albums: Blaze Foley, Oval Room," *BBC Folk and Country Review*, www.bbc.co.uk/music/release/x5f9/.

16. Susanna Clark, author's interview.

17. Andy Langer, "Townes Without Pity."

18. This would have been the show at the Great American Music Hall the previous November. Guy Clark confirms Townes' version of the writing of this song in the film *Be Here to Love Me* (2005).

19. A dozen tracks were released in 2001 as *Texas Rain: The Texas Hill Country Recordings* on Kevin Eggers' resurrected Tomato label.

20. Neil Strauss, "The Pop Life" (column), *New York Times*, November 24, 1994.

21. Michael Timmins, author's interview, January 18, 2000.

22. Townes Van Zandt, interview with Larry Monroe, KUT radio, December 1993.

23. Michael Timmins' comments in the author's interview suggest that Townes was "cheating" somewhat, at least during the later part of the span. Bob Moore, in his interview with the author, states with authority that Townes was sober for eleven months after his release from the Huntsville treatment center.

24. Keith Glass, personal correspondence with the author, 2002.

25. The author knows of no other live recordings of this song.

26. Michael Hall, *Texas Monthly*, "The Great, Late Townes Van Zandt," March 1998.

# Chapter 14

1. The author was privileged to view the wrapping paper during Danny Rowland's interview, April 22, 2001.

2. Bob Moore also observed his poor physical state: "I was selling vintage denim ... and he would tell me he needed a certain size of pants, and it was tough to find them because he had a 34-inch inseam, and it hit the point that he got down to below a 30-inch waist."

3. The sources of comments and observations on Townes' live performances here and elsewhere are in the recordings listed in Audio and Video Sources.

4. Reviews of shows from this period indicate the depths to which a performance could sink. This one is from 1994:
   This was a tough show for me because it became pretty clear that at this stage in Townes' career, sobriety is a physical problem.... It's likely that Townes will see better days. Until then, be forewarned. bigstar@augustus.csscr.washington.edu (J Paschel), "Review: Townes Van Zandt in Seattle," Article 36249 from Newsgroups: rec.music.folk, May 23, 1994.

5. Will Van Zandt remembers with fondness touring with his father: "Some of my first memories are real good stuff.... I remember Yellow-

stone and seeing the buffalo and stuff like that. And he would stop at every historical monument and tell me the whole story. I think that's probably why I'm into world history now ... he drilled that into me." Will Van Zandt, interview by Ruth Sanders, May 9, 2004.

6. Mickey White, author's interview.

7. Quoted in "Talkin' Townes" by Mark Brend, *Record Collector Magazine* (UK), February 2002. It is not clear what band she is referring to that "Townes fired."

8. Ibid.

9. The fourteen songs comprised the contents of the "Townes Van Zandt Songs" catalog, which was the publishing arrangement under which the most recent songs were published, including some not yet recorded. Titles fifteen and sixteen in that catalog are particularly interesting: "Houston, They Made a Fool of Me (50% held by Remo Circo)" and "When They Wing (50% held by Remo Circo)." Remo Circo is a Tennessee politician.

10. Hall, "The Great, Late Townes Van Zandt."

11. Townes Van Zandt, interview with Larry Monroe, KUT radio, December 1993.

12. Ibid.

13. Will Van Zandt, Ruth Sanders interview.

14. Royann Calvin provides this account based on her later conversations with Townes on the subject, as recounted in her interview with the author, June 26 and June 27, 2001.

15. Jimmy Gingles, author's interview, February 9, 2001.

16. Bob Moore, author's interview.

17. Townes made this statement during a live performance on the TV program *Texas Connection* (1993).

18. Jim Calvin, Royann Calvin, Susanna Clark, Jimmy Gingles, Bob Moore, Lyse Moore, and others, author's interviews.

19. Royann Calvin, author's interview.

20. The divorce decree was signed on April 1 but not fully processed and officially delivered until May 2, 1994.

21. Susanna Clark, from the author's interview, March 28, 2002.

22. "Townes last moments—report from Jeanene," Aug. 2 1997, http://ippc2.orst.edu/coopl/tvznotice4.html.)

23. This speculative opinion was offered on background only.

24. The DVD version of the film *Heartworn Highways* features an outtake of Guy and Susanna hosting an inebriated Christmas-time "song pull" with Rodney Crowell, Richard Dobson, Steve Earle, and others.

25. Townes Van Zandt, interview with Larry Monroe, KUT radio, December 1993. In the interview, Townes says he'll be leaving for Ireland to make the record on January 3, then recording in mid-January. In fact, he did not embark to make the record until that May.

26. From "Talk Townes," an article by Patrick Brennan, February 1995. It is not revealed which song Townes said he wrote with Shane MacGowan in mind.
27. Shane MacGowan discusses "piss artists" and many other topics in *A Drink with Shane MacGowan* (New York: Grove Press, 2001).
28. Patrick Brennan, "Talk Townes."
29. Jeanene Van Zandt, from the liner notes to Jonnell Mosser's 1996 album of Townes covers, *Around Townes*.
30. Townes had a large collection of Bo Whitt's paintings; Jeanene has some in Smyrna, as do Rex Bell and Jet Whitt in Galveston.
31. The album is *Daddies Sing Good Night: A Fathers' Collection of Sleepytime Songs,* released in 1994.
32. Neil Strauss, "The Pop Life."
33. Ibid.
34. From "An Interview with Townes Van Zandt," by Aretha Sills, *Cups* magazine, August 1994.
35. A recording of parts of this show—minus Emmylou Harris—was released in 2001 as *Steve Earle, Townes Van Zandt, Guy Clark Together at the Bluebird Café* on American Originals Records.
36. Quotes from Interview with J.T. Van Zandt, Son of the Late Great Townes Van Zandt, Lone Star Music, 2001, www.lonestarmusic.com.
37. Bayorischer Rundfunk radio interview, November 20, 1995.
38. Quotes from the author's correspondence with Claudia Winterer, January 2002.
39. Townes Van Zandt, interview with Larry Monroe, KUT radio, December 1993. Susanna Clark said that Townes' phone bill one month was $2,300 (Susanna Clark, author's interview).
40. Bayorischer Rundfunk radio interview.

# Chapter 15

1. Quoted in Hall, "The Great, Late Townes Van Zandt."
2. Claudia Winterer, correspondence.
3. Townes is referring to "Snow Don't Fall." See Paul Zollo, *Songwriters on Songwriting.*
4. Joe Gracey, from correspondence with the author, June 2002. The resulting Kimmie Rhodes album, *West Texas Heaven* (1996) is highly recommended.
5. Some tracks were eventually released in 2002 on *Absolutely Nothing,* on Normal Records.
6. Jim Calvin, Bob Moore, and Claudia Winterer all confirm the story of and the existence of the bruise, from the author's interviews and correspondence.
7. The accounts of Townes' last weeks related in this chapter are from the author's interviews with Jim Calvin, Royann Calvin, Susanna Clark, Jimmy Gingles, and Bob Moore, plus the account in "Townes last moments—report from Jeanene," Aug. 2 1997, http://ippc2.orst.edu/coopl/tvznotice4.html.

8. Matt Hanks, "A Gentleman and a Shaman: The Last Days and Sad Death of Townes Van Zandt," *No Depression*, Jan.–Feb. 1999.
9. Titles of the songs Townes intended to record include "Harm's Swift Way," "Old Satan," "Carolina," "Southern Cross," "The Meadowlark," "Apt. 213," "Cascade," "The Deer," and "Long Ball Hitter."
10. The attending physician, Dr. Michael McHugh, noting that his patient is a "chronic alcoholic," reported that "The patient did have alcohol on his breath at the time that he consented to the surgery, however, his wife was present and he did seem to be understanding of the description." A handwritten note initialed by the doctor and dated 1/20/97 says "Later I found out she was actually his ex-wife."
11. Will Van Zandt, interview by Ruth Sanders.
12. This could have been a seizure from alcohol withdrawal, indicating that Townes could not "sip" enough to get his blood alcohol level high enough.
13. Forensic specialists consulted on general background regarding the autopsy report include a chief medical examiner, a forensic chemist, and a professor of medicine and law at a major school of medicine.
14. The autopsy and the autopsy report are problematic, having been conducted and reported not by the Davidson County Medical Examiner, but by Dr. Miles J. Jones, an Indiana pathologist working with a private company, Forensic Medical, to whom the county had contracted its autopsies. An article in *The Tennessean*, "Public Autopsies in Private Hands," August 1, 1999, details the many serious problems that this arrangement engendered.
15. The diphenhydramine in Townes' system at the time of his death has been a matter of some controversy. The 0.62 ug/mL level listed in the toxicology report indicates that Townes took more than four Tylenol P.M. tablets. Jeanene Van Zandt later recounted that "I went to his nightstand drawer and found a bottle of antihistamines from Europe and all I can figure out is that while I was at the store for the Tylenol he must have found them and thought they were pain pills and took a bunch and it freaked his heart out." ("Townes last moments—report from Jeanene," Aug. 2, 1997, http://ippc2.orst.edu/coopl/tvznotice4.html.)

Jeanene, in a post on her public e-mail discussion site, later expanded on this story, calling the pills in question "Harold's antihistamines" and saying "Harold [Eggers] had the allergies and the labels were in German and somehow when they parted ways after the last tour Townes' Ibuprophen, which he took almost every day got switched for Harold's allergy medicine and ended up in his nightstand drawer which was the only place he could have gotten them from while I was at the store buying him what he needed...." (http://groups.yahoo.com/group/AboutTownes.)

However, Jim Calvin recalls, "But Royann, to this day, she'll tell you there wasn't no damn pills in there, she had just cleaned that whole place just a day or two before, and there weren't any kind of pills of any sort in there." Royann, in fact, reports: "[Jeanene] claims there was a bottle of European-made Benadryl in his drawer. I know for absolute certain that there was not. Because I cleaned everywhere; I even knew where her little hiding place in the bottom of his thing was, and I looked in there even, and I dusted and moved the table.... So I know for a fact that that did not exist."

The Calvins' recollections do not preclude the possibility that, in the brief time he was at Bayou Self when he dropped Townes there before being driven to the airport to catch his flight back to Austin, Harold Eggers might have left a bottle of pills in Townes' drawer, for whatever reason, or somehow by mistake. But, Jim Calvin makes this further observation: "Hell, [Townes] wasn't capable of grabbing any pills. Not unless somebody gave them to him and stuck them in his mouth. He was having trouble enough hitting his face with his pieces of roast beef and cheese. He was too weak to hardly do anything like that, I don't think. But I don't know."

16. By all accounts, Lara Fisher was Townes' fourth child—his second-oldest—unacknowledged except through the exclusionary gesture in the final version of his Last Will and Testament. The following recollections of three of Townes' friends are relevant to this statement:

"I know he had a will, and I know he cut his illegitimate daughter out. You should probably try to find that little girl and ask her what she feels about having such a famous daddy who treated her like shit. It was his blood relative. Townes had no reason to treat this kid bad. If you saw her, you could tell that she's his kid. I know Jeanene had him cut her out because she didn't want to have to deal with it." —Peggy Underwood, author's interview.

"He told me that he had an illegitimate daughter, and this had all happened with a woman he just met at a gig somewhere—in Texas or Louisiana, I think—and that the mother didn't want anything from him, but he was so upset about Jeanene taking her out of his will. He was a good man, you know, and wanted to provide for this kid, but she wouldn't allow it. This was not long before he died. He was so angry, and so sad, really. She was a teenager at the time, when he talked to me about her. It just went against everything he wanted, to cut her out like that." —Bianca DeLeon, author's interview.

"He told me this chick came up to him at a gig one time, and just told him she was madly in love with him and wanted to have his child. And they jumped in the truck and did it, and it worked, and she came back about eight months later, pot-bellied, and said, 'It worked, and we're gonna have a baby, and I'm not gonna bother you or anything, but I thought you might want to know that you got a kid out there.' And he was not overjoyed, because he'd never had time to really think about it, she just would pop up and leave. And then she showed up about seven years later, with this little girl. And she showed up at the funeral, but nobody spoke to her. Cindy also showed up at the funeral and no one spoke to her. I didn't know either one of them, and I had Claudia with me, so nobody would speak to me. But he made his will, and wrote this child into his will, and Jeanene would not abide by it. This child was supposed to get some money, at some point, somehow, and Jeanene wouldn't hear of it. But there is a fourth child out there that he knew about and was happy to know about, and when he told me that [mid-1996], he said she must be about sixteen now. And he said the kid was undeniably his, just from the face. I know for a fact that he wanted to provide for that child, and wrote up papers. But Jeanene didn't go by what he wanted with that." —Royann Calvin, author's interview.

17. From the Richard Dobson Archive: http://nativetexas.com/_dobson/ archive.html#35.

18. Actually, Jeanene had Townes' body cremated in Nashville; she kept some of the ashes, so only the remaining ashes were buried in Dido. The other family members in the plot as of the time of the author's visit on January 1, 2001, were H. P. Williams, March 18, 1866–July 25, 1904; William Lipscomb Van Zandt, February 3, 1875–April 8, 1948; Bell Williams Van Zandt, June 30, 1882–February 24, 1965; Infant Twins, December 6, 1904; Martha Ann Van Zandt Perryman, May 19, 1908–February 10, 1998; Jack Van Zandt, February 8, 1911–November 20, 1916.

# Audio and Video Sources

*The following listing documents Townes Van Zandt's recorded legacy in its original form, as first presented on his "official" U.S. album releases (not including reissues) and on various live recordings and collections issued on labels in the U.S. and Europe during Townes' lifetime and within the first decade following his death.*

| Date | Title | Producer | Label/Catalog # |
|------|-------|----------|-----------------|
| 1968 | *For the Sake of the Song* | Jack Clement/ Jim Malloy | Poppy/PYS 40001 |
| 1969 | *Our Mother the Mountain* | Kevin Eggers/ Jack Clement/ Jim Malloy | Poppy/PYS 40004 |
| 1970 | *Townes Van Zandt* | Kevin Eggers/ Jim Malloy | Poppy/PYS 40007 |
| 1971 | *Delta Momma Blues* | Ron Frangipane | Poppy/PYS 40012 |
| 1972 | *High, Low, and In Between* | Kevin Eggers | Poppy/PYS 5700 |
| 1972 | *The Late, Great Townes Van Zandt* | Jack Clement/ Kevin Eggers | Poppy/PP-LA004 |
| 1977 | *Live at the Old Quarter, Houston, Texas* | Earl Willis | Tomato/ TOM 2-7001 |
| 1978 | *Flyin' Shoes* | Chips Moman | Tomato/TOM 7017 |
| 1987 | *At My Window* | Jack Clement/ Jack Rooney | Sugar Hill/SH1020 |

| Date | Title | Producer | Label/Catalog # |
|------|-------|----------|-----------------|
| 1987 | *Live and Obscure* | Stephen Mendell/Townes Van Zandt/Harold Eggers | Sugar Hill/SH1026 |
| 1991 | *Rain on a Conga Drum* | Wolfgang Doebeling | Exile/EXLP02 |
| 1993 | *The Nashville Sessions* | Kevin Eggers | Tomato/ 598.1079.29 |
| 1993 | *Rear View Mirror* | Townes Van Zandt/Harold Eggers | Sundown/ SD2100-2 |
| 1993 | *Road Songs* | Townes Van Zandt/Harold Eggers | Chlodwig/ 7432113007 |
| 1994 | *No Deeper Blue* | Phillip Donnelly | Sugar Hill/SH1046 |
| 1996 | *Abnormal* | Townes Van Zandt/Harold Eggers | Return to Sender/ RTS32 |
| 1997 | *The Highway Kind* | Townes Van Zandt/Harold Eggers | Sugar Hill/SH1042 |
| 1997 | *Documentary* | Larry Monroe/ Harold Eggers | Normal/N211 |
| 1999 | *A Far Cry From Dead* | Eric Paul/ Jeanene Van Zandt | Arista Austin/18888 |
| 1999 | *In Pain* | Townes Van Zandt/Harold Eggers | Normal/N225 |
| 2001 | *Live at McCabe's* | Townes Van Zandt/Harold Eggers | Return to Sender/ RTS32 |
| 2001 | *Texas Rain: The Texas Hill Country Recordings* | Kevin Eggers | Tomato/TOM-2001 |

| Date | Title | Producer | Label/Catalog # |
|------|-------|----------|-----------------|
| 2002 | *A Gentle Evening with Townes Van Zandt* | (no production credit) | Dualtone/ 80302-01119-2 |
| 2002 | *The Best of Townes Van Zandt* | Kevin Eggers | Tomato/TOM-2002 |
| 2003 | *Absolutely Nothing* | (no production credit) | Normal/N235 |
| 2003 | *In the Beginning* | Jack Clement | Compadre/ 6-16892-52402 |
| 2004 | *Rear View Mirror Volume Two* | Townes Van Zandt/Harold Eggers | Varese Sarabande/ 302 066 608 2 |

*While Townes Van Zandt's recorded output includes numerous live recordings from various periods released by various record labels, there is a further rich body of independently recorded performances that circulates among collectors and aficionados to which the author was privileged to have access. The following is a list of those live recordings that are directly referenced in the text or directly inform general statements made in the text.*

## Audio

| | |
|--|--|
| 10/20/70 | Bob Fass radio show, WBAI-FM, New York City |
| 9/30/75 | *Austin City Limits* |
| 5/6/78 | East Lansing, Michigan |
| 6/24/81 | Anderson Fair, Houston |
| 4/22/84 | Anderson Fair, Houston |
| 5/31/87 | *Mountain Stage* radio show, West Virginia |
| 10/31/87 | Steewijk, Holland |
| 7/30/88 | Speakeasy, New York City |
| 4/1989 | BFBS radio |
| 8/1989 | San Marcos, Texas, studio sessions (rough mixes) |
| 3/11/90 | KUT-FM, Austin |

## Audio

| | |
|---|---|
| 8/10/90 | York Winning Post |
| 12/28/90 | VPRO Studios, Hilversum, Holland |
| 8/29/91 | Barbican, York, U.K. |
| 7/17/93 | Community Theatre, Lawrence, Kansas |
| 7/17/93 | KJHK-FM, Lawrence, Kansas |
| 11/21/94 | Munich, Germany |
| 12/9/94 | Manchester University, U.K. |
| 5/8/95 | Band on the Wall, Manchester, U.K. |
| 9/13/95 | Bluebird Cafe, Nashville |
| 11/20/95 | Bayerischer Rundfunk, Germany |
| 12/9–10/95 | Borderline, London |
| 10/13/96 | KUT-FM, Austin |
| 11/30/96 | Bochum, Germany |
| 12/3/96 | Borderline, London |

## Video

| | |
|---|---|
| 11/02/91 | Dutch MTV show |
| 11/02/91 | De Melke Way, Amsterdam |
| 11/28/94 | Ljubljana K4, Slovenia |
| 7/11/95 | Wein, Germany |
| 11/25/95 | The Drum Room, Kansas City |
| 11/24/96 | Munich, Germany |
| 1987–98 | TV shows: *New Country* (1987); *Nashville Tonight* (1987); *Bobby Bare Show* (1987); *Texas Connection* (1993); *Solo Sessions* (1995); Cactus Cafe tribute show (1997); Bottom Line tribute show (1997) |
| 3/28/98 | *Austin City Limits* "Celebration of Townes Van Zandt" |

# Index